DELICATE MISSION

© CONRAD O'BRIEN-FFRENCH, 1979
2nd Impression, February 1980
ISBN 0 7050 0062 1
Printed in Gt. Britain for Skilton & Shaw
(Fudge & Co. Ltd.), London.

DELICATE MISSION

Autobiography of a Secret Agent

Conrad O'Brien-ffrench

SKILTON & SHAW
52 Lincoln's Inn Fields · London

to M.C.

CONTENTS

1. Villa Torlonia 7
2. A Solitary Cloud 23
3. 'Pickelhaube' and Barbed Wire 38
4. The Lightning Out of the East 52
5. The High Himalayas 67
6. The Image of War 82
7. James Bond? 107
8. Black Ore for Death 121
9. Trans-Siberia 134
10. Rudolfo 149
11. The Passing of Monivea 158
12. Art and Alexis 168
13. The Sun Rises in the West 179
14. The World Catches Fire 192
15. Lure of Patriotism 204
16. Censorship Amid the Palm Trees 215
17. Out of the Frying Pan 230
18. How the Rest Was Won 243
19. The Great Beginning 259

I

Villa Torlonia

In the middle of the nineteenth century my grandfather, Acheson ffrench, left Ireland to seek his fortune in Australia. He had been preceded by his exiled cousin William Smith O'Brien, MP, the Irish patriot. In Australia he prospered as a sheep farmer, raised a family of eleven children and called his station 'Monivea', after his home in Ireland. It was here that my father Harry was born.

His early life had been spent on his father's station and later, when his schooling was completed, he travelled throughout Australia and the South Seas. He was ambitious to see the rest of the world and, in particular, Ireland, the land of his forbears. So, accordingly he set out.

On reaching London, Harry learned that his eldest cousin and head of the family, Robert Percy ffrench of Monivea Castle, in the British diplomatic service at the Court of Naples was, at this time, in residence at his London home in Lower Grosvenor Street. Harry, never doubting that he would be warmly welcomed, presented himself to his kinsman. While waiting in the hall before being taken to his cousin, Harry had noticed a number of visiting cards on a silver salver bearing the names of people from a walk of life that was entirely unknown to him – Lord Leighton, Princess Vigiano, Sir Humphrey Nugent, etc., etc.

Robert Percy ffrench, who kept pace with the cream of European society, was visibly disturbed when his butler announced the presence of this junior member of a colonial branch of the family and, so one might surmise, was Harry on being told that 'Mr ffrench is not at home.' This obvious rebuff came as a shock to Harry but he was soon to discover how intensely exclusive the upper crust of English society could be. But Harry was not disturbed for long. 'Upper crust,' he snorted, 'just a lot of crumbs holding together,' and with that he put the whole incident behind him.

Robert Percy ffrench had been married to a Countess Kindiakoff who had borne him a daughter, Kathleen. She lived in great splendour

with her mother in the largest of her palaces on their Simbirsk property
by the Volga, while Robert, who was a consumptive, lived the life of
a dilettante in various European capitals and was known to be amusing
himself with a Neopolitan princess.

It is hard to do more than guess what my father did with himself
during the year that followed this unfortunate episode, but he appears
to have been more determined than ever to acquire a social status.
Eventually he developed delusions of grandeur which was paradoxical,
for he was of ancient if not royal lineage. To my father all outward
pomp, subtly disguised as it might be, was rather vulgar. 'If you know
who you are,' he would say, 'it isn't necessary to tell the world of it.'
Nevertheless, he wanted at all costs to be noticed and since coming to
England he fell into the same trap as many others before him and
became a seeker after recognition. He did it very gracefully it seems,
always avoiding the obvious, but nevertheless revealing a certain
insecurity by taking social status too seriously.

Moving in among some good country families at a ball in aid of some
charity or other, he met the two Miss Thursbys of Ormrod House in
Lancashire. As the younger of the sisters was shy he chose the elder, a
gay blonde named Hilda, and they pranced around the ballroom to the
strains of a polka. Harry's dancing, however, lacked the necessary
polish, so Hilda soon found the exercise fatiguing and an aggravation
to a tiresome cough she was troubled with. He later led Winnifred, the
younger sister, out into the throng and perhaps the bewitching strains
of a new Strauss waltz put life into their evening. In any event they
both lost themselves in a dreamy rhythm from which they scarcely
emerged by the time they returned to the chaperones in the palm court.

Harry soon asked permission to take both sisters to the Royal
Academy, stressing the fact that Lord Leighton, its president, was a
friend of his cousin Robert Percy ffrench. Reports of the young colonial's attentions were going the rounds of the family and it was decided
to send the girls to Malta for the winter. Hilda's health had been
causing some anxiety. As the Miss Thursbys were orphans, minor
heiresses and not yet of age, it was well to get them away from 'fortune-
hunting Australians'. But Harry was not easily thwarted and no sooner
had they reached the Mediterranean island than he turned up. By the
end of their visit, Winnifred, or Freda, as she was called, was engaged
to be married to my father.

I was born at No 5 Montpelier Square in London but soon afterwards my family moved to Villa Torlonia in the Albany hills, east of Rome. It was there I spent the first eight years of my life, carefree and happy. The country surrounding Rome and Frascati is romantically beautiful, the inhabitants of a sunny disposition, their natural charm infecting and blessing those with whom they come in contact.

My grandfather had visited Frascati while doing the grand tour in 1834, recording his impressions in his diary:

> I started after my *collatzione* [breakfast] passing the Villa of Adrian which I could not enter, not having permission. I walked through by road and field to Frascati where I arrived at three o'clock and without drawing breath got a *ciceroni* to conduct me to the ancient Tusculum about three miles from Frascati. On our arrival there the guide, after making borrowed speeches from Roman stories respecting the surrounding country exclaimed, '*Ecco le miserabili ravine d'una citta anticha.*' So much for the site of the ancient Tusculum. First he showed me the remains of an amphitheatre, then the section of the city which is exceedingly beautiful indeed and on the other side the Mediterranean stretching far away to the westward. On this stood considerable ruins of Cicero's villa. Further on were the remains of a theatre in good preservation. I returned to my *albergo* at five, where I am lodged in a solitary bed for the night.

My grandfather mentions brigands who terrified the countryside during this period and I too associated them with my early childhood.

> We have sat over a large wood fire in a wide kitchen-like grate relating stories of brigands which put me in mind of the tales of travel which I read some eight or ten years ago written by Geoffrey Cayora concerning the very place in which we were.

Shortly after he wrote . . .

> Well, thank God I have passed the most dangerous road today without molestation. Before I started from Rome numerous friends endeavoured to dissuade me from making the journey on foot owing to the danger of likely attack from brigands, the chief of which appears to be Gasparoni.

My grandfather was not the first of our family to visit Italy. My branch of the family had intermarried with the O'Briens of Thomond and one of these, Donough O'Brien, came to Rome to obtain pardon for having killed his brother. He died there as a monk in 1064 and was buried in the Rotund Chapel of St Stephen's. Then in the seventeenth century a descendant of Donough's, one Moirough O'Brien, swept Ireland from end to end with fire and sword, burning the cathedral of Cashel with all the priests and people who had taken refuge therein. He professed his repentance on becoming a Catholic and by way of propitiating Pope Alexander VII, who was opposing his appointment as Viceroy of Catalonia, erected a monument overlooking the lake of Bolsena to the memory of this Donough. From the epitaph on that monument, 'Rex Cashel et Thomond', the property took its name, by local corruption, Castel Thomond. So became known the owner of it. Shortly after my birth my father, following a law of second-geniture, inherited the title of Marquis of Castel Thomond.

The ffrenchs were lineally descended from Sir Theophilus ffrench,

> a most valiant knight who accompanied William the Conqueror in his expedition to England and who was present with him at the great battle of Hastings. He derived his pedigree from Sir Maximillian de ffrench who was the son of Harloven junior, son of Harloven, son of Rollo the strong, alias Rollo, first duke of Normandy.

After Hastings the branch of the family to which we belong accompanied Strongbow to Ireland in the twelfth century, and after a sojourn in County Wexford settled in the city of Galway. One enters the ancient city by the Great Gate and once within its walls continues westward towards the bay, the harbour, its wharves, warehouses, and then, close by the source of their magnificence, the great families of Galway had their mansions. Here my branch lived and were known as the ffrenchs of Monivea Castle. Monivea, once a stronghold of the O'Kelleys, was purchased by Partick Begg ffrench who died in 1630 and passed his estates on to his son Robert. Robert acquired more land, developed the property into an attractive country residence with extensive parkland, encompassed by a wall and five rows of enormous beech trees. Here my ancestors lived in the style adopted by other members of the fourteen tribes of Galway and entertained lavishly.

The ffrenchs had the reputation of being elegant, socially prominent in whatever locality they lived. My father was no exception. He enjoyed the adulation of an admiring circle of friends whom he frequently invited to the house. Sensing a possible protest from my mother he would say, 'My dear, I am really doing all this for your sake, you know. You have never seen a motor car and the Costas are bringing their De Dion Bouton, and will drive it around the garden for us to see.'

The visitors' book in our home was filled with signatures of famous Roman names, princes of the Church and members of foreign nobility. Yet high life did not really appeal to my mother who wanted only to live quietly with her beloved Harry amid the bewitchingly beautiful surroundings of Villa Torlonia. 'Ach,' he would scoff, 'women are as natural as hens; they choose a good nesting site and then the only thing that interests them is clucking over their chicks.' My mother was strikingly beautiful, graceful, slight of figure, but erect with great dignity in her movements. Her manner towards others, however, was rather stiff, for she had that well-known English reserve.

The beauty of Villa Torlonia had but one true conveyance and that was the soul of the beholder. It could not be caught by words alone. Deep in the woods in a land as yet undisturbed by machinery the music of water echoed as did the haunting voice of the nightingale, making a deep and lasting impression upon me that it possessed the kind of peace the world so sadly lacks. Perhaps all of us born before the age of the motor car have a different kind of resonance, closer to nature than is known in this modern age. Walking or riding from place to place is not the same along a hard surfaced road built for speeding cars. The whole tempo of life was more in rhythm with the beat of the heart; moreover, there was time to savour the kindly gifts of mother earth.

Life was mostly tranquil in our rose-covered villa. My nurse, settling me down at night, would open the window, letting in the limpid air of the hills and would lavish true Italian affection on me as she whispered the caressing words, *'felicissima notte carino'*. French windows opened from our drawing room on to a terrace and I could hear my father at the piano within, his touch strong and resonant. Having finished a Schumann arabesque he would accompany my mother in some Mendelssohn songs: her voice not strong but true. How happy this music made me as it floated into the summer air.

As warm and reassuring as these moments were, there were also sights and sounds which appalled me. Looking over the north wall of the property into the sunken Grotto Ferrata road I could see the horrifying spectacle of beggars with their grotesque expressions, their wailing voices or noseless faces, and the absence of limbs on their bodies. The lot of overburdened beasts, driven by merciless blows from ignorant peasants, climbed the dusty road from Frascati. These things disturbed and haunted me during the darkened hours.

Life on the standards my parents had adopted was very expensive and soon there was evidence of domestic strain. As children we were not directly conscious of all this as our immediate needs were adequately cared for, but we suffered from lack of harmony in our home: my father's frequent emotional outbursts and my mother's complete inability to cope with them. I later grew to suspect, and not without cause, that the presence of Kenzie in the house, her interference in my parent's relationship, was a major cause of the trouble. Kenzie was well equipped to be a governess, her brother a school master and her background strictly middle-class Scots. Her responsibilities were more or less self-imposed. She ran the house, the servants, the children and the two nannies: a Swiss girl and a picturesque Italian *balia* (or wet nurse). She also organised Father Rosignioli who was hired as a tutor to my elder brother Rollo. She decided what walks we should take and when we should return, which would have been alright if she had not also run my mother's life as, indeed, she had done since her birth.

My father frequently went to Rome on social or business matters and sometimes as a special treat he took me and my brother Rollo. As a preliminary to these excursions we would attend an early Mass at the cathedral in Frascati where, upon the steps of the tomb of Prince Charles Edward Stewart's heart, we would sit with impatience waiting for the moment to catch the tram. The tram, horsedrawn and open at the sides, left for Rome about eight o'clock in the morning and we would excitedly rush to get seats on the right side of the car because the left side was usually hung with curtains to keep out the sun and, of course, that meant we could see nothing. Moreover, the high road from Frascati to Rome ran parallel to the right of the tram lines.

As the tram descended into the warmer climate of the Campagnia the cultivation changed in character and we would pass out of the seemingly endless vineyards, which ranged themselves like echelons of a peaceful army about the foot of the hills, and through masses of pink-blossomed nectarines or almonds, then trot alongside the normal road traffic with its gaily decorated Frascati wine carts, drawn by tassel-festooned horses with eye fringes dangling from their coloured browbands. White oxen, too, drawing loads of vegetables, plodded slowly, their shiny black horns curving gracefully upwards. It was all a joyous pageant progressing through a broadening landscape as we passed by the gently undulating land of corn and olives. The country here was crossed by ancient aqueducts, arches after arches in an endless line which once conveyed the waters of Tivoli, Frascati, or Sabine hills to a thirsting Rome. When we reached the capital we would become swallowed up by the populace and its traffic. The crowd generated in us a strangely infectious rhythm which, after the seclusion of the Villa

Torlonia, was very exciting. When the noon cannon from the walls of St Angelo echoed above the city, it would set off a chorus of frantic bell ringing from all the churches, a signal for Rome to halt, come to rest and repeat the Angelus prayer of rededication to a higher power. Our thoughts would later turn to the midday meal and a siesta in a more tranquil mood.

At *mezzogiorno* we invariably found ourselves in the vicinity of Piazza Navona, close to a restaurant popular amongst the Romans called Il Pazetto where my father liked to go, and to whose *padroni,* Sor Grovannino, he was well known. Whisking his napkin violently at flies and crumbs alike, Sor Grovannino would clear the cane-seated chairs, and setting a carafe of wine on the table would soon fetch the choicest Roman fare for us together with *nespolis,* or cherries, or whatever fruit was in season. Refreshed, we would then sit under some shady pergola or by the adjacent fountain of Neptune until the afternoon programme was set in motion. After the heat of the day had abated and my father's business completed, we would take the tram back to Frascati, trundling through the umbrella pines catching glimpses of the blue hills through the archways of aquaducts as we gradually approached the foothills. Home, tired, we were ready to submit to the soft concern of our mother and the dragooning of Kenzie and her two nursemaids.

The hot summer days were sometimes spent in a hotel in a small fishing village on the Ligurian coast where, on the sands of the now well-known resort of Viareggio, we played and bathed in absolutely nothing but a large straw hat, catching fish and sea horses. Meanwhile Kenzie, from the protecting shade of her parasol, mounted guard over us. Above the tide level and beneath the maritime pines fishermen mended their nets and made ropes of tarry oakum – a smell always henceforth associated with those happy days by the sea and with its own particular odours fanned by a breeze from the distant Appenines.

But this time of freedom was to come to an end as little by little the bearing rein of traditional authority tightened. The time for education and an end to sweet independence was approaching. My parents rented a house on a place called, somewhat ironically, Piazza della Indipendenza in Florence, close to the elementary school to which we were to go under the headmastership of Mr Begg. Attired in traditional mortar-board and gown he was to me, at all events, as beautiful a symbol of authority as the pictures I had seen of Jesus Christ; moreover, he had a small divided beard and classical features. Here the

Kenzie at 86

initial stages of our indoctrination began and we were taken on educational walks around the city. We even visited galleries like the Uffizi,
or went to the top of the Campagnili of Florence's cathedral to get a
bird's-eye view of that historical city. From here we could trace the
River Arno which flows through the ancient city and under its beautiful
bridges, though these were not connected in my mind with their
historical or picture-postcard importance so much as with picnic
lunches.

My father would take us to a small country inn on the Arno's banks
outside the city. There the innkeeper's wife would let down an enormous net into the river and almost immediately it was cranked up, full
of whitebait, which was thrown straight into a frying pan and within
minutes of being caught would arrive on our table in a large dish,
brown, crisp, and savoury. Of course the environment had much to do
with the experience – the swift-flowing river, the sun-mottled tablecloth under the vine pergola, the heavy grapes that hung over our heads,
the dew-covered jugs filled with cold water from the well and the poetry
of the repast in prospect.

Our initial steps towards enlightenment were halting. A French tutor was also hired, but he suffered from a nervous stomach and was so frequently absent that he was eventually dismissed. Jemma, the butler's wife, used to announce him as *il Signore con mal di pancia* (the man with the stomach ache). Finally the time for a more English education had come, for Rollo and I were nine and eight respectively. We moved to England and to a large house in Sussex Square Gardens, a fashionable part of Brighton renowned for its terraces, crescents and squares in the Regency style, with the classical columned entrances facing the gardens. Their lawns were carefully tended by unseen gardeners and fenced by imposing iron railings and laurel bushes. The owners of these homes were given keys which enabled them to use the gardens whenever they liked, and as Rostellan, our new dame school, was on the opposite side of the square, it was easy for us to cross each morning through the garden by the gates. This school was run by two Irish sisters, one plump and rubicund, the other dark and thin. The elder one carried herself always at the chin-up position and was the positive half, while the other inclined to be over-conscientious, stooped, and bore a worried look.

My sister Yvonne was about a year old when my mother, a Protestant, availing herself of canon law of the time, had Yvonne baptized into her faith. Whether this was the true reason for my father's departure from our midst, or whether he merely used it as an excuse, the fact remains he became so angry that he picked up his hat and walked out of the house never again to return. With my father's departure the atmosphere at home changed. My mother became better off financially but the situation was not, of course, ideal for we boys were growing rapidly and in need of masculine control. I always found Rollo a great support in all these domestic upheavals and I accepted his leadership unquestionably in all we did together. Through him I eventually regained much of my self-confidence lost during my father's tempestuous outbursts, which were especially devastating for the pitiable effect they had upon my mother.

After a few terms at Rostellan I joined Rollo at the Wick, a large preparatory school in the Hove district of Brighton. It was there that I first encountered discipline and its mate, devilment, but about the only recollection that I have of my actual schooling is that I had difficulty with my reading and was subject to occasional violent headaches.

The ordeal of reading out loud before my classmates was nerve-wracking. An absence of self-reliance and an almost total lack of interest in what was being taught, together with a constitutional phlegm, contributed little towards academic success. I came to accept failure as a depressing fact and knew that I could never qualify for an exam to enter a 'public' school, an imputation I accepted with resignation.

There were fights, of course, among the boys at the Wick and corporal punishment. Although I escaped the cane I heard of frequent whippings. It was there I first met with cruelty and sadism and not only among the boys. But as frightful as children can be to each other, there were also times of deep devotion when an elder boy would champion and protect a younger. The tender feelings thus aroused were sublime, not only of the elder for the younger boy, the stronger for the weaker, but they called out in the younger boy something akin to hero worship, a lofty feeling perhaps never again to be experienced. The need for love is fundamental.

Self-control was strange to me and I learned my lessons painfully. On a summer day or in late spring, in spite of the beauty of the English countryside, I would long for the carefree life I had known at Frascati and would turn more fully to Rollo, who shared the love of our childhood home, its woods and fountains, its sunlit security. Rollo did well at school. He became a prefect, a member of the college rugby team, joined the cadet corps, was a lance-corporal and a senior drummer. On the other hand, I shrank from competition, was hopeless at things academic, the mere sight of an examination paper causing my mind to go blank. I was, however, intuitive with people and could size them up immediately. My impressions were seldom wrong.

Having now no one to look to as the senior of our clan, I transferred my attachment to Rollo, yielding him the deep abundance of my affection. Rollo was, furthermore, my only true link with a carefree life at Villa Torlonia. He and I had been playmates from the beginning. He was much more than my elder brother; he was leader, generous and tolerant of my shortcomings, but positive withal. I was timid of taking the initiative if I thought Rollo would do so, yet if something arose which was obviously my responsibility I was naturally slow to act but eager to follow through with it, sometimes aggressively. He was quick-witted and clever, I emotional and inclined to be slow and dreamy, yet if angered could be frighteningly violent. I am sure a professional psychiatrist would have an impressive name for my condition and thus assigned I would travel through life with that label. But, thank God, no such thing ever happened. I was left to evolve, to change and mature, and the former things drifted out of sight or were eclipsed by new and exciting events. For the most part I was controlled by my emotions and my devotion for Rollo became a binding and blinding rather than a liberating force, and caused an imbalance in my vision; but then it is hardly fair to judge an adolescent, for I hardly knew reason from emotion nor either from spirit.

In retrospect it seems that relationships in a family are governed by a process of emotional stability and an increase in awareness as the journey of discovery progresses — opening up, as it were, new ground in one's self. But at that stage one is like a green shoot taking its ground roots for granted, and seeking only to blossom, and the blooming is in turn its means of attracting attention to itself. We do not gather flowers for the sake of their roots, yet without them there would be no gathering. And least applauded of all is the impulse of life which underlies the whole process. I loved nature because of its design and design was my mentor.

At that time I took religion for granted. Discipline, unquestionably, had its place, a means of providing rules to follow. I was thirteen and did not stop to reason but followed the rules of my training. Obedience to a dogma, and belief in a state which relegates rather than leads, seemed to me comfortable enough. Fear of death was part of the animal state in me, but guilt, the devil, or a fiery furnace was not. I sensed no paradox nor stopped to doubt and in my state of delusion I was content.

My great aunt Sophie lived at Brighton where she owned two houses. She occupied the one facing the sea on Brunswick Terrace – it was part of an imposing array of houses in the Regency style. The other, called Montpellier Hall, stood further inland and we lived in that one. Though not up to the standard of those on Brighton Parade it was nevertheless large and comfortable and had a garden of its own. Our next-door neighbour was a retired coal merchant whose name was Nye. The importance to me of Mr Nye was that he was master and huntsman of the Brighton Foot Beagles. Though he seemed quite old, he was actually in the prime of life and I soon made friends with him and got him to show me the kennels and to let me help in any way I could.

It was then that I first awoke to the instinct of the hunt – the sound of a pack of hounds in full cry. Mind you, not everyone is touched by that kind of music, but for me at that stage it was sweeter than church bells and stirred my deepest instincts. Before long I had paid my first subscription and proudly wore the hunt button on my tweed jacket. I was, from that time on, 'in rapture and in sweet oblivion lost'.

But beagling is a winter sport and during the summer holidays we

usually went to some Devonshire farm where we could ride ponies
over the moors and indulge in Devonshire cream on our breakfast
scones, 'chudlies', as they were called. It was our custom to travel to
the west via London. We always stopped at the same hotel in Harrington Road where the old porter, Fisher, helped us unload our baggage
from the growler. A growler was more of a family cab than a hansom.
It had room for four inside, and maybe a fifth on the box. There was
a luggage rack over the back axle and plenty of room for a large trunk
on the roof. It was not an uncommon sight to see boys or even fully
grown men running in the wake of a growler in the hope of earning a
sixpence for helping with the fare's baggage at the end of the journey.

The hotel was conveniently situated a short walking distance from
the Natural History Museum, and the horsedrawn buses stopped at
the corner by a chemist shop which displayed large bottles of coloured
water in their windows. We often went to Harrods on the 'favourite',
a blue bus, and raced to sit next to the coachman on top. What a joy
it all was.

From the Wick school Rollo went to Wellington College and I was
sent to St Aubyns, a prep school in Eastbourne, and from there I went
to Bradley Court Agricultural School.

Bradley Court was a nineteenth-century mansion on the outskirts of
the Forest of Dean. It had been the private residence of a squire and
was now converted into an agricultural school for about sixty students.
Some say that a boy should be buried at the age of fifteen and not dug
up again until he is past twenty. Well, that is understandable enough
if somewhat absurd. Admittedly boys go through a ghastly stage of
uncertainty during which they are neither children nor grownups, and
I was in just that stage when parents say despairingly, 'What to do with
the boy?' But that hurts the boy and serves no purpose. Perhaps it
hurts his ego but most of all it causes grief on account of what he is
doing to the love he so much depends on.

The headmaster of Bradley Court was a retired naval man who
loved discipline and was down on any form of slackness. He drew up
a daily schedule, which he called the Rota, and saw to it that it was
properly enforced and amply fulfilled. There were courses in practical
farming, horsemanagement, engineering, carpentry and poultry
management, and those in charge of these departments rendered daily
reports on the students' progress. But with all this the aptitude of each
student was carefully studied, and it seemed that my leanings were
towards gamekeeping on the estate. The property consisted of some

hundreds of acres including fox coverts, and woodlands in which there were pheasants. There were rabbits galore, and even the occasional Fallow deer from the bordering forest, yet what delighted me most was the sight of a woodcock flushed from the thicket.

As 'keeper' I was able to carry a gun, train dogs to retrieve, and work with the guns. I kept ferrets for rabbiting in the fence-rows, and so on. At first I contented myself with a collector's gun purchased through Gamages mail-order system, but later graduated to a 12-bore double-barrelled shotgun for which I learned to load my own cartridges. It was a second-hand gun but it had Damascus barrels and was the pride of my life. But my cocker spaniel, Nell, shared my heart with Tita, a white ferret, from which I was seldom separated. I would carry her in the poacher's pocket of my Norfolk jacket from whence her white head with pink eyes would peek out during lectures. Boxer was my next acquisition, a Springer spaniel, but unlike Nell he was younger and wilder, and I used to couple them together for purposes of stability.

Much of the joy of the out-of-doors was the smells of rotting vegetation – the unctious mould in the undergrowth and the roar of the winter gales in the leafless trees; the chatter of jackdaws and the lofty chorus of the rooks among the upper branches of the elms; the lapwings and the curlew on the fallow fields, and the placid eyes of recumbent cattle.

After the end of the shooting season when the snowdrops were showing on the banks and the primroses by the rides, I was told to spend time in the stables. This interfered with the setting season, a time when I would borrow broody hens from Mr Howes, the poultryman, to hatch out pheasants' eggs.

I had always liked horses so learning to muck them out was no chore; in fact, the ammoniated aroma of stables has a distinct appeal. I learned to groom them, remove their shoes, and above all feed them, and then ride them. I was a bit scared of one of them, a chestnut, who liked to buck, but on the whole they were a quiet lot. As well as hacks and hunters, there was a team of Cleveland bays that went with the four-in-hand, a couple of Suffolk Punches, as well as a pony or two. There was the tackle too that I was responsible for, and when I say tackle I mean also the four-in-hand harness which had to be oiled and polished.

In my second year I was allowed to follow the hounds. The district was hunted by the Ledbury Fox Hounds whose master was George Thursby; he was a cousin of my mother's which gave me a slight sense of prestige even though he probably didn't know of my existence at the time. George had been well-known as a gentleman jockey and had ridden his brother's horse, John of Gaunt, in the famous Thunderstorm Derby. John of Gaunt was the favourite, but a flash of lightning caused him to turn about and he lost twenty lengths. Nevertheless, he caught them up and came in second.

The summer holidays of 1909 were spent as usual on the Devonshire moors and we camped with some college friends of Rollo's on the banks of the river Tamar, but it rained so persistently that we were driven indoors to the farmhouse where my mother and younger brother and sister were. Here we sought our own amusement with games or books which Kenzie always brought, and seeing that I was still backward in my reading Kenzie would read out loud to us from such volumes as *Fifty-two Stirring Stories for Boys* by G A Henty.

When finally the time came for us to return to school I was the first to leave and Rollo saw me off at the wayside station. I was strangely attracted to him as if our parting was final. He waved to me until the train had disappeared from view and I slumped into my seat struggling to control my tears. Rollo would shortly return to Wellington, to higher mathematics and Greek exercises, while I was destined to grasp a pitchfork and simple instructions in the four-course-rotary system in agriculture.

It was November and rain, and I had just turned sixteen. I heard my name called down the hollow corridor which led to the headmaster's study. As soon as I entered this sanctum of authority Mr Gandy began telling me something which my mind seemed unwilling to grasp. He repeated it several times like an axeman persisting with cruel blows. Finally the staggering impact of his words began to get through to me. Yet still he continued to drive them home. There had been an accident to Rollo during a game of football and he was dead. The vision of a hurt to Rollo, a fatal happening, seemed too black a thought to grasp, for it would, it seemed, destroy forever the joy of living. Perhaps it was well that it numbed my perception for, otherwise, it would have crushed me completely. It took a long time for me to realise to what extent I had become dependent upon him and now that he was gone and I had lost my sun, I was going to have to find in all the space of loneliness a consolation, another point of orientation.

After all this it was thought best for me to return home. The Christmas holidays were, anyway, not so far off. But home seemed a hollow shell, echoing recollections of him. Moreover, it was not long before it became noticeable that a great change had come over my mother.

Her beautiful face now revealed signs of strain and her youthful buoyancy seemed to have been drained away. She no longer joined us in our outings.

I left my agricultural school to study practical farming with a Mr Gazalet, a Worcestershire farmer in the Evesham Valley. Living in his house was his sister-in-law, a Mrs Hodges, who knew more about horsemastership than most of those who write books on that subject. She used to give me a lead over the fences out hunting and show me how to keep on good terms with hounds when most of the field had lost them. I fell under her spell with enthusiasm and eventually learned a great deal about riding to hounds, the care and management of hounds, and could ride across country, leaping fences, ditches, water, and even gates with alacrity. I was sixteen years of age and life for the first time was coursing wildly through me. The lamentable death of Rollo had, in a way, lifted the lid off my own self-expression. The ecstasy I now felt, galloping my steed, the wind in my face, the bursts of energy in my horse as he raced at his fences, the thrilling moment of suspense in mid-air as we hurled to an unpredictable landing and then on in ever-quickening pace in the wake of the fleeting hounds, the music of their cry, the echo of the horn in the copse, a breather as they check to find a lost line and then on with the mad rush.

At the Gazalet's farm Nell was my constant companion. I lavished all my affection on her, frequently taking her for rabbit hunts. At this time my mother lived with Kenzie and my young brother and sister in Folkestone. This was for the good of my mother's health, for the bracing climate of Kent would stimulate her. And I joined them for Easter.

That year Easter came early, the gorse was in bloom, a yellow mass covering the hills contrasting with the deep blue of the English Channel beyond. It was all very typical of a spring day with a slight east wind, seagulls drifting high against endless ranks of scudding clouds. It moved in me a feeling of restlessness and a longing for a new horizon. The traveller feels he is leaving a part of himself behind when he journeys from one point to another; the land, the water, rush by him and somehow he associates this with that which is passing away, from which he would escape. I wanted to get away from the haunting thought of Rollo and the finality of death. I wanted to get away from places and things that brought him back into my memory . . .

I took Nell on to the downs for a possible rabbit hunt. And it was there that she picked up another dog. The other dog, an ugly mongrel, was springing about excitedly. An oldish fellow with rugged features appeared above the brow of the hill and when he saw me gave a friendly greeting.

'Guess our dogs have started a jackrabbit hunt!'

This man came from the unknown vastness of a country beyond the horizon. He had a free and easy manner and like the seagulls was accustomed to spacious living.

I asked, 'Are you American?'

'Well,' he replied, 'I'm from America alright, but I'm Canadian.'

We were at the opposite ends of life; I eager for adventure, he ready to retire. The dogs were yappingly in pursuit of their quarry. The old man and I walked along together.

'Funny looking dog, ain't he?' he mused, 'belongs to my sister who lives here at the cemetery.'

'That's an odd thing to do, isn't it?' I questioned.

'Well, she's the caretaker's wife.'

I changed the subject and was soon pelting him with questions in reply to which the old man told me all about his ranch in Saskatchewan. He was no longer very active as a rancher. The government had made him Justice of the Peace.

'Say,' he said suddenly, with renewed enthusiasm, 'why don't you join the Mounties? They're a wonderful bunch of fellers, and they're looking for recruits.'

My decision was not hard to make and by the following spring I was on my way out west. The J.P. had invited me to Buffalo Lake Ranch with, 'You come along to see us. We'll look after you until you're ready to join the Mounted Police.'

There followed a short correspondence with the Royal North-West Mounted Police headquarters in Regina, Canada; some formalities to be gone through and a visit to the Canadian Pacific Railway offices in London. Then in April 1910, at the age of seventeen, I sailed on the *Empress of Britain* bound for Quebec.

2

A Solitary Cloud

Arrival in Canada was a mixture of excitement and loneliness, finding myself in a vast land where people spoke, thought and acted so differently. However much I wished to harmonise with my surroundings, there seemed to be fear of letting go of that to which I was previously attached. Moreover, my life in Europe had been a comfortable one surrounded by goodwill and consideration and Nell, but here in the west it was each man for himself and a question of survival.

The transcontinental trip on the Canadian Pacific Railway, while thrilling, only deepened the sense of the vastness and loneliness of the land into which I had ventured. In order to reach Buffalo Lake on the open prairies of Saskatchewan, I was obliged to transfer on to a loop line at Moose Jaw, at which station the transcontinental stopped at 2 a.m. A black porter on board the sleeping car helped me out on to the dark track – for there was no platform – and handed me my five pieces of baggage, including an old banjo. I watched the tail light of the train disappear into the west. It was very dark. The sky was overcast and the newly melted snow had filled the night air with a smell of damp earth, for winter had released its iron grip and the ache of impending rain was relieved in a goodly shower. Alone, out on the prairie 6000 miles from home, with my baggage at my feet, I realised I had begun a new life.

I still had a desire to feel out the tone of my environment and having now removed myself from the protective dominance of my family, my immediate concern was to adjust to the new set of circumstances; in fact, I didn't know what to do. A thought passed, haltingly, through my mind. In this land of 'equality' had the sleeping car porter expected a tip?

Someone in the distance was approaching with a lantern. Perhaps he would help me with my baggage, I thought, and hailed him with a 'Hey! Porter!' The man approached, examined me quizzically by the light of his lantern, then, in the strong western drawl with which I was

23

to become so familiar, he said, 'I ain't no porter, so if you want your baggage carried you'll have to carry it yourself!' His light went out and his receding footsteps were swallowed up in a blackness filled with uncertainty and a faint smell of chewing tobacco.

When my eyes had become accustomed to the dark, I walked across the tracks to the station building. From there I followed a wooden sidewalk leading up an incline towards a beam of light cast across the dirt of the trail. On reaching the light which filtered through a screen door, I pushed myself in against a slight twang of resisting springs. The door slamming behind me, I found myself in the lobby of Moose Jaw's only hotel. At first it looked like a doss house. Some men were sleeping in chairs and others, lying full length on the counter, hid the room clerk from me. On hearing the door slam he woke up. 'Full up,' he said from behind his cigar stub. The fly screen slammed again and, loaded with my baggage, I staggered down the hill and back to the station, there to count the chilly hours until the arrival of the train that would carry me to Tuxford. For those who loved their creature comforts, western Canada was a good place to avoid.

The sun was high when the train reached Tuxford where I got out to face the last stretch of my journey to Buffalo Lake by road. A livery barn was across the way, the open door exposing a teamster lying full length on a straw pile. Though he was very much asleep his hand still grasped a bottle. If my destination was to be reached, this man had to be awakened! He looked tough, was repulsively smelly and his language when he 'came to' proved blistering. But he got his team hitched to a democrat and we set off together. 'I'm Mac,' he grunted curtly, wiping away the molasses of his chewing tobacco trickling from the corners of his mouth and through the stubble of his unshaven chin.

Yellow meadowlarks perched on the fence posts. The trail skirted a slough. The wheels sunk in and the democrat overturned. Passengers and baggage were pitched into the mud! I had never heard language of this potency! One of the 'tugs' was broken – obviously the leather was perished – but he soon mended it with twine.

On topping a rise we saw Buffalo Lake below us. It was not a very large lake, but it certainly looked good to me. On the edge of it, surrounded by poplars, stood the ranch house, it's barns and corrals grouped around it picturesquely. The teamster grinned and pointed with his whip.

'There she be. I expect you ain't sorry neither.' Inside the ranch house a true welcome awaited me.

'Come on in,' said the JP as his son helped the teamster with the baggage. His daughter-in-law came forward wiping her hand on her apron.

'You're very welcome,' she said, as a rather hard mouth stretched into a sincere smile, 'we figured you'd get here in time to eat with us at noon.'

Then, without further ceremony, her voice cracked out again, 'Come on Pappy! Get your preaching done and let's sit up before this dinner gets spoiled.'

Such was my introduction to western Canada.

At Buffalo Lake, I pottered about, found my feet, learned much and, above all, recovered from my journey before presenting myself at Regina for medical examination. The interlude at the ranch passed all too quickly, but everyone there seemed so occupied I spent much time by myself. Over and over again I thought with a sickening stab in my heart, 'How would Rollo have reacted in this situation.' But then, pulling myself together, I decided to force Europe and all its associations into the background and try not to think about them.

Presenting myself as a prospective recruit at the Regina barracks of the Royal North-West Mounted Police was a curious experience, something of a mixture of exaltation (for the Mounties had a terrifying reputation) and concern at getting caught up in a conventional machine which imposed on its men the strictest discipline in the world. My first step was a medical examination performed by Surgeon Bell, a small man with an imperial beard. Yes, I was fit alright and then I had to fill in some papers before the adjutant, parade before the commanding officer, take the oath of allegiance to the Crown, fetch my kit from the quartermaster's store and finally report to the corporal of the day.

There was a certain amount of readjustment going on at the barracks as a troop and their horses were being sent to London to represent the R.N.W.M.P. at the coronation of King George V. They were a very fine body of men, but since 1899 when 245 members of the force had volunteered for service in the Boer War in South Africa – in Larry Herchmer's 2nd Canadian Mounted Rifle and Sam Steel's Strathcona's Horse – the total strength of the force was now only 440, putting a big strain on those left behind. Recruits were rushed through their training in five months and sent out into the field, sometimes to far-flung detachments.

From the time I received my scarlet jacket and stetson hat to the day I was posted to a detachment near the U.S. border, I was under intensive training. A Mountie was given to understand that he might have to tackle any job at any time and under any circumstances. Above all he would have, at all times, to use his own discretion as to when he was or was not on duty. Issued with a revolver and taught how to shoot, he was never told under what circumstances it was to be drawn or used. The less conflict there is in any situation, the less likely that situation is to develop. The less guns are drawn the quicker the problem is solved. In other words, a policeman's identity was with his sense of right rather than with any arbitrary code. It takes a bit of courage to enter a bar which is rapidly being reduced to shambles by an angry or drunken mob, but it is courage and coolness together with a trust in the indestructibility of right and not firearms that have created the reputation the Mounted Police enjoy.

It was not all work, however; after five, the recruits could go on pass into Regina. There I met Doreen. She was only thirteen, but girls of that age in Canada were more mature than in Europe. Blue-eyed and blonde, as cute as a button, she was really someone worth polishing up for. Almost every day when I was able to get a pass I would meet her. What we talked about would not amount to much, but in the long summer evenings I would buy her a sarsaparilla and then look into her face with the same fascination as some stare at the moon.

It was Saturday evening and we had arranged to meet and go to the baseball game together. But I was always on duty. Just as I was polishing my buttons to go the alarm sounded. A prisoner had hacked his way out of the guardroom by way of its tiny wooden courtyard and had escaped. Patrols were immediately detailed and I was ordered to ride out with two others, Inspector French and Rogan, and bring him in. We scoured the country to the west until midnight, picketing during the darkest hours and were then in the saddle again until the next afternoon, finally returning with the prisoner. Doreen never forgave me for standing her up. But I looked upon this, my first 'manhunt', as a bit of a spree. It taught me a lot about conserving a horse's energy. As for Rogan's mount, we got him home alright but he died in his stall.

In the late summer I was posted to a division in the Cypress Hills, where I arrived in the small hours of the morning. The guardroom corporal, a morose individual with all the earmarks of a traditional turnkey, issued me with some bedding, handed me a lantern and directed me to the barrack room. He seemed to be the only one in barracks and it evidently annoyed him – perhaps he was missing something special. There was no vacant bed to be had, so I put my palliasse on the floor and prepared to sleep. I was shy, too, about meeting new people *en bloc*, and it was a relief therefore to find that I was currently the only occupant of the room.

In those days a western town consisted of a handful of dwellings, a church, theatre, livery barn, a saloon bar, pool-room-cum-barber shop, some stores and, outside the town limits, a brothel. The latter was against the law and fines were imposed upon the proprietress whenever things got too rowdy. This was the signal for the brief dispersal of the girls who, after a holiday, would return invigorated and eager to be back on the job. While this house was closed a state of despondency descended on the town.

The proprietress was usually a kindly woman and when things got out of control or a customer ran out of cash, he would be gently but firmly put on the road. She was especially lenient with the Mounties, but even so there was the right time for everyone to quit.

It was some hours before dawn when the occupants of the barrack room came home. There was the usual drunken argument about the time. A clock hung upon the wall. It was faintly visible; being the subject of interest, its large dial like a full moon suggested itself as a wonderful target. Someone opened fire! For a while the night was filled with flashes and lead. Their undiscovered comrade hid his head under the blankets. I was appalled, frightened and embarrassed. I decided to play possum and introduce myself in the morning. They were, I thought, all too drunk to know the difference. But before dawn, wishing to relieve himself, one of them fell over my prostrate body and a few choice words were added to my rapidly expanding vocabulary.

I was not long at divisional headquarters, but was posted to a detachment at Battle Creek in the heart of the cattle ranching country, some seventy-five miles north of the international border. The only other policeman there was Sergeant Quinn, a relic of the Boer War, who was a stickler for discipline. Bizarre as it seemed to meet with such conventions in the wilderness, nevertheless the old fellow had a non-commissioned rank and he did not wish it to be forgotten. He insisted on as much spit and polish and standing to attention when addressing him as on the square at Regina.

Another character of a different type was Sarchi, the Cree half-breed who used to hang about the post office store at Rusthorn, at least it was there I usually saw him, his pony hitched to the rail and the couple of hounds that always accompanied him sniffing around the ash cans at

Sarchi

the back of the log building. I envied him those dogs for they were swift and hardy and related, I supposed, to Scottish deerhounds, though goodness knows how remotely. Sarchi was enjoying a good year with his trapping and hunting and he and his longdogs were having the best season ever with wolf and coyote pelts at $5 each, as well as the bounty since Red-deer Smith and his ill-starred flock passed through and were caught by the early snows. The predators had followed them up from Montana devouring those sheep too weak to continue the trek. Smith had started out with 10,000 sheep and by the time they had reached the Battle Creek area there were only about 6000 left, and he was less than halfway home. The freeze-up had come in mid-October.

Sarchi and his daughter lived north-west of Battle Creek among the pine trees just where the creek flowed out of Ross Coolie into the open country.

Throughout that merciless winter when the thermometer dropped to 60 degrees below zero and cattle died by the thousands, I was very busy. But the frequent sight of wolves or herds of antelope lent colour and interest to my lengthy rides. There were a number of newly arrived settlers in the Kelvinhurst district who were mostly of Scandinavian or German origin and towards February their condition became desperate. Certainly things would not have been so bad had there not been a fuel shortage due to the local mine owners refusing to operate their mine. I came to the realisation that it was up to Sergeant Quinn and myself to keep them from starving, and we were often on patrol for days at a time keeping in touch with them, and owing to the vast area we had to cover we rode out singly.

While I was doing evening stables a constable from Maple Creek came to the barn. He had ridden all day and his mount was tired out. I went to take his horse from him but he told me he had come on an urgent mission and that he was to report immediately to the sergeant. It appeared that Sarchi's daughter was married to a notorious horse thief who went by the name of Harrington, whom she had not seen for many a month. And now Harrington had stolen a team of bays and a team of greys and had last been seen heading south down the Ross Coolie, evidently hoping to reach his father-in-law's ranch, rest and set off again with the horses under cover of darkness, his objective being the U.S. border. 'Go get him,' roared Sergeant Quinn, pointing to me. My heart was beating fast. In a short while I was in the saddle and figured on reaching Sarchi's ranch after dusk, my scheme being

to intercept Harrington in the Coolie north of the ranch. It was 19
November – what a way to celebrate my birthday, I thought, as I
approached the ranch on foot seeking out as best I could all traces of
strange horses but, finding none, I continued the trail up the bottom
of the Coolie. The going was heavy as there had been a good deal of
new snow. The beauty of that ride by the light of a failing moon was
striking.

At a bend in the river where the willows were thickest I halted. It
must have been shortly before midnight and my horse started pricking
his ears and snorting. I pushed him on but he seemed restless and
unwilling to continue. Then on the far side of the bend I saw the bodies
of four horses lying bloody in the snow within a few yards of each
other. A fifth horse had crossed the creek and headed west up the steep
incline and on to the open prairie. I followed these tracks south and
reckoned them to be Harrington on his Indian cayuse. For some reason
he had shot the stolen horses and, having performed this shocking
deed, was riding with all speed towards the U.S. border. I jumped to
the ground and with bare fingers felt the snow inside the tracks and,
judging them to be over two hours old, slackened off my speed. The
tracks led me right through Willow Creek not far from the R.N.W.M.P.
detachment from whence he had continued over the border towards
the city of Havre in Montana. I was only a kid and no match for this
seasoned gunman, but I derived enormous support from the uniform
I was wearing.

As soon as I arrived at Willow Creek I alerted the constable there
who was able to telegraph the sheriff in Havre. Harrington had earned
himself an international reputation as a rustler and was also wanted in
the United States. A deputy sheriff rode out to intercept him and on
meeting a rider on a cayuse, answering to Harrington's description,
attempted to stop him. The man drew out a gun and shot the deputy
dead. Sometime later Harrington was caught in a British Columbia
logging camp by two constables of the Force, who worked as loggers
in this camp for two months before apprehending the man. He was
eventually hanged.

A month later while on patrol it was brought home to me more
vividly than ever the character of the land I had chosen. As I left the
house of a rancher where I had spent the night, I noticed that it was
a dark day with a rising wind and falling temperature, but dismissed
it. Some miles from any habitation I found myself finally overtaken
by a blizzard and was soon enveloped in blinding whiteness through

which I sometimes could not even see my horse's ears. Fear I had felt for a bunch of trigger-happy drunks was nothing compared to this. It was as if one was in a white hell. Instead of being roasted by a continent of flame, one was being consumed by white tongues of ice from above and below and from all sides. I felt too numb to think for the cold seemed to freeze my brain. Dropping my reins I left it to my horse. After about an hour of plodding and floundering through snow drifts the exhausted animal came to a standstill. Dismounting, I tried to lead. But my fur coat became caught in a barbed-wire fence which I now followed hopefully along until we reached a gate. Eventually we found the ranch house. It was the closest tangle I had had with death and I was lucky to have escaped. How did the animal find his way to safety, I wondered, was it sheer luck? Was he possessed of a kind of compass which directed him? Certainly it was not his sense of smell in that shrieking icy wind. How often in those days did a Mountie owe his life to his horse or dogteam.

After my horse had been cared for, I was grateful for the warmth of the kitchen. I could not but muse on the incident for the circumstance suggested for the first time to me the possibility of living intelligence beyond my own, a new unknown. Next day the wind dropped and I completed my patrol.

Once a week the mailman drove through the district by sleigh. It was an occasion I usually looked forward to but one day a letter arrived from my mother, her usually generous and expressive writing now shaky; her health had declined and she wrote that she did not wish to say anything which would distress me but that she was seriously ill. "I can tell you now", she wrote,

I was very ill again last summer. The doctors were frightened and another operation was out of the question, so they tried radium treatment. It is frightfully dear, 50 guineas each time. I had five treatments and now, thank God, they say I am practically cured, but it was a near thing. I wasted to a shadow but mercifully the evil has been averted, and I am now fat and well, though I dread any shock or trouble which might bring the mischief on again. You know our darling's death, and the shock began my illness, and then I can't help thinking that your going too made me very unhappy. I always bear up at the time and repress my feelings and then it tells on my health. So if you can come back I shan't be able to stand another parting, I just feel I can't bear it. Can't you be content to live happily on a little farm where we could all be together, or does it sound too dull after your exciting life, etc.?

So had the message of my beautiful but frail mother run, and I read it with eyes ill-attuned and emotions unable to grasp its appeal. So dull is youth. Since then with more expanded vision I have wondered who among such ladies was one so pitiful and fair.

My sense of humour which had stood me in such good stead through many scrapes was nil, for the issue brooded of no escape and awoke in me a deep feeling of responsibility for the first time, not only as an eldest son but in response to feelings as yet not experienced in my youthful heart.

I had by now fallen in love with the west and knew I would return to it later, but in the meantime I was impelled to return to England. To be by my mother's side? Yes, to some degree. That was natural, but I knew the 'spell of the west' had been broken and that I was free to be myself. All this new vision opened up as I sat re-reading her letter outside the Rushmore store. Each time I read it the chord that it struck in me deepened and I realised that in all this rugged challenge I had ignored – and all but lost – my focus on her acts and lovely graces. But this was not all. I knew well there were other reasons, although momentarily they were eclipsed, and I have since known that I was right in my decision to return to England. I immediately applied to purchase my discharge. The application took months to go through and in the meantime I was recalled to divisional headquarters. While there I made a lengthy patrol into the dry belt north of Maple Creek, on this occasion riding 386 miles to Montgomery's Landing on the South Saskatchewan River to settle a dispute between two families which had immigrated to Canada together from Galicia.

It seemed that they had settled on quarter sections of land bordering on each other and, knowing nothing about surveying, had come to an amicable agreement about the division of their land. One family planted potatoes and when these were ready to be dug the neighbouring family found that a potato furrow had wandered on to their land. All went well until the planters of the potatoes started to dig them up on the other's property and so the quarrel had begun. First they argued and then they fought. Sides were taken by their neighbours and armed with pitchforks and scythes they were ready to march against one another. At this point I appeared on the scene and as soon as they saw my stetson hat coming over the horizon they were reminded of the Cossacks in their own homeland and fled with the utmost speed into their picturesque white dwellings where they barricaded themselves in. At first it was difficult to communicate with them, but gradually I impressed upon them my need for water and food for my horse and they finally opened up and agreed that we should get together at a round-table conference. This was done by signs as I spoke no Russian at that time and they spoke no English. A table was placed out of doors and black bread and beer set upon it as an initial gesture of goodwill and then both parties being present I indicated that the potatoes which had been planted on the wrong side of the line should be harvested by the owner of the land where they had grown and then shared equally between both families. This plan was accepted and resulted in general handshaking and jubilation as I rode off towards the north.

The weather was clear and the sandhills shimmered in the heat. I was hoping to make a cabin on the far side of the dry belt by nightfall, but lost my trail and spent that night out under the stars, my head cupped in my up-turned saddle with the horse blanket as cover.

My horse was easy to catch as I had hobbled him and I set off again at dawn, but had still not found my way and both of us were in need of food and water. I continued on towards the north, however, closely shadowed by a persistent coyote who was ever silhouetted atop each sandhill behind me as I pressed on over the next. In the late evening I saw the outline of a cabin close to a slough on the northern limit of the sandhills. In true western style the door was unlocked for it was the custom of ranchers to leave their dwellings open to riders in need of shelter. Usually there was food in the cupboard and I was not disappointed in this instance. The blankets on the bed did not look too inviting so I rolled myself up in my horse blanket and slept on the floor. I was devoured by bedbugs during the night, but was grateful there had been no lice.

On the following night I reached a small settler's home. A Pole and his young wife had recently built themselves a one-room shack, a barn and dug a well. They were poor but their welcome was rich for they were most hospitable and after caring for my horse brought me into their home where the woman provided a plentiful fare of corned beef and beans. I was then invited to share the only bed – a mattress on the floor occupying almost half the floor space. I suggested I could sleep on the strawpile in the barn but they would not hear of it. The wife lay next to the wall, her husband then crawled in leaving the remaining third of the bed for me. In the early dawn the man got up to attend to the stock and I found myself for the first time in bed alone with a woman.

My Polish host having put me on the right trail I made short work of the remainder of the journey and reached Montgomery's Landing

in the late afternoon. This ranch, on the banks of the South Saskatchewan River belonged to an old timer, Geoff Montgomery, who lived
alone and was the local Justice of the Peace. Here I made my bed in
the tackroom where I could ward off the cooling night with a small
wood stove.

There had been only one felony that year in the district and the
crime was theft. A pile of rails belonging to a rancher, who intended
using them for building corrals, had allegedly been hauled away by an
Austrian settler and used for firewood. The rightful owner, having
discovered the culprit, laid a charge against him and it was therefore
my duty to bring him to justice. I had little difficulty in finding the man
and at once brought him before the JP.

A book, *The Criminal Code*, was part of the normal office equipment
of a JP's office, but Montgomery had not the vaguest idea of what it
contained and accordingly relied on my advice as to what punishment
to mete out to the accused whom he had already decided was guilty.
It was not my business to oppose his judgement but it was encumbent
upon me to carry out the sentence insofar as it was feasible. In my own
heart I was satisfied that the accused was no criminal in the common
sense of the term. The penalty, according to the criminal code, was a
$250 fine or six months' imprisonment in default. If the prisoner was
unable to pay the fine I would accordingly escort him to Maple Creek
in handcuffs – a four or five day's trip. The man had some land and
a few head of cattle and the problem was what to do about them if he
was committed to gaol. Apparently there was plenty of hay on his
small ranch, so I took the law into my own hands and now made the
following proposal to Montgomery. I assessed the prisoner's team of
horses as being worth at least $200. These I said would be impounded
until the spring and both the Austrian and his horses would remain
at Montgomery's ranch until that time – the man acting as chore boy.
Provisions were to be made for him to feed his stock as circumstances
permitted. Not only was this plan acceptable to both the JP and the
prisoner but I heard later that it had worked out to the satisfaction of
all concerned. With a light heart I now rode back to Maple Creek and
on arriving there found instructions awaiting me to proceed to Regina.

I had a way with horses and was now employed by the riding master,
Corps. Sergeant-Major Tom Dann, breaking broncos for the force.
Bronco busting is not every man's ambition, but I had already tried
my hand at it on the neighbouring ranches at Battle Creek and was
able to rope, throw and saddle a 'bronc' with a reasonable chance of

sitting him when he did his worst. The riding master was a tough guy who was intolerant of poor horsemanship or the lack of discipline. The abuse he hurled at the recruit who allowed himself to be unseated made hurt pride and bruised muscles feel like gentle caresses by comparison. If they objected to his language, he would invite them to put on the boxing gloves in the gymnasium. He usually got the better of it there, too, but not always.

Broncos are often as round as barrels when they come in off the range. I had broken a little mare and, wishing to accustom her to a ride, took her into the riding school where the riding master was putting some recruits through their paces. The sight of other horses galloping gave the range mare a happy thought – down went her head! She started bucking as only she knew how! The ride became disorganised; the recruits reined in to watch the fun. All might have gone well had not the mare's saddle begun turning; another two bucks and it was under her belly and I was on the ground. Bucking and squealing, she now weaved in and out of the recruits while the riding master grew almost apoplectic with rage. 'Get up on your blasted horse!' he roared. 'Who the hell told you to dismount?'

To fill a gap I was temporarily sent to Prince Albert where a French Canadian commanded a small detachment of police. Inspector Genereau had a beautiful white horse called Cordite which was put in my charge. A few days after my arrival a half-breed with a grudge against the law let the veterinarian's black stallion loose in the barn where we stabled our horses and when I went to feed them in the morning I found that he had wreaked his fury on all our geldings during the night including Cordite. I found the white gelding in a critical condition; he had kicked one leg right over into the next stall and was suspended on the partition with one hind leg dangling on either side of it. It called for all my resourcefulness to get him off the partition and all my horse-mastership to restore him to health – a most rewarding task, for Cordite responded to treatment in the most amazing fashion.

On unofficial occasions we wore cowboy boots and chaps and one such time while saddling Cordite for exercise I was called to the office. Thus, improperly dressed, I had to face my commanding officer. There had been a murder on the outskirts of the town. The inspector eyed my boots and chaps but without comment ordered me to take his horse and go down to the scene of the crime and arrest the murderer. Fetching my sidearms and tightening the cinch on Cordite I vaulted into the saddle and rode at full gallop to the scene of the crime. A small crowd of excited citizens was gathered outside a neighbouring house. One of them shouted, 'He's got a loaded gun in there.' I dismounted and with gun in hand advanced on the cabin. Hammering on the door I ordered the man inside to open up and to come out. At first there was no reply. I repeated this a few times and then heard a gunshot, followed by the thud of a body falling to the floor; the hard clatter of a gun as it hit the naked floorboards was unmistakable.

Stepping back a few paces I fired two bullets into the lock of the door and with all my force hurled myself at it. The door crashed inwards but was prevented from opening wide by the body of a man lying on the floor. Once again I charged the door and this time, before I could regain my balance, I fell over the body into a darkened room. The man had taken his own life. His wife, whom he had also shot, was still alive but died in hospital shortly after.

The case was dealt with on the same day as a coroner's inquest upon the bodies of a couple of railwaymen who had been killed in an accident in the freight yards involving a caboose. Thus in the brief space of two days I had seen death at close quarters for the first time. Taking witnesses and relatives to the mortuary was the worst part of it and the vision of the mutilated bodies which had suffered so violent a death haunted me for years. I dreamed of the waxiness of their flesh, the sightless stare of their eyes, the evidence of vacancy of human remains after the withdrawal of life! On that day something in me was deeply moved by the pitiable plight of human beings, for I could not reconcile the exuberance of life with the apathy of death.

After this experience I was not sorry to learn that my application to purchase my discharge had been granted and not much later I was on my way back to England. But I could hardly suspect that I was moving into a closer embrace with the image of death.

My trip across the Atlantic, which was made shortly after the *Titanic* disaster, was uneventful and upon arrival in Liverpool I went directly to Esher in Surrey where my mother had rented a small house on the London and Portsmouth road, and my sister Yvonne and Kenzie were with her.

The atmosphere, as soon as I entered the front door, was one of impending doom, for once again the dread disease had flared up.

The ravaging process of mother's illness, the worry it occasioned, and the strain of the lengthy vigil, was showing now on Kenzie. Her indomitable features, her eyes and mouth revealed the acceptance of coming tragedy. Too frail to hold in my arms as I had so longed to do,

I planted a filial kiss upon my mother's brow and whispered some of my feelings of love for her in her ear. It would have been impossible to say all that welled up in me at that time, for words seemed to choke me. She died the following summer and we laid her to rest in a grave next to Rollo's.

In the meantime I had joined a special reserve battalion of the Royal Irish Regiment and being satisfied that my little sister was duly cared for, I went into camp with my unit, once known as the Tipperary Militia, and a wilder month I have never spent.

3

"Pickelhaube"
and Barbed Wire

Carlyle and Gregsons were renowned for helping army exam aspirants over their fences and literally crammed them on subjects calculated to meet their needs at the examination table.

Kenzie's brother was headmaster of Uppingham College and education was her strong point, not that she knew anything about military matters, apart from admiring uniforms, but she was a wonderful support to me during that time. C and G's classrooms were not far from the hotel we usually stayed at on our visits to London, and it was in the heart of South Kensington and near the Natural History Museum which I liked visiting. Of course we had to apply ourselves during class, but at weekends a fellow student, Denis, and I used to 'do the town' together, and Denis who had a wealthy background, knew the ropes. He drove a sports model Rolls Royce and was dating Gaby de Lys, who was at the top of her music hall career, and I was much impressed.

On Saturday afternoons we sometimes went to Brooklands race track where Denis introduced me to his motor-racing friends, one of which drove a twelve-cylinder Sunbeam and took me for a test trial at what seemed to me to be an incredible speed. It was there I learned to drive and furthermore bought a car. This vehicle, which I got from a mechanic, was a Mercedes-Simplex, chain-driven, two-seater, 1909 model. It looked harmless enough when I got it, but I souped it up to resemble a racing car and although I doubt it could have done 60 m.p.h., I loved every bolt in it. Occasionally a sprocket would come off and I would have to go back looking for the chain, but it was all part of the game.

Denis also introduced me to the joys of the Empire Theatre where one could mingle with top-hatted youth and fashions of the metropolis.

It was here I experienced my first date. She was obviously liberal with
her affections but I now had an allowance from my mother's estate
and effected such places as Odanino's and the Piccadilly Grill, or
hung about the stage doors in search of chorus girls. It was there I met
Gertrude who was playing the leading role in *Kiki*. Looking back at
that period I am inclined to shudder but it was fascinating while it
lasted. My experience prospered in these matters for I learned faster
from Denis than I ever did at C and G's.

My next date was a girl whom I met under more formal circumstances. She was the younger daughter of Harrington Mann. The
Manns lived in Eaton Square in Belgravia and Cathleen and I went to
many parties and social gatherings together for, being a well-known
society portrait painter, Harrington was well-connected. At his studio
I met Rex Whistler, Augustus John, Singer Sergant and the Laveries
as well as many others and my consciousness of art in an academic
sense increased. So far as C and G were concerned, whether I passed
or not was luckily irrelevant, because at the outbreak of the First
World War I was automatically gazetted to the regular army, arriving
in France in good time for the Battle of Mons. It was a walkover for
the Germans and a victorious retreat for the British, depending upon
whose story you listened to. But for my part it landed me swiftly in a
prisoner-of-war camp in Germany. My role in the fighting was short
and inglorious. It actually ended from the moment my regiment, the
Royal Irish, moved out from its reserve position in a gravel pit close
to the bleak imposing structure of the Mons Insane Asylum. Our
orders were to advance over the hill on which the asylum stood and
down towards the Nimy Canal, which was to have been held by advance
units of our brigade. The air was heavy with a clinging mist and charged
with the muffled concussions of exploding shells.

The odds were altogether too great. On the way we met a squadron
of the 5th Irish Lancers and I watched grimly as a young subaltern,
flushed with his first brush with the enemy, brandished a bloodstained
lance above his head. An artillery horse, shot through the lung, snorting
scarlet froth through his nostrils, careened through our ranks as if
thrust from the netherworld. It all happened so quickly. We pushed
forward over the hill and found the Germans were isolating it with
intensive shell fire, backed murderously with machine-guns.

Marching in front of my platoon in traditional style, I was leading
my men to almost certain death. But what was one to do? The earth
on the hillside was being mashed by enemy shells while machine-guns

raked the ground we were crossing. Deadly detonations cratered splattering earth in all directions. The noise was deafening. Within a few minutes not a single officer in my company remained. Captain Mellor and three of his subalterns were killed almost instantly. Captain Barry-George and I were stricken with severe wounds and were carried painfully to the improvised dressing station prepared by nuns in the asylum. The inmates, terrified by the din, now burst from their confines and ran screaming into the battlefield where they mingled indiscriminatly with the soldiers. The asylum, our only place of refuge, now in a state of pandemonium, was being directly shelled and finally caught fire. As it burned to the ground the conquering hordes swarmed over the devastated land.

So ended 23 August 1914 and as the beauty of a summer's day reddened in the west and the melancholy notes of the German cease fire faded over the havoc around me, I kept thinking about the men I had lost contact with in that terrible battle and of my initiation into a world of death and destruction. A few of us wounded were moved to a small pub and from the floor of the tap room I could hear the moans and groans of many others in that darkness. In the early hours of the morning a priest loaded as many of us as he could into a car and took us to a hospital on the outskirts of Mons where for weeks I remained unmolested. It was, as it were, a backwater in a tumultuous floodtide of invasion. My memory remains soaked in gratitude for the tender care we received from the nuns who staffed that hospital. The cream of the land drifted in through the back door of that institution rather than fall into the hands of the invader. I watched a great raw-boned Irishman in a bed next to mine dying of wounds and witnessed the Sacraments of Peace being administered to him as gradually the essence of life ebbed from his Celtic frame leaving only an aura of stillness and peace.

Weeks later a monk came and sat by my bed. He was about to walk, he told me, to Antwerp which was still in Allied hands. I would be provided with civilian clothing and he would take me with him. We fixed a date and from then on I increased my daily walking exercise so as to be fit for the journey. In my ignorance, however, I broke what I afterwards learned was the golden rule of escape – I shared my plan with another. This other was Major X, a British military doctor who had been appointed by the Germans to visit the British wounded in the area. While he examined my wounds I asked him whether I could do the trip. His reaction was unexpected and violent for he saw the project as a violation of the Geneva Convention and held that while I was under the care of the Red Cross I should not endanger the lives of the nuns and medical staff by provoking reprisals. He had a point, but in my mind it conflicted with the duty of a prisoner to escape if and when he could. The enigma was, however, solved a day or so later when a party of German troops came to the hospital and took me away. I was then placed in a cattle truck train filled with British wounded bound for the German fatherland.

Next to me in the boxcar lay Stiven, a wounded lieutenant in the Royal Scots who wore a gold-rimmed monocle amid his unshaven red whiskers, and this on top of all the lies spread in the German press about the British being 'unkultured' savages who used expanding bullets, my comrade at arms presented a terrifying figure to the simple country folk who were our guards.

The trip to the fatherland took us five days owing to Germany's reverses on the Marne and we were constantly being side-tracked to make room for the reinforcements they were rushing to that front. The weather was very hot and at Aachen a very unfriendly reception awaited us. We had, up to that point, received neither food nor water since our departure from Mons. Nurses were ladelling water out of buckets for the benefit of the guards and I, noticing that Stiven's condition was desperate, his splintered shinbone having become gangrenous from lack of attention, asked for water for him. A nurse appeared at the door of our boxcar. Frightened by his appearance, she hurled the water in his face screaming, '*Englander Schweinhund*', and fled for safety.

At Minden on the Weser we were removed from the train and Stiven and I were taken under heavy guard to the military hospital where in a prison ward we were later visited by the staff doctor. This man declared me fit to go to a prisoner-of-war camp, but he looked at Stiven and said he couldn't go unless he was able to walk. 'I'll walk,' said my Scottish companion, but he quickly fell and that was the last I saw him, for he died shortly afterwards. From here I was sent to the Bismarkian fortress of Torgau.

Up to this point I had still clung to the hope that the debacle I had witnessed was only limited to our particular brigade, but when the guards opened the great doors my gaze fell on a depressing scene and my disillusionment was complete, for there seemed to be here assembled on the parade ground the whole of Britain's expeditionary force – a vast crowd of officers in khaki uniforms among whom were many French and Belgians.

I remained in German hands until I was interned in Holland in 1917 and during that time made various attempts to escape, but was checkmated with every attempt. Finally I contented myself with the thought that perhaps after all I was of more use where I was, for I had begun to consider and develop ways in which I could establish some form of intelligence system within the German encampment.

Most of my confinement was spent in Burg bie Magdeburg, a camp containing a handful of British, some Frenchmen and many Russians. Life was full of privations and irritations. The English were rather exclusive, the French full of cares, but the Russians, taking things philosophically, were extremely good company. Many of them were quite wild. There were men from Georgia, Turkistan, Siberia and the Ukraine. They were full of character and hospitable to a fault. To those who were not too conscious of the disadvantages of prison life, or over-concerned with keeping fit, it offered opportunities to learn languages or to study any other subject that came to mind. Many of these Russians were aware of that and took advantage of the chance of an English or French teacher. I found a Siberian, whose name was Docia Logwinoff and about my age. We agreed to reciprocate in teaching each other our languages. He had that sort of gentle yet forceful character, a power which came from within and drew me irresistibly to a point of common awareness of something excitingly profound and at the same time beautiful and of which he was quite unconscious. To me he epitomised the whole simple character of the wide Siberian landscape, yet he was no mere peasant of the soil. He had a deep yet natural brooding wisdom, but like the things of nature had a defencelessness against the evils of civilisation. He loved as only a child of nature can and was vulnerable through his heart. I flew into the friendship with him as a bird escapes into the vastness of its element and we found in each other a comradeship never to be repeated. Had this been on a more physical plane it would have been unnatural, but as it happened it was the truest form of expression imaginable. Together we read Milton, Tolstoy, Pushkin and Shakespeare in their own rich languages.

Docia was not always happy with his English lessons. He thought in Russian and the English language was too complicated for his pleasurable reading.

'Peter the Great,' he was fond of saying, 'said you can speak French to your lovers, German to your enemies, English to your shopkeepers, but Russian you can speak to anyone.'

'But,' I reminded my pupil, 'Russian is not a universal tongue, while English is becoming so.'

Docia smiled wryly, 'Why is it so complicated – why do you write Manchester and pronounce it Liverpool!'

Nevertheless, he learned to speak English fluently, though the formation of his sentences remained somewhat quaint.

Whatever social background he had he owed to his grandfather who, until he was banished to Siberia, had been a government servant. Together we played Lopka for physical exercise and chess to activate the mind. We smoked Russian cigarettes, played the balalaika, sang songs and drank endless glasses of tea. The months rolled on and the war reached a deadlock. Then, unhappily, this pleasant interlude came to a sudden end.

In the spring of 1916 a handful of British prisoners carrying their small belongings were marched out of the camp. I was among them. Winston Churchill, first Lord of the Admiralty, wishing to put a stop to the sinking of neutral shipping on the high seas by the Germans, had declared that any member of the crew of a German submarine captured while engaged in such warfare would be treated as a pirate. Shortly after he had made this dramatic announcement, two German subs, the U8 and U12, were sunk in the North Sea and thirty-nine of their crews were taken prisoner. On landing in England they were placed in naval detention barracks at Dartmouth where they were, according to the British reply to a United States Government enquiry, 'treated with humanity, given opportunities for exercise, provided with German books, subjected to no forced labour and are better fed and clothed than British prisoners of equal rank now in Germany'. Nevertheless, German reaction was swift. They chose, out of their great numbers of British prisoners-of-war, thirty-nine officers with names similar to those in high positions in Great Britain. Although my name is spelled differently to that of General Sir John French, then Commander-in-Chief of the British Forces, it came close enough for propaganda purposes and I was accordingly chosen for this particular reprisal.

Our prisoner-of-war camp was close to the small town of Burg where there was a gaol. This was now converted into a 'military detention barracks', by the simple act of having a sign painted and placed at the entrance which read *Garrizone Arrestanstalt* and here five of us were locked up into individual cells from which we were let out only once a day for brief exercise in the prison yard. Like circus horses round the sawdust ring we were made to walk for thirty minutes at five paces from each other in complete silence and without stopping. Nevertheless, the fresh air did us good and we were happy to see one another, even if we could not converse. For the balance of the day life was rather dull and uncomfortable as our beds were folded up against the wall, leaving only a prison stool to sit on. Besides the bed and the stool the only other article of furniture in the cells was a small washbasin, an earthenware crock and an inadequate corner cupboard. For company I had none except at night when the cell became alive with bedbugs which lived in the crevices in the wall.

About a month after we had been gaoled, the door of my cell was opened and I found myself face-to-face with a dapper little man in a blue overcoat, holding a bowler hat in his hand. Behind him stood the camp commandant, the gaoler, and a collection of officers of the German General Staff.

'I am the American Ambassador,' he said, 'have you any complaints ?'

To think in terms of complaint was absurd – where, after all, was one to begin ? Then it came to me and I answered slowly,

'Well, sir,' I replied, 'if this is supposed to be solitary confinement, I would like the bedbugs removed.'

The Ambassador's face never moved a muscle but his answer was positive.

'I shall see to that,' he said, as he departed.

That very day I was moved to a new cell and our general circumstances improved.

The fearful part about the organising abilities of the Germans, that made itself abundantly plain, was that they seemed so imperious, impersonal and inflexible with no more wisdom than a piece of machinery. What was worse they depended upon this organisation to win them the war. Their trust in the infallibility of these mechanical means of procedure caused them to adopt a kind of logic which resulted in the most appalling atrocities and belied their natural goodness of heart.

Late that summer, Churchill's place as First Lord of the Admiralty was taken by Arthur Balfour who saw fit to repudiate the arbitrary measures inflicted upon the German U-boat crews and had them sent to ordinary P.O.W. camps. Consequently, we were treated in like manner. We had been nine weeks in solitary confinement and upon returning to our P.O.W. camps we found many changes. To begin with I found that Docia had been removed and though I enquired after him I never saw him again.

Because I had now become implicated in several abortive escape
attempts, I was sent to a newly established camp in the north of Germany called Augustabad, presumably escape proof. It was about five
nights' walk from the Baltic and such neutral countries as Denmark
and Sweden and consisted of two large villas each in their separate
compounds known as Camps A and B. I was placed in B which was
full of possibilities from an escapee's point of view.

As mentioned, during my cramming period in London, I had made
the acquaintance of Cathleen Mann. With her I had developed a
sentimental attachment mostly taking the form of undemonstrative
admiration.

She was a very pretty girl and, above all, she had the talent of a
quick wit. She wrote to me regularly during my four years absence
as a prisoner-of-war. I conceived the idea of establishing a secret mode
of communication with her by which I could reveal things I did not
wish the censor to know of. In writing to her I employed three steps
in constructing a code, each step providing the key for the next. The
final step involved the use of a secret ink, made from a potassium
iodide solution which I acquired from the hospital orderly, ostensibly
to treat my wounds. A previous letter, written on glossy paper, referred
to my aunt, Mrs. *Washit* of *Inink* Road, *Bath*, England. Of course,
that meant wash in ink bath.

Having established a reasonably safe way of communicating with
her, I was now delighted when she wrote saying that she had landed
a job in the War Office. Many R.F.C. pilots shot down over the enemy
lines had undelivered reports which they had memorised and such
valuable facts as troop movements or gun emplacements, etc., were
worth relaying on to the girl for transmission to the appropriate
department. I felt that in this manner I was doing even more good
than being in the trenches. At first the War Office was sceptical and
unable to believe that anyone could be so foolhardy as to undertake
such a mission, and refused to accept even the hottest information
on troop concentrations as genuine. Time, however, caused them to
change their attitude.

While this was going on the British, wishing to deliver their first
big Handley Page bomber to Air Command headquarters in France,
entrusted what must have appeared as a monster plane to a young
test pilot who had never been out of England. The weather report
was fair. Nevertheless they ran into an electric storm over the Channel.
The instrument panel was put out of order and the plane was therefore

flying blind. The pilot decided to land in a field so as to make enquiries. He probably circled around the area before finding a good landing place. Both pilot and observer then set out in search of human life and each chose a different direction. A German patrol came out of an adjacent wood and captured the plane and also took the two members of its crew prisoner.

This, from the British standpoint, was a calamity but its sequel in some measure redeemed the incident.

The two prisoners-of-war were then sent to Augustabad in which the test pilot told me the whole story. It seemed that the German General Staff, wishing to exploit their good luck, had taken the pilot to where they were building their own bombers, specially designed to bomb London, so as to compare the two bombers' various features. They made the mistake of showing the test pilot their blueprints. Having a photographic memory the pilot memorised in detail what features he thought would be of value and together we now compiled a report which was in Cathleen's hands in less than two weeks' time, when she in turn took it to the War Office. In this way also the pilot was cleared of suspicions that the new Handley Page had been handed over to the Germans intact by one of their agents. His German name which had, however, for many generations become associated with Ireland, tended to substantiate treachery.

My secret ink was put to another purpose. I planned an escape and included this pilot in my scheme. I wrote for German money and maps and solicited a means of getting out of the country by boat.

The prisoner-of-war camp was situated on a lake in northern Germany among some well-wooded hills. It consisted, as I have said, of two big villas, called Camp A and B, each encircled by a high barbed-wire fence and about 300 yards apart.

Escape from a prisoner-of-war camp was one thing but getting out of Germany was a much more difficult one. In any case the project needed guts and very cautious planning.

Con (as I now called my pilot friend) and I agreed to go together. Cathleen had sent five one hundred mark notes concealed in the false bottom of a biscuit tin. The camp was guarded by a collection of old reservists called *Landsturm*, most of whom were farmers and peasants who were not too keen on militarism. Fritz was one of these, a kindly son of the soil. Of course he loved the fatherland but was completely unimpressed by war lords and their ambitions which resulted in frightful austerities for the ordinary people, depriving them of their

sons and imposing the strictest regime on their diet. Germans are by
nature a submissive race, ruled by overlords for millennia but this was
the twentieth century and they were no longer serfs. In any case a
hundred mark note to Fritz was a fortune. We had already primed him
with tidbits from our weekly Swiss parcels, things like coffee, butter,
or canned meat which were unobtainable in the stores due to the
British blockade. Fritz was posted at the entrance gate of the camp at
night every two weeks. It was arranged that he would turn his back at
a given signal from us; furthermore, he had purchased with my money
two second-hand bicycles which he had concealed at a certain point
in the surrounding woods.

Con and I were ready to go. We had collected some plain clothes,
concentrated foods, maps, and had trained around the camp grounds
so that we were fit to walk so many miles a day. We now only waited
for instructions from the War Office regarding getting out of the
country.

It was a Sunday and the leaves were falling off the trees. Geese,
with an ease I envied, could be seen taking off from the lake on their
way south. Fritz, on duty on the outside, jokingly aimed his gun at
them as they circled overhead. He would not be on duty at the gate at
night for another five days. At the daily roll-call one of the orderlies
employed in both camps gave me a written message from the other
camp. It read, 'Come at once, I must see you,' signed S.B.O. Now the
Senior British Officer in Camp A was Captain, the Hon. Barry Bingham,
who had won the Victoria Cross at the Battle of Jutland. My only
means of getting to him was by handing in my parole card – this
facility had only recently been extended to us. We had been issued with
cards each bearing the signature of the bearer and also that of the
Commandant, and by handing the card to the sentry at the gate one
was automatically on parole. One could go to the other camp but was
unable to escape or in any way violate the laws by helping others to
escape. If I had escaped while on parole the British government would
have to send me back.

On reaching Camp A Barry Bingham took me to a bench in the
garden between the villa and the lake. There had been frost and all that
remained of the allotments, where vegetables had been grown, were
bamboo sticks.

'See those bamboo sticks,' began the Captain. 'They are vents for
a tunnel we have dug during the past months. My gang numbers
sixteen. The tunnel is entered by a cupboard in the dining room and

its outlet reaches the bank at the lake shore. We have postponed the breakthrough pending the arrival of instructions from the Admiralty with whom I have been in contact. The instructions for getting out of the country finally reached us yesterday.'

He pulled out of his pocket a piece of paper no bigger than a postage stamp. It was a minute photograph of a typed message and it could only be read with a powerful magnifying glass.

'I received this message,' continued Barry, 'hidden in a prunestone.'

'But why are you telling me all this?' I enquired.

'Because your name is mentioned as one of the men I must take with me.' He then continued, 'The problem is that now we have received our instructions I cannot delay any longer. It's been tough on the boys waiting this long; besides winter is approaching and it will be cold sleeping out at night.'

I saw immediately what this meant to our own plans and, being on parole and in a different camp from Barry Bingham (which the Admiralty obviously knew nothing of), I had no alternative but to return to Camp B and prepare for the inevitable search following this escape.

That night the whole party of sixteen got out through their tunnel. Barry and two or three with him were captured within a short distance from the camp, and for the rest they eventually reached a small wood on the shore of the Baltic Sea, a short distance from Rostock. Here they hid, and following the Admiralty's instructions they sent the only German-speaking member of their party to the fishing harbour of Rostock where he was to contact the captain of a small yacht flying a certain burgee. From there on this captain would take over and sail to a point on the shore where the party would embark for a neutral country. But on reaching the fishing harbour this emissary found it completely encircled by a barbed-wire fence and in seeking an entrance he was accosted by a plainclothes man and arrested.

After waiting some time the leader of the party sent a second man, but his fate was no better than the first and as the party had by then exhausted its food supplies and was suffering greatly from the cold they gave themselves up.

The *Kriegsministerium* in Berlin were furious at this escape and drastic changes were immediately made in the camp personnel and life thereafter was full of privations and reprisals. Censorship too was tightened up. A new fumigating box was distributed to camp censors into which all letters would have to be put before being expedited. This would disclose all secret inks.

One morning my pilot friend came into the room.

'What have you done with that letter you wrote last night?' he enquired anxiously.

'You mean . . .? Yes, why, I posted it this morning!'

'Well, we must get it back at once or you'll be in between a wall and a firing squad!'

The censor was just leaving for his midday meal and I caught him as he was locking the door of his office.

'Going for your lunch Herr Censor?' I enquired.

'*Jawohl.*'

'Would you care for a can of butter for your bread?'

'*Ja.* I agzept mit bleasure.'

The man beamed, for they were very strictly rationed and we prisoners received weekly parcels which were kept in his office. He opened the door again and led the way into the parcel office. I took a rapid look at the fumigating box which stood wide open in the centre of the room and could see my letter hanging inside it by a clip. I whipped it out while the censor was in the parcel room.

'Und here is your box, Herr Kapitain. You have just one can of butter left.'

'You are entirely welcome to it, Herr Censor,' I assured him amiably.

Shortly after it was agreed between the belligerents that all prisoners-of-war who had been three years in a prison camp should be sent to a neutral country for internment until the end of the hostilities. It fell to my lot to be sent to Holland where I remained until the signing of the Armistice in 1918.

Scheveningen was chosen as the district to which British interned prisoners-of-war were to be restricted under a Dutch commandant. However, it was my very good fortune to escape this tedium because the doyen of the diplomatic corps at the Hague, Il Duca di Calvello, who was acquainted with my father, invited me to come and help look after the interests of the vast numbers of Italian prisoners still in Germany. To this end a bureau was opened at his legation and I was to take charge of it. Naturally I was anxious to do what I could to relieve their unhappy lot. In my spare time I used to take the Duke's younger son Paul for outings and we became life-long friends. After the restrictions of a life of confinement the social amenities of the Hague were most enjoyable.

But there was another side to the matter. The long years spent in captivity, which included, as I have related, months in solitary confinement, had vanished and liberty now gave me a strange, almost terrifying sensation of freedom and for a while I was unable to cope. Women! I had almost forgotten what they looked like and here in Holland they were wonderful: wonderful service was rendered to us internees by Miss Vulliamy, Baroness van Breenan, Sir Francis D'Arcy Osborne, Lady Susan Townley, and others. The last named was the wife of the British Minister Plenipotentiary to Holland – a woman of great ability and determination who, however, was sometimes too impulsive. While declaring the new Hexham Abbey Y.M.C.A. hut open at the Hague she threw out her arms to an audience to British internees.

'Men,' she said, her voice trembling with emotion, 'since you came here all we women have become mothers.'

Then seeing the double meaning of her words, she turned to the press and asked them not to record what she had said. It, however, speaks well for her sense of objectivity that she later wrote a book called *The Indiscretions of Lady Susan.*

It was in connection with my Italian prisoner's bureau that I once paid a visit to the British Vice-Consul who, as it happened, was engaged in contra-espionage in Holland. The web of my connections grew and I found myself, almost without a conscious decision, establishing patterns which would influence my future role in the European drama.

At this point in the war there was much smuggling out of Holland of materials needed by the Germans and though it was done in an air of desperation there were often amusing consequences. There was a shortage, for instance, of rubber due to the Allied blockade of Germany and bicycle stealing became very highly organised; since bicycles were the common means of locomotion in Holland and were to be found everywhere propped up against walls and street curbs, the deft thief could easily rip off the tires and then throw the rest of the bicycle into the neighbouring canal. The tires were then brought to central collecting points, the rubber melted down and smuggled out to Germany. On one occasion, while incidentally noting the loading of a consignment of green peas to Germany, one of our consular staff saw some of these falling from a burst sack and found that when they struck the ground they bounced unnaturally high – they were all made of rubber. Bulbs, too, were found to be going to Germany in unusual quantities, but this enigma was quickly solved when we learned that they contained acids valuable for making explosives. But these were but the final hours of the war, most of mine having been spent, I felt, in constraint on the periphery of the drama.

The process of readjustment in the aftermath, when the young have been deprived of natural outlets and the old frustrated in many ways, is not quick. Concepts had to be overhauled or scrapped to suit the level of the nation's advance. In an outer sense a prison life was a retardant; the progress of a people under pressure of active warfare, rapid. I felt out of it, bewildered and nervous. I was not ashamed. I had done nothing shameful, but all the same there lurked a strange feeling of guilt and the beginning of much soul searching.

War effort is spurred on by propaganda machinery. I had been subjected to propaganda, too, but it had fed my mind on depressing facts and all too often, lies. It had tried to discredit the Allies and enlarge upon their failures while ignoring their successes. Those at home had seen one side of the picture only, now they rejoiced over their victory. A returning prisoner saw a different picture in the back of his mind. For my part, I felt I had missed out on an important segment of history. I just hadn't taken part in it. I had been passed over. From a military standpoint, experience, seniority and so forth, I was finished and should have quit right there. But I was so mixed up in my mind that I did not know what to do. Indeed, I hardly knew any more who I was and my sense of purpose and direction was largely shattered.

4

The Lightning
Out of the East

My cousin, Rosamond ffrench, invited me to Monivea Castle and I was glad to accept. The old family home, which had been the property of Robert Percy ffrench, had been inherited by his only child Kathleen and since she lived on her enormous estates in Russia she permitted her uncle 'Atchie' and his unmarried daughter Rosamond to live there.

Kathleen, known as the wealthiest Britisher in Russia, had been imprisoned by the Communists and her estates confiscated. Atchie (Acheson) having died, Rozzie lived on in the castle alone and was regarded by the country folk in Galway as the chatelaine. She had, in fact, lived up to the role for so long that she felt she belonged there as a fixture. In the so-called 'bad times', she had not been molested and the castle survived a rash of burnings and pillagings which spread all over Ireland. As much as Rozzie was popular, Kathleen was looked upon as an absentee landlord, in fact a *persona non grata* in Ireland. Such was the situation when I returned to the family home that Christmas of 1918.

To announce the homecoming of a Monivea ffrench, a hunt was called and Rozzie invited the Galway Blazers to meet at the castle. This was the red-carpet treatment and after the intervening years of uncertainty meant a great deal to me. There was, however, a vast difference between riding to hounds on a pancake saddle and sitting on a bucking bronco with a Western outfit. I hadn't sat on a horse for five years and the stone walls which divided the fields of Galway filled me with a sense of insecurity and foreboding. But I felt there was a challenge here and that the honour of the Monivea ffrenchs was at stake, so I rode with the best of them until I was stiff and sore.

When I returned Rozzie was awaiting tea before the turf fire in the big hall. She motioned me into a comfortable chair and in the warmth

52

of our old home my fatigued body grew relaxed. I fell to musing. Something in me attuned itself to the spirit of the family; an insurgent sense of belongingness welled up in my heart; a part of me belonged to the place and there awoke a deep feeling for it . . . to dwell in, to be identified with and to blend into this ancient home. The maid brought in the tea and some letters. One of them, addressed to me, was from the War Office and it contained interesting news, news that was to set the tone of my life for the next two decades. Someone in a special branch wanted to see me. It connected up in my mind with some information I had picked up in the press concerning the government's growing interest in what was going on in the new Soviet Russia. Europe's economy was vitally dependent upon its great eastern neighbour at that time and it was not geared for Russia's retraction into complete isolation. The trend of things there, much as it shocked the free world, was fraught with interest and had at all costs to be watched. And now diplomatic relations had been severed. These things I knew, but I had not anticipated having to play a part in England's relations with the Soviets. My time at home had come abruptly to an end.

The next day a jarvey car was ordered and when it drew up to the castle I found a shaggy two-year-old in the shafts steaming to be off. We covered the six miles to Athenry Junction at the gallop, but it was all to no avail for, as we sped over the railway bridge, I saw my train disappearing into the distance. According to the station clock the train was not yet due. I expostulated with Mr Clancy, the station master, whose glib reply was simply that 'the punctuality of the Irish Mail was often to the inconvenience of the passengers.'

I arrived in London a day late and found my way to the address given me in the letter. As I entered I speculated on what new phase of my life was opening up before me. The play began almost immediately. By roundabout means I was eventually shuffled on to another place in London where, high up in the attic labyrinth of a large building, I was greeted by a very pretty young lady.

'So this is where you've been hiding, Cathleen,' I said, recognising my friend, the artist's daughter with whom I had corresponded while I was a prisoner-of-war. She put her finger to her lips.

'Not a word,' she cautioned, and led me through an intricate maze of narrow passages to a small office. A youngish Colonel in the uniform of an officer of the Life Guards came forward to greet me. It was Colonel Stewart-Menzies later referred to by those who worked for him as S.M. My head was in a whirl as this unexpected meeting with Cathleen began to expose part of the picture.

'I have a job to offer you in Stockholm,' he began, 'holding a position as Assistant Military Attache. I expect you are anxious to get back to work. It will be no picnic and carries with it great responsibilities and is, of course, highly secret.' He went into further details which ended in a 'Now, think it over and come again tomorrow.'

I was ferreted back through the same maze of passages and in a short time found myself a little dazed looking at myself in a Bond Street window. My decision was already made and I was wondering what I might look like in some disguise – a beard, perhaps? England had no particular cause for secrecy with Sweden but with Russia, oh! *Eta buila drugaya riba* – that's another matter. My Russian was quite fluent, but I had never been on Russian soil. The thought of perhaps doing so gave me a peculiar feeling. The next day I was once again led into the Colonel's office.

'Well,' he said, 'I take it you have decided to accept the job?' I nodded in the affirmative and there followed a lengthy period of general explanation of what it entailed.

'I'll take you to see the Chief,' concluded the Colonel and this time I, who was over six feet tall, banged my head as we passed up some steps and through a lower passage than before. We entered a larger room than the Colonel's, crammed with such a number of intriguing objects that my gaze was distracted in many different directions.

The Chief, who wore the uniform of a captain of the Royal Navy, was busy writing at a roll-top desk. He was a thick-set man with weather-beaten face and was possessed of a thick shock of grey hair. He had lost a leg in some nameless battle. His features reminded me of a Roman Emperor for they were striking in their lines of strength; his mouth almost cruel in its determination. He did not ask us to sit down but, swinging around in his chair levelled his eyes at mine. It was a curious, unforgettable gaze which said, 'I'll never let you down – don't you ever dare do so to me.'

'You'll be under a Major Scale in Stockholm who will give you all further details about your work. The Colonel here will see to your transportation. Good luck!' he said cheerily, putting out a powerful hand to shake mine.

Sunday morning, after a harrowing sea voyage through a field of limpet mines, I arrived in Stockholm. It was a bright, cold January day in 1919 and the party which met me, consisting of Major Scale, his wife and secretary, was going out skiing. I was diplomatically attired in dark suit, overcoat, bowler hat and spats. But starchiness was not in the Major's line.

'Come on, get those ridiculous clothes off and come out with us,' he pressed. 'We have some extra skis for you.' I could not change my clothes because my registered luggage had not yet arrived, so I put the skis on over my London shoes, spats and all and in a dark overcoat and bowler hat very much enjoyed my first skiing experience. I got covered in snow as, of course, I fell repeatedly. The other skiers who saw me floundering about in such a manner could hardly believe their eyes; but I joined the Major's party in laughing until none of us could stand up.

The next morning at the office I was busy reading files and getting up-to-date with what was going on. Most of the important information about Russia seemed to come from an agent working under several assumed names, but known to us as Paul Dukes, secret agent S.T. 25. My designation was S.T. 36.

Paul Dukes was the answer to a spy-writer's prayer. He had knocked about Tsarist Russia as a boy, spoke the language perfectly although he had a slight accent, had a flare for journalism, a keen sense of the dramatic and a sensitive nose for important information. Above all he was intelligent, courageous and good-looking. Vladimir Pitch Mianor, alias Nicholas Lenin, who had been harbouring in Switzerland, had been wheeled in by the Germans to ignite a highly inflammable situation which had been first created by the half-measure merchant Kerensky and later Trotsky. Lenin then proceeded to put Karl Marx's theories into practice. He and his associates plunged Russia into the chaos and confusion of a violent revolution. When the latent elements of evil in a land are stirred by violence, the worst will always rise to the top and when the destructive phase is over the trick is removing them from their positions of authority without further revolution. It is these disreputables and fanatics that distort and debase such ideals as may have actuated the revolution and the result in this instance was the Stalinistic regime which eventually followed.

My superior, Major Scale, was tall, handsome, well-read, intelligent, with a debonair manner which endeared him to everyone. At his villa on the outskirts of Stockholm or at the office, I met with many members of the cast of perhaps the greatest single political drama of our time – Litvinoff, Generals Mannerheim and Udenitch, Gulkevitch, Bruce Lockhart, Arthur Ransom, Leslie Sharpe and, later, Lieutenant Agar who won his V.C. sinking the Communist fleet in Krondstadt.

The duties of an assistant military attache are varied and it fell to me to assist a couple of demobilised British flying officers to establish a civil flying school near Stockholm.

They had brought with them two Avro planes and were eager to initiate the novelty of civil aviation among the Swedes who responded to the idea with enthusiasm. To many it was a new form of sport after the restrictions of the war years.

However, my respect for the law of gravity was still beyond compromise. I was quite content to remain on terra firma. Nevertheless, my pride caused me to accept an invitation by these two intrepid Englishmen to lunch at their airfield and make a flight with them. I had up to then never been near a plane, let alone fly in one, and though the idea of making a maiden flight filled me with apprehension I was too proud to refuse the challenge.

I accordingly found myself climbing into the cockpit behind the pilot's seat, fastening my seat belt, fitting my goggles over my flying helmet and preparing myself inwardly for the takeoff.

The exhilarating rush of air upon the upper part of my body, which was exposed to the elements, was now bellowing my cheeks, obliging me to close my mouth tightly. With a sudden upward lurch and a feeling of complete loss of stomach the earth receded rapidly and fragments of cloud rushed down to meet us. The glistening Swedish landscape became a map slightly revolving beneath us. My head too was revolving but I thought I saw the pilot make a circular motion with his hand. Could this mean that he was going to loop the loop? We were still climbing when suddenly the plane took a sickening nose dive and then as if every ounce of me had been loaded with lead the plane turned upwards and over. The rapid change of weight from feather to pig-iron seized me – from drop to climb. I looked up and saw the map of Sweden, then over and down until it seemed as though my destination in slow motion was the sky. The plane righted for a brief second then down again in a crescent curve until the nose of the plane pointed to the sun, and then losing all speed we slid backward, tail first, down and up, in a curve until the tail looked at the sun and the propellor was making magic circles of light towards the earth. This was, I learned later, a 'falling leaf'. But this rocking chair progress downward was suddenly turned into a spiral nose dive, during which the whole landscape revolved rapidly over my head and the plane spun to earth. Thank heaven the pilot flattened out and landed in good order as if the whole fantastic exercise had been commonplace.

With staggering gait I reached the hanger where my pilot's mate had prepared a picnic lunch. I looked at the fare of sandwiches and beer and wondered when my stomach would catch up with me.

Some months later a flotilla of flying boats belonging to one of our southern allies came to the Swedish capital on a propaganda mission and advertised that they would fly under a bridge close to Stockholm. It was Sunday and the weather being fine large crowds had gathered to witness the spectacle. The said bridge spanned a deep canyon-like fjord and the people upon it blocked all traffic. But the gallant commander of the flotilla decided that the wind conditions were not ideal. A lengthy delay caused the tense crowds some frustration. Then all attention was suddenly diverted to two specks in the sky approaching from the direction of our British pilot's airfield. The two Avros now commanded the attention. They were not content to fly under the bridge but had to loop the loop over and under the laden structure and then disappeared into the distance as fast as they had come.

The impact upon the watching crowds was one of utter amazement. A worthy citizen seeing this feat of bravado exclaimed, 'Some propaganda!'

This improvised incident became the subject of a good deal of diplomatic interchange and a lot of smoothing down of irate feelings, but it was eventually forgotten.

During the year I was in Stockholm, the centre of the political drama had moved to Finland, where Major Scale transferred his office in the autumn of 1920. Up to then my experience had taught me that, from a state of well-being, I had to be able to accept humility – even degradation – and now I was in the process of learning how harmful human thought could be, spurred on by revolutionary zeal lacking in wisdom. Communism seemed to me rightly conceived, wrongly centred and, accordingly, a danger to itself and to the world in its execution. At first I thought its abuses were caused by individuals misapplying their powers. Both love and hate it seemed to me were opposites of the same force and controlling factors in the life of man and I disliked such domination.

If Communism rose up as a power it would, I reasoned, inevitably challenge a civilisation based on personal gain. They might even cancel each other out. If at the back of Communism there were those manipulating power, so also behind the non-Communist countries was a gang of international financiers in control and it would ever be so while man's values were dominated by greed. A change of heart, I reasoned, was needed and until that took place it was idle to compare the different brands of ideals being expounded, for they were all various states of a revolution. I realised with a certain despair that probably nothing would bring about a change of heart but an epoch of frightfulness and devastation. And I began to wonder about the role in which I was finding myself in the midst of all this. At that time I tended to look upon Communism as an irresistible force and upon anti-Communism as an immovable mass because, it seemed to me, the principles upon which my childhood beliefs had been based were themselves immovable. Yes, my period of retardment had come to an end. I was receiving a kind of mental kick in the pants and was better able to accept responsibilities. Oohna was the Major's private secretary and her office efficiency was what we all grew to rely on. Quick-witted and pretty with a keen sense of humour, she was a very reliable woman to whom we all easily related. When the time came for the office to move to Helsingfors, as the Finnish capital was then called, it was Oohna that we all looked to for details.

At the time Major Scale's outfit moved to Finland the White Russian offensive against the Reds had just about collapsed. This, of course, need not have been, but they did not get real support from the Allies who had little trust in them. In that respect Lloyd George was astute. The chief anxiety of the British arose from an erroneous idea that Russia was a country swelled with an abundance of cereals, lumber and other products so badly needed in post-war Europe. The facts were otherwise. It has taken Russia over sixty years to approach a state of industrial stability.

There was now a great deal more work at the office, but also more freedom and fun. After Stockholm, Helsingfors seemed alive. Paul Dukes describes it as one of the unhealthiest spots in Europe and a feeling of tenseness was certainly predominant. There were many Swedes and Russians as well as Finns, the Swedes mostly belonging to the pro-German group. The great meeting place was a first-class hotel called the Societets Huset and there I liked to go and meet people in my off time.

Following Britain's recognition of Finnish independence, Lord Acton was sent to Helsingfors as Minister Plenipotentiary. He was three-quarters German, being the son of the famous historian and of a Bavarian mother. Clever and farsighted he lacked, however, candour, and his first appearance in public eventually cost him his job. It was on the occasion of a banquet and being the guest of honour he should have kept to non-controversial subjects. Instead he chose for his theme, 'The lightning cometh out of the East', and thereupon aired such opinions as the inevitability of Communism. The next day the papers reacted so furiously that Lord Acton kept to his house. On 27 February, while crossing the market square in Helsingfors, his car was fired upon, the first of numerous incidents which, luckily,were without casualties. Lord Acton was too German to be British, too intolerantly 'efficient' to play the game of 'muddle through' to gain time. He saw no future in Finland as an independent state and was merely telling them that eventually their fate depended upon Russia. Whatever the case, it was, perhaps, an unhappy moment to say so. A month later he was recalled.

News, which had diverse ways of reaching me, arrived from Moscow regarding my cousin Kathleen ffrench. She had been at her palatial residence on the Volga when the tidal wave of the Revolution had broken over that district, and she had been dragged off to the common gaol while the rabble ransacked her property. Many art treasures of national importance had been saved for the public museums, but hundreds of smaller objects such as miniatures, of which she had a famous collection, were looted; her gold plate, which numbered no less than four hundred *couvers*, had disappeared.

She was I suppose autocratic, but kind withal and shared the beauty and grandeur of her estates with her friends. The local regiment of Lancers wore a magnificent uniform and were, in fact, as gallant and dashing a lot as could be found in the Russian cavalry. Their attendance at balls and other receptions at Kathleen's palace was frequent. Of their officers one in particular, Count Orloff, was Kathleen's friend. Some days after her arrest the Colonel, seeing his opportunity to join forces with Admiral Kolchak commanding the White Russian forces on the eastern front, decided to leave by special train and called for volunteers. His officers unanimously agreed to accompany him with the exception of Kathleen's friend young Orloff, who demurred. That evening he bribed the guards of the prison to let him speak to her.

'I will not leave you,' he whispered through the bars. But Kathleen persuaded him to go.

'I am British,' she argued, 'they dare not kill me, but you they will shoot for certain if you stay.' On her bidding he joined the troop.

After several days of halting progress the train reached Lake Baikal and stopped at Slyndyanka not far from the Mongolian border. One of the officers' wives, rather than suffer separation from her newly-married husband, had dressed herself up as an officer in order to travel with them. All had become very trainbound and being unable to bear the confinement any longer she got out onto the platform to stretch her legs. Her husband, not wishing her to go alone, accompanied her. The uniform quickly attracted attention and soon they were surrounded by a mob of angry peasants. There were threatening words and some members of the Red Army joined in the scuffle. Seeing his friends in danger, Orloff rushed to their resuce. Grasping the seriousness of the situation and fearing that the rest of his officers might become involved, the Colonel ordered the train to pull out of the station which it proceeded to do with full steam. The last that was seen of Orloff and his friends at Slyndyanka were their prostrate bodies being trampled by the mob.

In 1920 Lady Marling, the wife of a diplomat, was in charge of Red Cross activities concerned with repatriation of interned British subjects in Russia. Her headquarters were at Terioki, close to the Karelian Isthmus. Normal communications between Russia and

Finland were at this time disrupted, for a state of open warfare existed between the two countries. A small river called Siestro formed the frontier in this sector and its one and only railway bridge had been blown up. Down by its ruins was a small hut occupied by members of the Finnish frontier guard. From this point, hundreds had set forth across the ice of the river in an attempt to reach the sinister city of Petrograd. A few had made it but many had perished after being hunted down by Red Guards. It was at this hut that exhausted refugees, many of them having narrowly escaped death, arrived and it was here on a cold March morning that I received a call that Kathleen ffrench had reached the safety of Finnish soil.

No longer was she the elegant lady of property, but a little old woman tired in body and spirit who had lived under the threat of a firing squad for three years. I met her and accompanied her to Lady Marling's headquarters. She was placed in a quarantine camp but was allowed out for walks. It was in this manner that she and I found ourselves sitting out on a sandbank by the Finnish gulf in a backwater of the flood tides of revolution. We looked out across the glaring sheet of snow-covered ice towards Kronstadt. It seemed as if spring was trying to come; there actually was a little warmth in the sun; the pine trees emitted a resinous smell. Slowly and deliberately she told me her story, talking about the ordeal she had been through and of her shattered life. I tried to understand the significance of it all in terms of my own experience, but it defeated me and I fell to offering sympathy though I felt that what I said was shockingly inadequate. It was not sympathy she needed, but friendship. How often those who are getting older are thrust through the eye of the needle. Deprived of worldly possessions and given the opportunity of going forward towards a higher plane, how few have passed the test, remaining involved with their worldly goods, mourning their loss, and finally going out with the things they had clung to – out into oblivion. Kathleen shuddered; she felt cold and, charging me with some commissions, returned to camp.

After this I had a very busy time. My chief was away, and General Udenitch's army had collapsed. Also General Scobalsine's northern White Russian forces had retreated into Finland and laid down their arms. The fight against Red Russia in the north was over.

Kathleen would be in London in the first week of April where she had a house. I wired Rozzie; her reactions were not favourable. Back in Helsingfors my pending tray was stacked high – a case of whisky and another of Madeira had arrived by diplomatic bag and the former had been shattered on the journey. It was a major disaster with St Patrick's Day so close. Madeira is too heady a wine for steady drinking and there were many casualties.

Among my opposite numbers in the other diplomatic missions in Finland was a Captain Quisling, a Norwegian, afterwards a prominent Nazi. We met occasionally and he always struck me as one in need of psychoanalysis, a form of treatment gradually becoming recognised at that time. My suspicions proved to be right.

Finland had been part of Imperial Russia and when the 1917 Revolution against the Tzarist regime exploded a considerable portion of the Finnish population had joined in. But Finland had been dominated by Sweden and their influence was still very strong and this now asserted itself. Indeed General Mannerheim himself was partly Swedish and had served in the army of Imperial Russia. He now accepted the leadership of the anti-revolutionary element in Finland and, forming the White army of Finland, allied himself with the Germans in pushing the Red Finns north into the region of Murmansk towards Petsamo.

Mannerheim's interest was to rid Finland of the Red Finns. The Germans, who were running short of war materials, hoped to capture the enormous Allied munition dump at Murmansk, an ice-free port in northern Russia.

Disorganised elements of the Red Finnish army were retreating into the area at Petsamo where a Canadian colonel was commissioned to organise them into a unit calling itself the Finnish Legion. These men were under British military discipline and were put into British uniform and made excellent soldiers.

While all this was going on negotiations for the recognition of the independence of White Finland were in progress – it was a bizarre situation. But just as the drama had reached its zenith the Germans signed the 1918 Armistice and their troops in northern Finland were withdrawn. The independence of Finland became an accomplished fact on 6 December 1919, and everyone thought the time had come to rejoice under the regency of Mannerheim the Strong. But for us there was a problem, what was to be done with the men of the Finnish Legion ? We approached the Regent who declared that if any of them set foot in Finland he would have them shot. Finally we reached a compromise by renting an island off the coast of Finland on which they could have temporary sanctuary. In order to ensure their safety we placed them under the supervision of a detachment of the East Surrey regiment. From here, and with some subtle negotiations with the

Canadian government, they were finally absorbed in that dominion; and as the president of the largest lumber 'company' in the West later told me, 'If ever we get trouble in one of our camps you can be sure of who had started it.' As wild as these Finns were I have always admired them for they are real men.

The stream of refugees to Finland and repatriated prisoners of war was increasing, the world was growing less tense and the more normal heartbeats of Lombard Street and Wall Street produced the natural flow of its commercial bloodstream. There was a note of optimism in the air. News reached me of secret plans for opening up trade negotiations with Soviet Russia.

In the spring of 1920 the time had come, it was thought, for Russia to send an envoy to Britain; the question was how to get him out through the ring of antagonised countries surrounding the Soviet state on all her frontiers. By now I was pretty well organised in a material sense, but was suffering from a delayed reaction after my imprisonment in Germany. Besides, political pressures on me personally were building up.

One bright, cold morning I got out of the train at Viborg and had bacon and eggs at the Hotel Andre while awaiting my connection to Terioki. The occasion was unique and I confided to my batman, an ex-sergeant of the Finnish Legion, that he was to use my V.P.K. camera with the utmost precision and discretion. The event was the arrival at Bielostrov of a trade delegation from Soviet Russia headed by M. Krassin and it had been left to me to make all necessary arrangements with the local authorities. It entailed a short and local armistice and all the arrangements for a special train to Abo where the delegation would embark for Sweden en route for England.

During breakfast my batman laid the morning paper on my lap. The headlines were about Krassin's imminent arrival. So! The news had leaked out! Even then, the full impact of the importance of the occasion did not occur to me. I was not given to contemplation or to study all the implications involved, historical or speculative. I was, as indeed it often fell to me to be again in the future, the one who triggered the initial step in a vast drama. My concern was to see that the staff work for which I was responsible went smoothly and this proved easier in the political field than on the military front. The military personnel were all members of Mannerheim's reactionaries.

As I have said, General Mannerheim had been leader of the forces of liberation from the Russian yoke; he was worshipped by the army but had now stepped down from the regency in favour of a peacetime government. The liaison, therefore, between the politicians, the army and the railway authorities was tricky.

On Palm Sunday a slight mist hung over the Karelian Isthmus from the Finnish Gulf to Lake Ladoga. Across this area the telegraph wires had been busier than usual as negotiations went forward between Helsingfors and Moscow for the transit of the Krassin delegation.

By 6.30 the following morning I, who had kept in touch with Lord Acton in Helsingfors, moved forward to the frontier and, after several false alarms, Lieutenant Daniels of the Finnish army came out of the hut with a white flag. The delegation arrived at the same time as a trainload of refugees. Lady Marling had enlisted volunteers from all the local services to attend to the needs of the new arrivals. The station of Bielostrov was indeed a busy scene and the advent of the first Communist delegate to the free world went almost unnoticed. There were twenty-five members to the delegation including one small boy. The party came down the snow-covered bank onto the ice of the River Siestro. Their papers were examined by a Finnish officer and then, under heavy guard, they walked to Bielostrov station where they got into their special train. There was no fuss, no press, no photographers other than my batman who used my vestpocket camera to photograph this epoch-making event. I travelled right through with the party to Abo and thus had a chance of a lengthy chat with M. Krassin. He was an extremely sincere Communist, a Leninist as opposed to the Stalinists, which he chose to ignore rather than criticise.

'The beneficiaries of our revolution will be those who today are three years old. It is idle,' he said, 'to criticise a movement such as ours by its offences against the traditions and concepts we are moving away from.'

He did not deny the atrocities or acts of barbarity which had shocked Western civilisation. These he referred to as 'peaceful acts'.

'When the sod is turned,' he said, 'we are no longer interested in that which was formerly uppermost but in that which is brought to light, for in that lies our potential.'

From what he said I formed a picture of Communism as it was to be applied, if the final aims were ever to be implemented. Peace meant world conquest and the formation of a utopian state on earth wherein there would be no needs and, consequently, no crimes; no wars; no sickness, yet the approach to this ideal state was to be utterly ruthless from any ordinary standards and ethics upon which my way of life

Harry ffrench from a
drawing made by the
author in 1928.

Winnifred (Freda) ffrench,
née Thursby, about 1900.

The terraces at Villa Torlonia. Ducal Villa in background. About 1894.

The author aged 5 at Villa Torlonia, *and right* aged 14 at Bradley Court.

At Cazalet's Farm, Worcestershire, age 16,
and below, two years later in the Royal North-West
Mounted Police.

"Boxing kept me fit while cramming for Army exams." London, 1913, aged 19.

CON FRENCH.

Below:

The R.N.W.M.P. Detachment at Battle Creek, about 1910.

Yvonne in the author's 1909 Mercedes Simplex, *and right*, Cathleen Mann (Charlie), Allahabad, 1916.

"The coffee was made from acorns."
and below
Burg bie Magdeburg p.o.w. camp. From left to right: the author, Docia
Logwinoff, Tyrrel, O'Malley, unknown, and a Belgian orderly.

Sir Walter and Lady Susan Townley, The Hague, 1917.

and below

Major Dymoke Scale, D.S.O., his wife and family, with
the author *(far right)*.

Above, left to right:
The author, Captain
Sydney Fitzgerald,
Oohna Stewart and
Major Scale, D.S.O.,
Stockholm, 1919.

Left: The station
platform at Rajajoki.
The author with M.
Krassin en route for
London for talks
with Lloyd George,
1920.

The Prince of Wales with Sir Harcourt Butler,
Lucknow, 1922.
and below
Christmas Shikari in the Terai.

Facing page: Rock of the midnight
climb in the Skoro La.

Maud and the
author in the
Austrian Alps.

Climbing in the Hohen Tauren.
and below
Kitzbuhel, 1935.

Monivea Castle
and below
Haus St. Franziscus.

A street and Buddhist temple, Harbin, 1936.

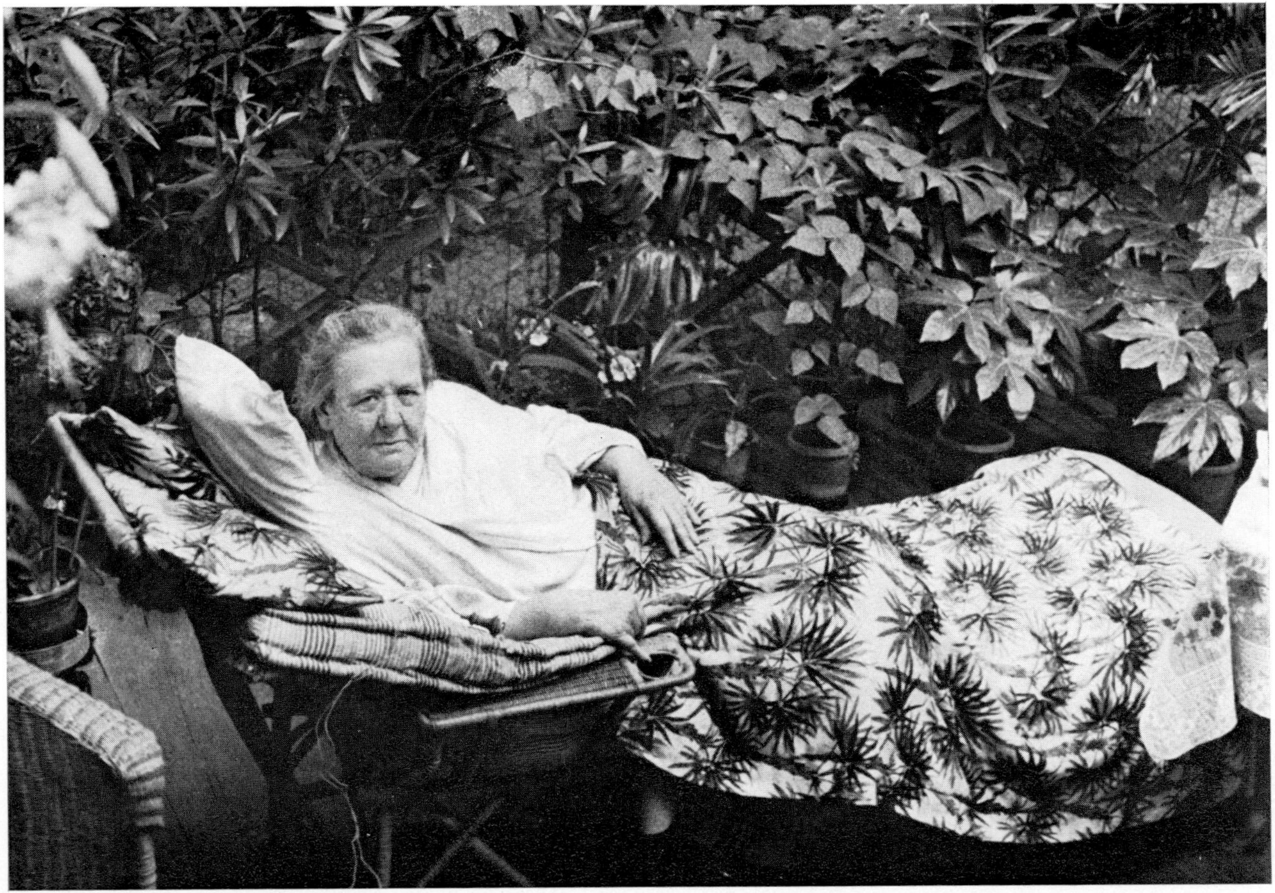

Kathleen ffrench of Monivea, Harbin, 1936.

was based. It was, as it were, completely out of the focus of my vision.

I simply could not take it in. They claimed to stand for universal peace which would be attained by arbitrary means. I was familiar with the kind of peace which human beings seek as an antidote to the turmoil which they have themselves initiated. Then there was that eternal and serene state which is brought about by the individual knowing spiritual oneness which could be called a divine peace. But here was a totally new concept to me of peace and it dawned on me that peace to a Communist was the state produced by the achievement of Communism's ultimate aspirations irrespective of the means, and that any act which brought that state nearer its fulfilment was a peaceful act even if it involved the massacre of millions.

Abo's Chief of Police, who was wearing his white plumed hat when he met the train, led the party through the passport control on the way to their embarkation for Sweden. After a reunion with his wife and three beautiful daughters in Stockholm, Krassin, his family and his party travelled to London where they took up residence in a Curzon Street flat. Curiously enough the apartment he rented was just above the one occupied by my brother Alexis. Krassin soon got in touch with Kamenieff and other roving Russians – there was the Arco scandel and the Clare Sheridan story and much more. He finally went to Paris as Soviet Ambassador.

Lord Acton's diplomatic career came to a sudden end on the first of May that year and this, together with the rumour that drastic cuts were imminent in all government services, caused me to consider that I was in need of leave.

No doubt I had greatly benefited by my experience while Assistant Military Attache. I had made good friends with my immediate chief, Major Scale, and also with the Actons whom I found mentally stimulating and, in Lady Acton's case, elevating. The position regarding Britain's interests in the Russo-Finnish sector had called for non-commital fluidity, qualities which Richard Acton did not possess. The Actons retired to their country seat in Shropshire and I, reading the writing on the wall, applied for leave.

My native city, London, was wearing a carnation in its buttonhole when I returned. The weather was fine and everyone was busy going to Ascot, Lord's, Wimbledon or whatever the accepted form of diversion happened to be. My first visit was to Kathleen at her father's old home in Lower Grosvenor Street facing the south wall of the gardens of Buckingham Palace. At this period I seldom did anything without

some self-interested motive. My interest was, of course, Monivea
Castle.

Kathleen had already visited her castle. She had been met there by
a resolute Rosamond. Her reception had been cold. Her cousin, still
handsome in spite of her age, took the attitude that it was thanks to
her good standing with the local people that the castle had survived.
Kathleen, on the other hand, as absentee landowner, had no standing
whatsoever in the Ireland of 1920. It was obviously impossible for them
both to inhabit Monivea and therefore, feeling herself unwelcome,
she retreated leaving the field to Rozzie.

Rozzie now rapidly consolidated her victory by turning against me
whom she regarded as being on Kathleen's side. Kathleen's legal claim
to her Irish estates was not in question, but she was no longer rich
and her health was much impaired by her experiences in Russia.

'Little did I think,' said Kathleen, 'that I would live through one
revolution only to find another awaiting me at Monivea.'

She made the excuse that living on board a cargo ship was cheaper
than living in London and the next that was heard of her was from
Manchuria where she had dug herself in on the outskirts of Harbin.

The situation at Monivea settled down to a status quo, but for me
there was need for a reorientation of interest or, at least, of approach
to the matter. I was still inclined to become emotionally involved with
situations and it took some time and effort to readjust my attitude
towards Rozzie and her supporters as well as my aspirations regarding
Monivea. It was obvious that Kathleen's legal rights did not match
up to her moral claim to Monivea. She was, in any case, unequal to
the conflict. She went into a kind of retreat during which time she
corresponded with no-one.

5

The High Himalayas

The Prince of Wales spent the winter of 1921-2 in India and I was chosen as an extra aide-de-camp by one of the governors whom His Royal Highness was scheduled to visit.

After England the social limelight of India was dazzling and easy to get in to. However, it tended to blind the young to the culture which that ancient civilisation offered. Caught up in the social pattern of the British Raj, India of Akbar and of the sages remained largely a closed book.

The Prince had gone out to knock the polo ball around with Fruity Metcalf. I had risen early to attend to their needs; the sun was not yet up and the poinsettias were still damp with dew. It would be some hours before the Government House party came down to breakfast and polite discourse and later to the races.

In the A.D.C.'s room there were still signs of the disorder of the night before. There had been a large reception. The remnants of caviar sandwiches beside an empty champagne bottle sat on a large silver salver on my desk. 'What nervous energy that man has,' thought I, as I called for a servant to tidy up the room.

It had been a heavy week with little rest for anyone, but governors and their staffs were geared for that kind of work. At dinner I occupied the humble end of the lengthy table with Lord Louis Mountbatten on one side and some other guest on the other. The Prince, with the Governor Sir Harcourt Butler, had Lord Cromer, Sir Lionel Halsey, Godfrey Thomas, Piers Leigh and a sprinkling of Indian princes and guests at the exalted end. The meals were extremely cheerful and no-one more in his element than the Governor himself. However, as there was usually some reception, parade, ball or durbar afterwards, my attendance at these meals was often cut short by the *Jemadar* Major announcing the arrival of the first wave of a tide of guests whom it was my duty to welcome.

'Not at all, Lady so-and-so, not a bit too early! You are just in nice time. You will find the cloakroom to the left.'

An A.D.C. is a fool, a footman and everybody's friend and though his life is strenuous it has its extremely interesting and funny moments. I had to have my tongue in cheek and some extra sustenance in the office or I would never have been able to carry it through.

This was the swan song of the British Raj, a time never to be forgotten or repeated. It was a time of triumphal arches and of boycott, of fabulous parties and political unrest. The Indian National Congress Party's influence was being increasingly felt. India of the Indians under the leadership of a saint and at the same time a shrewd politician was pressing, insisting upon freedom to rule itself. Gandhi and Nehru formed a powerful team: Gandhi the holy man and his adjutant, Nehru, whose English education had put a deceiving veneer on his pan-Indian aspirations. In February 1922, while shooting big game with the Governor in the Terhai, Lord Reading, the Viceroy, had sent for His Excellency to discuss the possible arrest of Gandhi; a fact which I had deplored because we were having good sport.

India's influences on me were subtle and unconscious, not to be realised until much later in life and recognised when I began to awaken to my spiritual side. Then I appreciated the unconscious part this Indian interlude had played and how many unclassified feelings and misunderstood events were brought into proper significance, focussed into a rich and holy pattern appealing to the imagination but above all deeply satisfying to my sense of being. At the time, however, I noticed none of this.

Apart from military, social and sporting activities, I was introduced to the greatest mountain range in the world. I took to mountaineering like a goat, yet never with a feeling of competition. There was a restlessness, a hungering and thirsting which I could not truly comprehend, but which compelled me to seek its satisfaction. The mountain was there; it was beautiful. My inclination was to climb, an upward urge, to reach a point as far from the centre of the earth as possible, up into the rarified planes of atmosphere where the light lingered longest and came soonest.

I came to realise this shortly after my arrival in India when I was sent up into the Chakrata Hills. From here I could see the gleaming snows of Nanda Devi. The higher altitude seemed to quicken the circulatory system, stimulating the lymphatics, accelerating every thought and movement until I felt inclined to shout with joy. I found others who loved the mountain too, and that they were likeable people with whom I had much in common. There was something about the native inhabitants of the upper mountains and plateau with which I felt at home. Anyone who has a close acquaintance with the Sherpas of the Himalayas or with those who guide and explore in the higher mountains of the world will know what a common love of a 'something beyond' they all have. I had the good fortune to enjoy the friendship of many mountain lovers including Sir Francis Younghusband, Frank Smythe and later Sir John Hunt and Sir Edmund Hillary. Should one borrow colour from one's associations, be influenced by the personalities of others? I was inclined to be jealous of their successes or, should one say, the recognition they received. This, perhaps, was due more to a feeling of inadequacy in myself than to an ungenerous wish to deprive others of their laurels. This was counter-balanced by a quixotic impulsiveness – the making of sudden decisions or taking breathtaking steps – for my deepest desire was to overcome my sense of limitation and to satisfy the growing longing.

After the departure of the Prince I was returned to duty with my regiment and, of course, I was soon found to be behind in routine soldiering. Most of my brother-officers had been allowed to go on leave and such irksome jobs as are necessary when the regiment is in a more or less relaxed state under a burning Indian sun were given to me. It was the preparatory season; those who are backward are given extra drills; men, horses, and equipment are brought up in readiness against the opening of the training season, a time eagerly looked forward to by the keen soldier, but dreaded by the rest. Cavalry training called for precision, accuracy and an arbitrary exactitude which were all foreign to my nature. It soon worried me so much that I could never relax, grew tense and in the end fell ill.

As the hot weather season reached its climax, I asked for leave to go into the mountains. My Colonel had not counted on letting me go. At first he refused but later rescinded. Mountains had always fascinated me but now the pure mountain air seemed essential with a passion approaching desperation. Routine soldiering had its points but, coming on top of a winter at Government House, it was to say the least, drudgery. Was it the heat or the pettiness of social life and the inevitable polo? No, actually all these apparent causes were secondary. It was a spiritual unrest capped by my lack of interest in soldiering. A medical board decided that it was a delayed reaction of war strain.

I reached Srinagar in the first half of July away from the heat, the dusty crowds, the persecutions of an ordered life, to the cool smell of the pines and the towering peaks and mountain meadows. I was glad for I felt my urge had been no whim. I was instinctively preserving my wits. I had feared a nervous breakdown and grew more desperate each day at the abyss of morbid apathy which seemed to open up before me.

By introduction I had got a guide or *shikari* called Habiba, a powerful man and utterly reliable. The *bundabust* (arrangement) had been made by him. All necessary supplies had been acquired and soon my little band of mountain men and I were gliding down the fabulous River Jhelum and out on to the Woolah Lake on the far side of which ponies awaited us.

We were twelve days out from Srinagar and the leisure of Kashmir, along the Gilgit road and up a certain side valley over the pass of Boorghi La. The prospect opened up upon valleys of gold and emerald, the gold of apricots and the emerald of young rice fields. With me was

Habiba, Aziza the cook, a band of coolies and faithful Scamp, my dog. We had reached a ravine called Scoro with a tiny hamlet and a friendly headman who promised his simple supplies. That evening, under the direction of Habiba and the headman, I dispensed liberal doses of one all-round remedy to the sick of the village. Sore eyes, goitre, rheumatism, all alike they received castor oil of which I had brought no small supply.

Next morning by break of day, camp was already being struck. The sixteen coolies from the neighbouring villages adjusted their loads

and we set off up the *nullah* towards the region of glaciers and eternal
snows. The going was rough and the volume of water in the stream
which ran along the bottom of the *nullah* increased as hour by hour the
strength of the July sun melted the ice and snow at its source. It was
almost unfordable by midday and we crossed it for the last time as
we climbed up to our hunting grounds 16,000 feet above sea level.
Here we made a permanent camp on the steep tilt of the mountain side.

We now turned our attention to looking for signs of game and on the
afternoon of the second day made two discoveries, the first negative,
the second positive. We were on our way back to camp after a fruitless
search for ibex marks when we suddenly disturbed a snow-leopardess
with two cubs that were sunning themselves on a ledge just below us.

The scruples that prevented me from shooting the mother of a
family was not shared by my *shikari* and for some time after we were
not at one about it. He explained that while there were leopards on the
mountain I could expect no game. Nevertheless, I was determined not
to disturb the cubs and so there was nothing to do but to look for game
elsewhere. Silently and at a little distance from each other we sat,
scouring the grassy patches on the mountain opposite. Nothing moved
save the shadow of an eagle that, like a speck below us, winged the
middle air. Habiba was the first to speak. He had for some time past
been peering across space to where the snows and rocks united. I heard
him mumble into his field-glasses something about brown objects
moving and I instantly joined him; yes, he was right. I could see them
myself now, five, eight, a dozen ibex at least, as they moved down a
ridge of snow towards their grazing grounds. They seemed so close
through the binoculars, yet to reach them on foot would take half the
day; there was nothing to be done but to wait until the morrow and
hope that they would again return to the same pasture; and with this
aim in view we returned to camp to make some preparations. Little
did we know what we would be undertaking.

It was still dark when Habiba woke me next morning, but in a little
while we were able to see well enough to follow a winding goat track
which led to the stream 2000 feet below our camp. The opposite
mountain rose steep and rugged for some 2500 feet before slanting
upwards into smooth stretches of pasture. We reached these just as
day broke. The great crags across the valley that in the pale grey dawn
had seemed like dark turrets of a giant's castle, now turned to molten
copper and then to gold – Hindu gods rising out of their cold white
lairs. At their feet the snow caught the sun's warm eye and in a minute

the grassy slopes beneath them showed up like emerald scales upon a dragon's side.

It was the boy Sultana who first distracted my attention; he had been watching a mackerel sky come drifting up from behind the mountain, the morning sun touching it lightly. There was something in it that displeased him. 'No good sign,' he said; but beyond this I could not get out of him what it was in the cloud that displeased him – not until later did the cause become apparent.

There were among the grasses enormous slot, or hoof, marks which had been freshly made. No ibex, however, could be seen. We pushed on uphill until the summit of the spur was reached; here we passed through a cleft in the rock and found ourselves gazing down into the deep abyss of a ravine 2500 feet below. At the bottom I could just see the thin frozen white line of a stream. By this long cliff we made our downward way. At first it seemed unreasonable to me that I should be expected to make its descent, yet even as the thought crossed my mind I found myself following my two companions from ledge to ledge, holding on with the tips of my fingers and hardly daring to look below me. Once, in an endeavour to keep my hold on a shelf of rock less than an inch in breadth, my khud stick slipped from my hand and I can see the shaft now glance once or twice off the bare surface of the mountain in its downward flight and then disappear.

As mountains go, the Himalayas are considered young, one of their characteristics being a tendency to landslides and avalanches; it frequently happens at these altitudes that the mountain side along which you come in the morning has completely altered its appearance through landslide by the time you return in the evening.

The sun was high in the heavens by the time we reached the frozen bottom. I stepped out on to the snow quite unsuspectingly, relying on my grass shoes, but the next instant I was lying prostrate, an object of ridicule to my companions.

We ascended a shale slope on the opposite side until by one o'clock we had reached an altitude of well over 15,000 feet and halted for the midday meal. It had grown oppressively warm. I found it difficult to find a shady spot at midday at the top of these mountains as the sun seemed to find its way around the largest and most sheltering of rocks, forcing me out to look for another patch of shade elsewhere. On the top of the shale was a huge rocky formation from which we could watch the pastures the herd of ibex had been making for the day before. Up this I now climbed and laid myself down in amongst the crags of rock to observe them. There was nothing to be seen with the binoculars, although I searched the rough country around us. But as it was still early, I decided to wait through the afternoon until five o'clock.

The air was dead still and it had grown very hot. To the west there was gathering a heap of sullen, sable-coloured clouds. I found it a strain watching the rock-strewn parts of the mountains for the movement of ibex, hour after hour, and turned to see what the other two were doing behind me. I found them squatting over a slanting slab of stone on which they had placed a heap of snow. By means of a V-shaped ridge of mud on the lower side of the slab, the melting snow was being conducted and was trickling out over a dockleaf which had been placed so as to serve as a lip. Thus they provided themselves with a cold drink. Later Habiba joined me in my observation post and about five o'clock things began to happen.

First to make their appearance were two female ibex accompanying some kids. They came over a ridge beyond the grazing grounds just

below us, still half a mile or more away, though through my glasses I could see them clearly. One of them climbed on to a large rock and from this commanding position surveyed the whole landscape for signs of an enemy. She must have given the 'all clear' to those below, for now several more appeared, old ones, young ones, males and females, fifteen or twenty in number. Kids frisking about their anxious mothers, young males nervously sniffing the air and one or two big, bearded *kale* (male ibex) keeping well in the background, rather more inclined to watch the others graze than to show any undignified haste in breaking their own fast.

They had all reached the top of the rise and were descending into the *nullah* which had separated them from their pasture. It was now our turn to move for they were out of sight. Cautiously but rapidly we dropped from our rocky hiding place and raced across the pasture land towards the bank of the *nullah* which had, for the moment, swallowed up the herd. There was no time to lose, yet I dared not risk getting out of breath; I might have to shoot very accurately in a few seconds at one of the biggest heads that was ever measured; might lose the chance of a lifetime by being too late. It was clearly a case where 'hastening slowly' was the best policy.

The rough, stony edge of the *nullah* was close at hand now and in another instant I should have an opportunity of using my rifle – I sank down between two friendly rocks and took a final glance at my sights and safety catch. My pulse beat a furious tattoo in my temples as I drew myself to the brink. To my left, Habiba was already using the binoculars. Brown forms moved in the *nullah* just below me within fifty yards – just so! They were females; one false move now or a stir in the breathless air might stampede the lot and all would be lost.

Quite unconcernedly, in almost his ordinary voice, Habiba now discussed the merits of a big head he had sighted on the opposite side of the *nullah* and as I contemplated this awkward shot at long range, the dull notchy horns of a male just below me attracted my attention. The head was down in a grazing attitude. It was quite a shootable one but he was endways to me and presented a poor target. I was in two minds whether or not to shoot, when suddenly the elements solved the problem; a stir came in the air, I felt the cool breeze on the back of my neck. Up came the head, the ears pricked forward in my direction.

There came an agony of indecision whether to shoot, just for a second. The odd remarks of casual friends, tips from shooting manuals, diagrams of the vulnerable points flashed through my brain. Then I aimed at the neck, my rifle kicked and my first ibex toppled, staggered and disappeared. There was panic in the *nullah* below us; none of the herd had really seen from where the shot had come and for a short while they could none of them make up their minds in which direction

to run. Thus it was that the big *kale* which Habiba had first sighted crossed the *nullah* towards us and met his fate. He was moving up the bottom a hundred yards below me when my second shot struck him amidships. He paused for an instant and then his heavy head fell backwards and with a snort he sank to the ground and started to roll down the side of the ravine, followed by a cloud of dust and shale. His white belly flashed in the sunlight at least a dozen times before he finally dropped out of sight.

The rest of the herd now made off up the *nullah;* high above the rattle of loose stones and shale which their feet dislodged could be heard the shrill alarmed whistle of the dams calling to their bewildered kids to follow. My last recollection of them as they zig-zagged their way up a smooth face of rock still fills me with wonderment, for it must have been almost perpendicular.

I went down into the *nullah* to take a look at the big *kale* which I had so luckily come by, while Habiba went after the one I had first bagged. I found the ibex lying on a narrow strip of snow some 200 feet below where I had shot him. He was a beautiful specimen with a handsome head measuring forty-eight inches.

I was putting away my tape measure when a peal of thunder caused me to look upwards and almost at the same moment I felt the blast of a moisture-laden breeze blow cold upon my face; a dense black cloud had settled over the mountain tops and Habiba calling to me from above confirmed my suspicions; this was the urgent meaning of the mackerel sky.

'Hazoor!' – there was anxiety in his voice – 'A storm is coming, we must stay no longer here.'

'But,' I replied, 'what about the *kale*?'

'Hazoori! I will come for them later, perhaps tomorrow; the first that was shot has carried on into the big *nullah*. I will find him with the help of the vultures when I return, but now there is not time to lose; these mountains are not safe when it rains!'

He was clearly concerned, so I joined him as quickly as I could and we set off together. It was now 7.30 p.m. Large drops of rain began to fall just as we reached the rocky hiding place where we found Sultana impatiently crouching beneath a sheltering slab. The wind increased and with it the rain and by the time we had reached our midday halting place, it was a downpour. We quickened our pace as best we could, but it was growing dark and the loose slates of shale were treacherous on a hideously steep incline. Once or twice I lost my footing and slid on my back for a considerable distance, clutching frantically at tufts of grass or digging my heels into the squelching earth to stay my progress.

At last we reached the snow-bound *nullah* which had been the scene of my undignified sprawl only that morning. How much more grim the spot looked now! We gazed up at the forbidding-looking wall before us, at the dark and dripping rocks; how bold and sheer they rose! Discoloured water ran from the cracks, oozing from the crumbling portion of the stone, gurgling and gushing out of the crevices. The mountain was not safe to climb. We stood, drenched to the skin, wondering what to do, whither to go. It was just possible that by following down the *nullah* we might with luck find some way out, perhaps into the main ravine which ran below our camp. How far that camp now seemed!

The rumble of shifting rock in the heights above decided us; down the *nullah* we must chance it. We slipped and slid down the narrow gorge; I missed my khud stick sadly, but nevertheless we made pretty good headway.

My thoughts changed to lighter subjects of chicken salami and custard puddings and other things Aziza could make so well. Surely there was still a chance of reaching camp for dinner? How dark it was getting. How hungry I was.

What was it in front that brought Habiba to a sudden halt? Why did he stand gazing up on either side of the sheer walls of the *nullah*? He turned to speak – there was despair in his voice. 'No good!' he cried. 'What's no good?' I said impatiently. As I spoke he pointed into the darkness in front of him and what I saw caused my spirits to sink below zero. Snow no longer lay in front of us, but in its place the swift dark current of the *nullah* swept on into the night.

Then as the storm drew breath for one short instant, I heard the boom of falling water far away in the distance beneath us – we had come to a waterfall!

'What now?' I shouted, for the gale had renewed its vigour. Through my sodden clothing the icy blast was cutting like a knife. It was clear to me that sleeping out at night 14,000 feet above sea level on a snow-bound *nullah*, drenched to the skin, meant death. Of course, there was nothing to be done about it but to turn back up the *nullah* and, I think, to do us credit, we all came to the same conclusion at once. It was a big undertaking, as we were, of course, pretty well exhausted now and going up the ice and snow was very different from sliding down it.

We had, however, not too far to go, for a noise as of the thunder of falling masonry, followed by the roar of shifting earth, caused us to stop. The spluttering of the advancing landslide grew louder. With ear-splitting reports I heard rock rebound off rock and finally, with an impetus gathered in a thousand feet or more, large boulders crashed into the *nullah* a hundred yards ahead of us. Then came the rattle of the smaller stones and shale subsiding into the narrow way like plastic clay into a mould. Overall, the tempest soughed supreme.

Silent and apart we stood, the one before the other like men doomed

to eternal darkness. The encounter had brought more fully to my mind
the seriousness of our position, how insect-like we were, trembling in
the vault of this bottomless ravine, helpless as flies washed down the
drain.

A sudden doubt came over me. Were we three no more to look upon
the sun ? A mad desire to make a final effort rekindled the failing light
within me. Looking around, I found a slender crevice in the rock down
which a stream of water trickled. It was no more than two feet wide
in places, but it reached up as far as I could see.

The rocky face oozed water and was unsafe, but, as I began to
climb, the unseen cliff assumed an abstract shape in the darkness and
my fingers, now numb, now throbbing, developed a kind of vision of
their own. My body, too, pulsated with a rhythmic throbbing, taking
a pattern which blended with the mountain, a form into which the
tiny rivulets, the mud and slimy surfaces were part, and beyond and
behind and above it all was a greater design to which the vast whole
found common dimensions. The mountain blended like a cell in the
whole of a body. Mountains of difficulty rise in the minds of men,
giants of opposition in which he seeks a crevice of solution and now
each ledge, each hold and each fissure became evidence of salvation in
that gradual struggle for life. The storm-lashed mountain induced
lucid concentration and an undivided heart in which all sense of fear
and doubt was washed away. And so the design of life and of the body
and of the mountain became in my nature one harmonious whole and
I felt imbued with a superhuman endurance and strength.

The darkness which had been intensified by the rain became our
ally, for in the daylight we would have been overawed by the nature of
the climb. As it was, our only problem was the next hold on the rock
as we inched our way upwards.

Our bodies, aching and bleeding in our tattered and wet clothing,
became instruments of contact between a dynamic power and the
mountain, as if a supreme force was earthing itself through us and
illuminating all that was unstable. The heavenly state was triumphing,
giving us the promise of life.

How we reached the top now seems like a miracle but this I know;
that the hours that seemed to drag on in that desperate struggle between
life and death will remain fresh in my memory until my dying day.
After about 100 feet I came to easier climbing and finally arrived at
the summit of the spur; the others followed close behind.

It remains a blur in my memory how we slid down the grassy slopes to the snow-bridge over the torrent which now raged at the bottom of the main *nullah*.

When we crossed over the water at the foot of the spur on which was our camp, I heaved a sigh of relief. But it was all too soon. Our path ran parallel with the stream for some distance through a dense jungle of wild roses, juniper and wild rhubarb which grew out from among the rocks. Through this wilderness we tried to find our way; we stumbled into holes and over boulders, sometimes climbing a rock ten feet high, at other times dropping into a blind chasm hidden by a tangle of undergrowth.

After wandering in this manner for what seemed hours, I at last yielded to the perpetual pleadings of the other two to stop for the night. By midnight it had ceased raining. Habiba and Sultana produced matches and some dried fir bark from somewhere and soon a fire was going. We gathered around it, making the most of its flicker and presently our tattered socks began to steam and a glow came into our exhausted limbs.

Towards morning the black cloud wrack broke away and through dispersing fragments of moisture-haze shone a ghostly moon. By her cold ray we found our way out of the jungle, away on to the bare mountain slopes where a friendly goat track took us back to camp.

From the servants' tent a large, brown chrysalis-like form emitted occasional grunts. This was Aziza; he had enveloped himself in our spare blankets and was slumbering peacefully. Two camp coolies were likewise enshrouded and asleep.

Only one member of the camp showed signs of sleeplessness and anxiety: Scamp. When first I caught sight of him, he looked indeed a miserable object, for judging by his appearance he had spent the whole night sitting outside my tent in the rain. His coat was wet and the cold was shaking him violently. As soon as he sighted us round the bend of the spur he crept into my tent, climbed on to the camp bed and pretended that he had been there all night. I was too tired to eat or think of anything but rest. The day promised to be fine, the wind had dropped and by the time I had changed into something dry the sun was throwing shafts of light into the eastern sky. I pulled my camp bed out of the tent into the open air and throwing myself down upon it lay for a while looking up into the deep cold sky. I felt a smile come over my face and deep down in me I knew that all was well.

When I awoke the sun was high in the heavens. I could feel the soft air on my face and hear the crackle of Aziza's fire. Turning my head a little I watched the slow fleecy clouds high up, drift across the sky. Something on the bed moved a little closer to me; I put my hand down and found it was Scamp.

On the way back to Srinagar over the Burzil pass, I found a large caravan in possession of the Dak bungalow. It belonged to Captain Samud Shah, a cousin of the Aga Khan and an important member of the Khoja Ismailis returning from a mission to the north of Gilgit with gifts from the followers of this sect.

Being tired after the long trek from Skardu which had taken us over the Bourghi La, a pass as high as Mount Blanc, and across the plateau of Deosai, we made camp on the moraine. But after a rest and one of Aziza's restoring meals, I put some soft Gilgit boots on to my weary feet and descended to Samud Shah's encampment. As I made my way through the pickets I noticed that most of the loads which had been borne by his pack animals contained collections of curios. There were precious rugs and carpets, horse furniture of great value, scimitars, boxes of food and spices and three superb Arab ponies.

When I went into the bungalow to pay my respects to Samud Shah, I quickly gathered that he had been on some sort of intelligence mission so did not press him for details of his movements. However, he did tell me that he had visited the Hunzas, a tribe of hillmen who were quite free from sickness and that many of them had lived up to one hundred and twenty years without ever having been ill. It seems that a Dr McCarrison, a pioneer in nutritional research, was stationed in Gilgit some sixty miles from Hunzaland and that his services, so much in request in and around the garrison, had never once been called for by the Hunzas. They were, he said, entirely free from any dyspeptic diseases. What had the Hunza people got that so-called civilisation lacked?

Perhaps the forbidding nature of their land, the towering peaks and passes isolate them from our more sophisticated consciousness and its media emphasising sensationalism and crime, cruelty and death. As it says in Proverbs, 'For as he thinketh in his heart so is he.' It is thanks to 'the Alpine Club' that I have known many of the hillmen of this world and some great mountaineers, and all have shown a desire for freedom from the destructive claims of the human mind and when I felt those pressures of routined existence upon me I have always sought relief among the hills.

But time was running out and I had to return to duty in Lucknow. The bonds of convention, the atmosphere of tradition and routine with their disciplines develop controls within certain limits, but in the end they tend to cramp natural expression and dull the soul.

6

The Image of War

Stow-on-the-Wold was wet and cold after the sun of India. The grey stone town amid the Cotswolds had collected a rustic crowd about its market place where they were holding a horse fair: shaggy colts from Ireland, cart horses, raucous-voiced vendors, all doing their best to shout down their competitors.

The bar of the Talbot Hotel was a busy place with its smells of wet-clothed human beings, beer and tobacco smoke. I shoved my way through the crowd and up to the sitting room which had been allotted me; behind me, still stressing the virtues of a five-year-old chestnut mare came my friend Kenny. We sat at the gate-legged table in the window while a buxom country girl set drinks before us. Another dealer from Dublin now stood in the door; he offered an iron-grey four-year-old for twenty pounds. There was a healthy thrill in horse dealing.

Outside a salesman had collected a gullible crowd and was handing out indelible pencils. 'Ere, give the gent a safety razor' – a sprat to catch a mackerel – but his voice was drowned in the sounds of 'Yes, We Have No Bananas' from a hurdy-gurdy.

I was wary. I had rented some stalls in the stables behind the Talbot and did not want to fill them with green youngsters, remembering what I had learned at the Indian Veterinary College at Ambala; I wanted good hunters and not the trashy stuff that mostly reached country fairs.

After military service, it was good to feel able to appoint one's own time and to dispose of one's life as one desired. Mr Phillips, the proprietor, lent me a horse and we hacked out together to see the country. The Evenlode, the Heythrop Valley; it all smelled so good and the soil rode light. It was the cubbing season and I had bought a horse from the local parson and so went out to the nine o'clock meets. During those autumn days I made many covert-side acquaintances while dog foxes were allowed to slip away; cubs were harassed in the echoing woods.

I sat my horse, occasionally tapping my boots with my whip and mused. Already my young life was overtly rich with experience and yet, emotionally, I was still immature and inwardly there was a great void opening up. Was it the spirit of failure?

Down in the bar the terrier man was treating himself to a glass of port on his way home. A cub, he said, had eventually gone away from Bank's Fee Gorse, past Ossington towards Morton-in-the-Marsh, but hounds had made little of him and had been taken home.

Hounds trotting home to kennels on a wet and misty evening – what a sight! With their sterns still high, their flanks spattered with mud as they cluster at the heels of their huntsman, a picture of triumph and anticipation.

There followed a year of outdoor self-indulgence. I thought of nothing but horses and hounds. I read Peter Beckford and Surtees, looked as horsey as I could and generally overdid it. I gave exaggerated recognition to a minor portion of my personality. It was a phase one grows out of, perhaps, but never regrets.

My Uncle Willie deserves mention during this time. He was my mother's brother and had my grandmother Johnson's good looks. He was a man of independent means and when not actively riding to hounds or hanging about Tattersalls in Knightsbridge buying or selling horses, he would be reading the *Horse and Hound* at the Bachelor's Club. He was what one could call a gentleman horse coper. I had many a good hunt on Uncle Willie's mounts and sometimes we would do a little horse-trading amongst ourselves, usually with excellent results. But on one occasion he sold me a brown gelding which I called Pullman, partly because he was comfortable to sit on but mostly on account of his hard mouth. The horse showed breeding though I could not call him good-looking because he always hung his lower lip and would stand by the hour with his head in the corner of his loosebox and look sulky. It was then that I suspected he was a 'puller'.

I took him for a hunt with the Heythrop shortly after I had purchased him and warned Jack, my groom, to put a gag on him in case I had difficulty holding him. I rode him 'second horse' and when I met Jack at the appointed crossroads the horse was white with froth and fretting to be off.

'He's awful hard to hold,' warned Jack as he held his head for me to mount. No sooner had I got into the saddle than I realised that I was in for a rough ride. Then with every powerful, increasing stride he took charge of the situation. I was utterly helpless. Hounds were running and he rapidly closed the gap between us and the racing pack. Objects flew past us, horsemen perhaps, I could not see. We overtook the field of some thirty-five riders starting with the stragglers. A groom with a child on a pony on a leading rein were in the lane ahead of us. Pullman parted them as he chose a course between them. My whole attention was riveted upon inescapable objects in our path. It was worse than being in an express train which had no brakes. We entered a lane with banks on either side which was full of the hard-riding members of the hunt, beyond whom I could see the huntsman and his hounds: twenty couples of them and all of the finest stock in Britain. Pullman cut through the steaming cavalcade, scattering and stampeding all in his way. I was tugging at his mouth with every ounce of my strength but to no avail.

The hounds had checked and were feathering in a ploughed field beyond the land. Leaping the bank Pullman landed in their midst and stopped so suddenly that I slid up his neck to his ears from which position I was unable to get back into the saddle. My horse lowered his head and deposited me on my back in the mud. Witnessing this undignified spectacle Ernest, the huntsman's only remark was, 'Get that horse out of here, Sir, PLEASE!' Eventually when I got Pullman away and back along the lane, past a score of angry riders, I found a large twelve-acre field and, entering it by the gate, I told that maddening animal, 'Now if you want to gallop here's your chance.' And I took him round that field at full speed until he was sobbing and ready to drop. Then back through the gate, but I had hardly time to close it when Pullman's head went up, ears pricked, he had heard the sound of the horn. It was a long way off but it made no difference. Off we went like a shot out of a gun and I swore then and there I would never take him out hunting again.

I later sold him to a subaltern in a foot regiment who won several point-to-point races with him. 'The trouble,' said the young soldier when next we met, 'is how to stop the horse at the end of the race.'

During this sporting interlude, I had a recurrence of phlebitis which I had first experienced in India. Sister Agnes Keyser took me into her nursing home in Grosvenor Crescent where the medical profession tried to pinpoint the cause. Consultation followed consultation, operation followed operation, until the exhausted patient, refusing to be cut up any more, said, 'You are trying to cure me by a process of elimination. Presently, I shall be as hollow as a drum and still suffering from the same complaint, because I feel sure the cause is not physical.'

As a matter of fact, the thing was not clear in my mind, but instinctively I felt that I was on the right track. My difficulties had a more obscure root. But as so often happens the antidote was at hand.

I met two people about this time who had a distinct influence on my life. The first was a society lady, a Christian Scientist, who said that her five aunts had all married peers while she, with her banker husband, lived in a beautiful country house in Norfolk. The other was a Czechoslovakian doctor in Carlsbad.

I recall the former in her context of grandeur and elegance. Her wealth enabled her to live the life of an idealist, romanticising herself and dramatising the lives of others as she indulged in an insatiable lust for matchmaking. There were weekend parties where youth and decorum were the keynotes; sporting and recreational amenities on lakes or in woods and in the formal gardens were available.

Happy were those who entered into the spirit of arcadia which prevailed. When I appeared upon this blissful scene the effects of my war experiences had finally overwhelmed me. I was lost in a desert of my own heart and was desperate for a horizon of hope, a respite from the belief that God sends tribulations to try His children. There were things stirring in me which I was far from understanding and before which I found myself helpless, the traditional stabilities falling away. A greater vision was outshining my previous concepts and beliefs.

I met at one of these weekend parties a nineteen-year-old American girl called Jane, the like of whom for sheer physical beauty I had not known. My obsession was complete. I was a fly in honey and could scarcely see through it all except in golden hues. The frustrations that had mounted over the years of captivity had engendered a sexual imbalance. I was literally intoxicated with sex. Jane was a little above average height, her blonde hair in pageboy style framed an oval face exquisite as a cameo. She used neither cosmetics nor undergarments and her silk dress clung to her lithe young body, causing her carriage and manner to be most arresting.

More than mere physical appeal she was to me an open declaration of oneness – no hidden fantasies, romanticism or cheap sentiment. She was the embodiment of sexual union, poised as it were before the male population of the world openly and directly challenging man to come out of his hypocrisy and accept the freedom of love, her basis for womanhood. And she was so completely honest that she made all who beheld her in judgement feel unclean.

I had passed through the anomaly of war and solitary confinement, years of frustration and readjustment during which I had not given thought to women, and now all of a sudden I was face to face with this bonus and was quick to harness my good fortune. At all events for me it was sex at first sight. Jane brought romance, sentiment, and desire to point like a flame and recalled a primitive yet aesthetic pang in me like a sound of war drums.

There followed weeks of happy and exciting sorties into the clandestine realms of romantic intrigue until, when we were both in Paris, upon one night in spring, I went without discerning and with no other motive to her room. I found my way in that old hotel by a creaking and ill-lit passage, believing that no other person might appear. I turned the handle of her door; it yielded with a sigh, revealing her naked body in relaxed contours. So bewitching was the sight that for a while, with knees melting, I stood transfixed by her beauty. A pale moonbeam played upon the whiteness of her skin. Half inclined to panic, I surrendered to desire and lay down beside her. She moved, half enveloping me in her arms and so I lost control. Melting ever closer, my face upon her breasts, I threw all care among the fruits and lilies of her charms, there to fade in ecstatic homage to the laws of life.

I lingered, so couched in the supremacy of satisfaction, the burning pounding of my heart abating till we sank to rest. Moments turned into hours, feeling naught but the lulling faintness of the midnight air.

Then, suddenly, in the harsh and callous dawn, our peace was shattered by a rude knocking on the door and in unmistakeable Bostonian accents, I heard her mother's voice. Brought sharply to my senses, the shock ran down my spine and exploded in my solar plexus. 'Mumsie' was already in the room, middle-aged and more pretty than handsome. I thought I saw cunning rather than anger in her face. Obviously she had handled the likes of this before and was anxious to regulate the circumstances without scandal, lest it jeopardise her own chances of remarriage to a well known senator.

'Bless you my children,' she said with the cool benevolence of one who assumes the control of potential mother-in-law. Collecting my only garment, I made my inglorious exit.

But my mind was still in too great a turmoil and my emotions too much in chaos to take a decision involving another's life. In fact my life progressed with a fluid, forward motion like a river conforming to circumstances as they were met, halting momentarily, then encompassing and pushing forward. It irked me to make pledges limiting my movements, for I felt at this stage that women were likely to involve me in limitations. They possessed a thousand little devices, some so subtle that no ordinary man could detect them and these little devices were like tendrils curtailing, clutching, holding back both movement and vision.

Having perhaps shamefully sidestepped the tendrils of marriage, I was once more loose in a vast field of possibilities to sample the delights of courtship, and with the demise of that Victorian symbol of decency, 'Mrs Grundy', it was amazing what opportunities there were.

My faith in Christian Science principles was transitory; nevertheless my spirits were buoyed up for a time. Religions were ways and means to an end, but what irked me about them was that they were all in disagreement with one another and none, so far as I was aware, was free from the distorting effects of concepts about the truth. They seemed concerned with knowing about whatever the truth might be, rather than experiencing a living revelation of it. I felt I alone would have to do that. The umbilical cord of orthodox Christian religion had been severed, for while it might set me on the right path the footsteps thereafter must be mine. I grew more tolerant of others, their viewpoints, their political aspirations, feeling that in season my own vision would dawn and the reality would become evident.

We are all born with a serene and directing spirit. The trouble is that so few become aware of it.

I admired my sister Yvonne. I had introduced her to the Actons and they became close friends. Richard Acton and his family now lived at Aldernham Park where his learned father amassed his famous library. There in this great collection of books Yvonne had immersed herself. She was an outstandingly handsome girl, striking in colour, bearing and intellect. Whereas she had a capacity for much reading and a discerning and appreciative eye for literature, I, on the other hand, had none of these talents. I suffered from uncorrected eye trouble during my childhood and became inclined to learn by experience rather than by mental application. Through Yvonne I heard of a German physician at Carlsbad in Bohemia who was popularly known as Dr 'Hunger' Meyer. He would work wonders with his gentle massage, his diet and the drinking of the saline waters. I resolved to travel to see him, for the possibility of a more natural curative approach to my phlebitis appealed to me.

Above Carlsbad the river winds through some wooded hills among which the town is situated. There is a law, it cannot be by chance, that dock leaves are found among stinging nettles. The antidote is always at hand. Thus, too, the inhabitants of that country, having a natural tendency towards adiposity, have the waters of Carlsbad which are renowned for their fat-reducing properties.

Dr Meyers was tall and handsome and wore a brown beard which gave him an air of great dignity. His consulting rooms were in a house called 'The Three Rings' and during the season he took his first patient at 6 a.m. From then on, every quarter of an hour was booked until late at night. By appointment I went to see him daily at 8 a.m. when he gave me a massage and told me to drink fourteen glasses of the famous Carlsbad waters each day. Apart from this the cure consisted of starvation, one's diet being limited to two glasses of milk a day.

At 7 a.m. large crowds would gather at the springs to begin their daily water drinking. There are several different kinds of waters, some more disgusting than others. In its initial stages the cure makes one feel ill. All sorts of people are present at the springs, from grand duchesses to orthodox Jews in clerical hats. The former are florid and gay, the latter wear black gowns and beards, including their cultivated curly wisps of hair hanging from either temple. There are a few English, a handful of Americans of all ages and dimensions and the rest are either Bohemians, Austrians or Germans, rich and poor. All carry a souvenir mug in their left hand; one old lady carried hers slung around her neck on a strap. On the whole they would have been a depressing sight if they had not been so funny. But the weather was fine and the municipal orchestra played Schubert. As the time goes on and the cleansing process continues, the water drinker grows more and more hungry and less tolerant until he reaches a point of crisis which is like a bad attack of flu. After that he enters a much happier phase. Life takes on a rosier hue and his brain is keener, his vision clearer and spirits brighter. At this stage he is even skittish at the springs.

I met a group of old Americans and I joined them daily for my simple meal. They had a permanent table in the Frieundschaftsalle, a restaurant by the river. Their table was set under an awning and, as they sipped their milk with relish and joked, the water flowed as it does by a ship. 'We'll foregather at the yacht,' they would call out gaily over their water drinking. They called each other 'Colonel' or 'Doctor' or 'Judge'. They were all from the deep south and dragged their Cadillacs, their valets, secretaries, chauffeurs and guides into their conversation. I was decidedly tickled by it all. They all had a knack of merging their yarns like links in a narrative chain, each inseparably joined with the next in such a manner that it was impossible to break away without appearing rude. I learned that the stories always ran on like a gramophone whether one listened or not and I would rise and make a friendly gesture of farewell with my hand and walk off. After all, Carlsbad habitues became quite accustomed to the unceremonious departure of their companions and nobody is so tactless as to ask, 'Where are you going?'

The crisis comes about the fourteenth day when the patient feels he would prefer death and is not so sure he is far from it. There is a dizziness, fever, sickness and a sense of void. Full of misery, his limbs tremble like pale, wilted asparagus.

I tried to think myself upon the firm silver sands of some tropic island with the waters of the lagoon lapping over my feet. It was an escape but it sometimes worked. The nights were full of terror. I dreamed short, fitful but vivid dreams: odd ominous shapes, dream agonies and exhausting horror that filled the room. Then, as the afternoon ripened, a host of problems and trivialities got mixed into my kaleidoscopic thinking and I laughed at their absurdities, but my mind was entangled by them. Somewhere a bell rang sounding a delicious note from a woodland belfry, where rusty-barked trees rose from purple ground. Up, up they went billowing in my mind until their cool leaves mingled in a cold sky and I drifted off to sleep.

I sent for the doctor who arrived in excellent spirits. 'Everything is fine! Go on drinking your water; the toxins are now loose and need only to be washed out.' From that moment there was rapid improvement. The sufferer leaps out of bed with a glad shout as if he had been delivered of an evil spirit. He feels like a new being. He must have been drugged for years and now it seems as if once more he is alive, alive to his past experiences yet alive, too, with the clear perceptions of a child.

My sight grew keener, my hearing and my sense of smell more acute, my thinking nimbler. I sat at the old table in the Freundschaftsalle by the river. The judge, the colonel and the doctor had left for Berlin and the U.S.A. They were all doubtless dining tonight together in luxury and profusion now that their cure was completed. I opened a continental *Daily Mail*. Lady Marling was dead.

The waters of the river flowed past and sang to me alone. I pondered. She was a remarkable woman and now all the chief personalities of that drama were gone. Lord and Lady Acton had died and so had Krassin. Like milestones in a race, who knows whither, or buoys in a channel, as I glided irresistibly forward towards open waters they had vanished from sight.

A little round man was eating an egg at the next table. He and his egg resembled each other. He introduced himself as Baron Max Ferdinand von Oppenheim, archaeologist from Cologne. I felt uneasy with Germans, but this man's interests were centred in archaeological research in the one-time Babylonian Empire. Max was friendly and talkative. He, too, had undergone the cure – 'a thorough autumn cleaning', and now, along the woodland paths under the changing beech trees, we strolled together and talked. He spoke of excavating a city on the lower reaches of the Euphrates and how, beneath its ruins, they had found the silt and debris of a great flood. 'The flood?' I asked, my interest thoroughly aroused. 'Exactly so,' was Max's reply. We spoke much of these matters and Max was inclined to stress that another flood tide of events was coming upon us. 'The future looks pretty black to me,' said Max, 'and being an escapist by nature I prefer to lose myself in the past.'

'What's wrong with the future?' I asked, with assumed optimism.

'Ever hear of one Adolph Hitler?' asked Max ironically. I had not. We came to a hunter's lodge amid a clump of chestnut trees. The time had nearly come for their leaves to fall, the vast blue sky could be seen through the rents in their foliage. A brown hen clucked as she scattered dead leaves. A September haze hung over the distant plain. One had to acknowledge autumn on every hand.

I urged Max to tell me more of this man Hitler and the National Socialist movement and why he was so concerned at its proliferation.

'We hear so much' I said, 'about "race" these days and the distinctions that are drawn and the antagonisms they generate.'

'By the way,' interrputed Max, 'the word "race" is of Hebrew or Arab origin, you know.'

I tried to look impressed.

Then Max continued, 'As for the Nordic claims of world leadership, I have seen passages from German, French, Italian, Roman, Russian and American literature claiming leadership of the world; what then is all this talk about the superiority of the Aryan race? These blue-eyed, fair-haired Nordics, have they not borrowed much from their darker neighbours in the way of ideas, speech, etc. Anyone who speaks of Aryan races and their physical characteristics is deluding himself.'

(After that I took the trouble of looking up the word Aryan and found that it was first used correctly by Sir William Jones, 1746-94, as a name for speakers of a group of Indian languages, but believe that its adoption elsewhere is discredited by any ethnologist of repute.)

'The Germans,' continued Max, 'now claim that the prototype of an Aryan race is fair, longheaded, tall, slender, unemotional, brave, straightforward, gentle, and virile.'

I have since recalled this description. Was Hitler physically longheaded, was Rosenberg direct or Goebbels tall or Goering slender or Streicher straightforward? Of the German people who claimed the pure Aryan origin none probably realised what it involved.

That evening I called at 'The Three Rings' and found Dr Meyer preparing for his departure. The doctor shook my hand warmly.

'You look a different man,' he smiled.

'Yes, I feel as new as a pin. By the way, doctor, what do I owe you?'

'Nothing at all,' was his reply.

'But you have given me your time each day for six weeks,' I protested.

'Well,' said the physician, 'you lost your health at the hands of the Germans and now I, a German, have helped you to regain it. Let us say that I do it for the love of humanity.'

I was overcome with gratitude. My subconscious distrust of Germans was cleared away and with it also dissolved one of the chief causes of my ill-health. I was cured both physically and emotionally which, compared to the methods of the knife was, to my mind, more satisfactory and closer to truth.

My thoughts still dwelt upon Dr Meyer's gesture when I left Carlsbad and started toward the south Tyrol. My diary reads as follows:

Now, close to the border town of Eger through which I passed, lived at Konnersruth a peasant girl called Theresa Neumann, who was said to have manifested on many occasions the stigmata of the cross. Every Friday she lost two kilos in weight and, lying exhausted in bed would weep. More from interest in watching the power of superstition over people's minds than in any religious motive, I resolved to go and see for myself. Reaching Eger, the frontier, I got out and taking a car for eighteen crowns, drove to the small German village of Konnersruth. On the way we passed many pedestrians trudging along in the keen morning air. The day was fine and young, for it was but nine o'clock. Omnibuses, charabancs, private cars and even trucks loaded with country folk were all making their way to the same quiet spot to see the phenomenon, as yet unexplained either religiously or scientifically. This young peasant girl of twenty-one had for two years borne marks of the wounds of crucifixion and was said also to bleed from them and to weep tears. Yet, on Saturday morning after the miraculous Friday occurrence, she returns to her habitual state, the bleeding with its odour of violets ceases and her weight returns to its accustomed measure. She is once more the delicate young girl that she was and remains so for the rest of the week.

As I approached the village it was already filling with people come to see her. The open, grassy space in its centre where the geese at other times fed and cackled around the pump, was covered by cars. The oxen looked bewildered at the invasion. By midday a great concourse of people had gathered before the house of the parish priests which faced the church in the centre of the village. It had been given out that the door of the house would not be opened to visitors until 12.30 noon. I took my place about that time and found about 600 gathered there and that they had begun to push and shout more like trippers than pilgrims. I was much disgusted and sought another way.

The crowd gave the impression of hypnotic hysteria, none of the expected reverence or abstraction, but more the evidence of idle curiosity. I suppose I was in a sense no better. Two women stood against the front door of the priest's house and started a pushing match, to the amusement of all. Shortly before 12.45 the door opened and a white-haired priest begged the crowd to stand back, but they paid no attention to him. They pushed and weaved, complained and cursed each other until the priest's entreaties were drowned in the din. With the help of another he let them in by sixes and sevens and I soon saw that in this seething herd I would be lucky if I reached the door within the time allotted to the visit. So, seizing the opportunity to fight my way backwards out of the mob, I stepped around to the back of the house where I had noticed those who had been to see the girl being let out.

I awaited my chance and then followed some priests in. A boy at the back gate remonstrated, but I took no notice of him and walked in through the garden and upon entering the house found myself in an ante-room in which a door stood open. By this door a priest stood with a policeman trying to control the inrush of sightseers. The latter noticed us coming up against the stream, shouted to us to go back, but at that instant his attention was distracted by the surging crowd, so I passed on into the room in which sat the maid.

She was dressed according to the fashion of the local peasants mostly in black, with a black shawl tied over her head, which accentuated the pallor of her features. Her face was round and her expression serene, but her eyes were hollow and her delicate hands rested in her lap. I noticed that the left hand which was resting on the right had a red mark on its back but no blood issued from it. I learned later from the crowd that there had been no bleeding on this Friday. But as to whether or not she had lost weight, I could not say. I am told, and this has been confirmed scientifically by medical observers, that she has eaten nothing for two years but half a Holy wafer of Communion bread which she takes daily from the priest. This is accepted as fact and was proven over a period of ten days.

So revolted was I by the vulgarity of the crowd that had invaded this pretty village with their litter of paper and bottles, motor horns and dust, that I was glad to get out of it. As for the 'miracle', I put it down to a case of hypnosis occasioned by the control of the emotional realm by passionately-held fixed concepts. Whether a concept be based on love or hatred, trust or distrust, it will manifest in the flesh to a greater or lesser degree according to the nature of the individual.

These thoughts ran through my head as the train bearing me away towards the south Tyrol trundled on into the night. The time had come for some travel, I felt, to make both new acquaintances and to renew some old. My interest had always gravitated toward Switzerland and Austria, so now I found myself entrained for the southern Tyrol.

At the Brenner Pass the train came to a standstill, hissing and steaming in the crisp morning mountain air. We seemed to remain there longer than scheduled and as the first signs of daylight were stealing into my compartment, the attendant appeared to explain that there had been a cloudburst and that part of the track had been washed away. An emergency train and seventeen men of the breakdown gang had fallen into the river.

Passengers were bundled out into the twilight and eventually transferred into smaller carriages in which we now travelled to the region of the disaster. The train could go no further. Here we stood by the railway track gazing into the narrow valley flooded with mud, uprooted trees and boulders that had been strewn by the force of the water. What a wild and chilly sight amid the grey light. The mountains stood impassive, shrouded in dark coniferous mantles and brocaded here and there by golden threads of light. They seemed almost to block a white array of peaks blurred by a hurrying mist. At our feet the muddy torrent raced on defiantly. We walked some few hundred yards over boulders, crossed an improvised wooden bridge to where a fleet of buses awaited us on the road under a rocky cliff. We got on the buses, not without a lot of shouted excitement on the part of the officials, and so proceeded on our journey.

We reached the scene of the storm which had devastated the valley, tearing up vegetation and causing general havoc in the gorge. Here the road was washed away and there it was covered by thousands of tons of sand, mud and rocks. At several points the road had completely disappeared into the river and a new road was being cut into the hillside by a gang of labourers. Then we were all told to get out and walk, as the road was not safe for a loaded bus. On the opposite side

of the river ran the railway. The rampaging waters had washed away
the grade in many places and, at the point where the train had fallen
into the flood, hundreds of yards of rail had disappeared. Further on
we saw where the deluge had gutted the mountain side, washing away
with it a railway bridge as if it had been a woodcutter's trestle. Nature
in one of her cataclysmic moods makes man's efforts at destruction
pale by comparison.

Salvage work was in progress and we saw the twisted remains of
what had once been a railway carriage lying in mid-torrent beneath a
pile of boulders. It was now broad daylight but the sky was still grey
and threatening. We got into another train further down the valley
and after a half-hour's run arrived at a small station where we once
again entrained for the south in whatever luxury our tickets entitled
us. While I was writing a description of this journey to my sister at
a table outside the Hotel Grifoni in the piazza at Bolzano, I was conscious of the fusty, friendly smells surrounding me. The pigeons that
basked in the sun at a confidential distance indicated the heat of the
day and the hour of the siesta.

In the late afternoon a small electric train, threading its way through
the vineyards, took me up to the village of Wolfgraben in the foothills.
I was weary when I reached the small guesthouse there and after a
night of restful oblivion awoke to the noise of magpies in the larches.
An echelon of light upon the wall told me the sun had risen and I lay
for a time saturating myself with the beauty of the morning. I had
always been an early riser and had heard it said that the night was
made for love or work or the hatching of plots, but the morning was
for joy! My watch ticked as if it had grown into a clock overnight.
Everything else was so still. I drew the blinds and saw the jagged
tooth of the Latimer silhouetted against the morning sky.

Seeking out my rucksack, my nailed boots and my thick socks, I
pulled a sweater over me and sat and ate my breakfast upon a bench
out of doors. It consisted of groundwheat boiled in milk and eaten
with salt, butter and boiled eggs. The air was bracing and resonant,
the view perhaps unsurpassed in Europe. There was a small lake
within sight of the Dolomites: spires and blades that are ruddy at
twilight – a challenge to the mountaineer and to the artist, an orgy of
sentimental splendour.

Except in the subtlety of the imagination, the play of colours as
sunset flushes red among those peaks is hard to describe. And, alternatively, when the colour has died out of the crags and they are left cold

and forbidding against an orange sky, the fibre of the Teuton melts and he turns with melancholy joy to the *Weinstübe*, there to muse with Wagner and Goethe over a ruby glass of Sud Tiroler.

I was frequently in Bolzano. I had many friends there now and it was the starting point for many excursions. I always put up at the Grifoni, for it was an old-established and extremely well-run hotel and I liked the temperament of the people. I rose with the sun and if not climbing the mountain would stroll through the market in the colonnaded streets of the town. Under awnings, Tyrolean peasants in green-checked coats sold sage, millet, bay leaves in bundles; or onions, eggs, hares and partridges; masses of golden apples; brown heaps of potatoes; *pommedore*, limes and turnips. Their asses and jennets waited patiently by the pavement.

With pipe dangling from his mouth, a fishmonger at his trestle board chopped up tunny fish next to a mound of silver whitebait or a mingled mass of eels. An old woman in black bodice and grey shawl raked together her remaining *fungi*, orange and gold. Posto 51 had a stack of cheeses to sell: square hunks, round lumps and a jagged rock of parmesan; strings of sausages hung from his rickety booth. An old pedlar covered from head to foot with dangling bootlaces hawked his wares. This busy sight was at seven on a frosty morning. The day had just begun.

A sweet smell of roasting chestnuts popping and crackling in the charcoal ovens wafted through the street. Climbing in the Sella group was excellent, although a great deal was good steady plodding. Since guides were expensive luxuries, I seldom did anything spectacular but, on the other hand, gathered a lot of climbing experience by perseverence, patience and observation. Usually I climbed alone, but occasionally encouraged a companion to join me. I always watched other climbers closely, especially those whom I recognised as veterans. Techniques never came easily, but I had a natural instinct for it. More than anything I enjoyed long rambling tramps over the mountains, sleeping in wayside inns and following paths rather than roads. I walked with a brisk step, drank in the beauty of the scenery with ecstasy, stopped frequently to look at alpine flowers or butterflies and took a tolerable interest in their names. Above all I loved birds. I had never forgotten all I had learned from Rollo about them and now added extensively to my knowledge.

As well as English, Russian and French, I now spoke Italian and German fluently and if I fell in with congenial company would walk with them and exchange ideas.

Once when walking in the Dolomites I picked up a professor from Bergamo University who, like myself, was walking for the pleasure of it from Trento to Como. I learned much from my academic companion. He had a dog and the three of us walked together for two days. It was late autumn and the peasants were busy in the valley below as they drove their oxen to and fro from the vineyards, with their loaded wine carts creaking.

We spent the first night of this walk at an inn above the dust and heat of the valley. A guitar and a mandolin had played dance music late into the night; nevertheless I awoke early to a fresh breeze blowing from distant mountains to the south. I sought the church and as I emerged from its incense-laden darkness into the bright sunlight I met my learned companion who pointed in the direction of the dazzling snows of the Presanella group.

'Let us walk together over the Tunale Pass and I will there show you where I spent my war years fighting the Austrians,' he offered, so we continued on together.

At noon we stopped at a small inn. The girl-of-all-work showed us into the dining room, but the host, taking me for a peasant, sent us to the commercial room where the local people take their wine and cheese. It was rank with stale wine but was preferable to the pretentiousness of a bourgeois lounge.

I felt close to the peasants for they were more indigenous to the country and imbued with greater measure of its spirit. The professor knew a lot about them and their history and specialised in the ways and customs of the people of the Venetian Empire. We strolled round in the hot afternoon to see the local castle and the various architectural influences it displayed. Here we were joined by the parish priest, a portly man in a very discoloured cassock. The two Italians now vied with each other over historical information. And so the professor and his dog led on . . . towards the mountains to the south-west.

The battlefields of eight years ago, still strewn with barbed wire, steel helmets and here and there an unexploded shell, were our prospect. A small herd of chamois on the edge of the snows above the pass watched us as we threaded our way in the direction of Ponte di Legno in the west towards beautiful Lake Como.

Calming, recuperative days in a world seemingly at peace. It was a placid phase before the gathering of forces towards fresh growth. The mountains remained my relaxation, but I was beginning to feel that I had to do something and was beginning to wonder if I wasn't, perhaps, wasting my life. There are conventions drilled into all of us, and I wished to leave a mark in some material form so as to lay claim to having made a 'success of life'. A big bank account, to figure in the honours list, a book, a collection of art – any claim to fame that satisfies the ego has been the object of such aspirations. I reasoned now that any avenue I explored would ultimately produce patterns of association which would be useful, though I could not explain why I felt so nor define in my mind the nature of that usefulness. It was simply a compulsion.

While passing through my 'horsey' phase I had done a few water colours of my hunters. A hunt secretary, looking for talent in that field, had commissioned me to do a set of hunting scenes for his opulent master. They had been a success and their reproductions were subsequently published in a book. Encouraged by this I considered the life of an artist.

The Slade School of Art was comparatively easy to get into in those days, its chief instructor Professor Tonks. I enrolled as a student and though I profited by this contact I transferred to the Byam Shaw for three years where I studied under Ernest Jackson, from whom I learned much. Then, partly to break away from the academic style, I went to Paris and to André L'Hote's Academy of Modern Art where I remained a further three years.

L'Hote was a great theorist, but he could also teach better than most in the world of art and I eventually left feeling myself better qualified to take a place as a painter.

My friend, Simon Elwes, had not long left the Slade and was, like thousands of others in Paris, an obscure painter. He introduced me to an inexpensive restaurant called Chez Rosalie in the Rue Compane Premier. Rosalie had a soft concern for artists and provided soup, entrée and dessert including wine for six francs. Many of her customers, having no money, paid for their food with sketches, some of which later became very valuable. One of those who achieved fame, it was said, had given her hundreds of sketches in exchange for his keep; she had placed these in the cellar for safety. Realising they were now worth thousands of francs each she lumbered down to fetch them but, on finding the box, she discovered them to have been gnawed to shreds by rats.

Another friend was Guy Arnoux. His studio was a veritable museum of naval trophies and relics. It was hung all over with cutlasses, telescopes and model ships. He had a vast collection of the type which were cunningly put into bottles. a library of books on naval history, charts of the Caribbean Sea and coloured plates of early naval uniforms. His nautical period had been brought on by a commission to decorate the interior of the 26,000 ton *Ile de France*. This had followed on the heels of a Buffalo Bill phase, remnants of which, such as stock saddles, six-shooters and lariats, were evidence of the time when Guy used to trail his spurs across the pavements of Montparnasse or roll Bull Durham cigarettes at the Dome restaurant. But that craze came to a sudden end when in his over-emphasis he roped a butcher boy peddling along the sands of Deauville and dragged the unfortunate lad, bike and all, until he was finally able to rein in his drugstore cowpony.

Fuggy, noisy, excitable Paris fitted my mood for it stimulated my mind and rudely jogged me out of my dreaminess which the serenity of the Alps seemed to sustain. I acquired a studio in the Parc Monsouri district and did a lot of work living there while attending art school. My student friends were Elena Mumm, a pretty Russo-German girl whose father was in the champagne business and, also, Henri Cartier-Bresson, a talented young French photographer.

Paris was having a late autumn; her trees were still covered with dried foliage. It was the time of the 1930 depression and I had just become fit to be launched as a full-blown artist. The cost of living rose sharply and it became almost impossible to sell a picture. Streets were filled with unemployed and soup kitchens were set up to keep them from starvation. I went into commercial art as did most of the well-known artists, so competition was very keen. But my father, with whom I now corresponded, suggested our going to Jamaica to escape from the winter. I jumped at the chance and took my paints with me.

It was my father's idea in the first place. Christmas, he said, was fine on a card with suitable greetings, but far too chilly in England. In fact, he used to avoid that tight little island until the August sun had aired it. But here we were already in November, and he had lingered on with an old friend in Sussex. My home, if it could be called so, was my club in Mayfair, a part of London dominated by Piccadilly.

Negotiations had been going on for some time, until finally we agreed to spend Christmas in Jamaica and perhaps remain there until the trade winds died down in March and the heat became intolerable. Neither of us had any ties at the time and so were free to come and go as we pleased.

Modern hotels, apart from their expense, were to be avoided, as were tourist resorts. We both wanted to see old Jamaica, Jamaica of the days of sugar estates. I had heard of two maiden ladies, known as the Misses Fisher of Mahogany Hall, who, having belonged to one of the old sugar families, had, like so many others, been ruined by the uprise of the beet sugar industry in Europe.

Elder and Fyffe had switched to carrying bananas and so were still in business. Their boats sailed from Avonmouth once a month for Kingston and could also accommodate fifty passengers. The corresponding boat-train left Paddington Station at 11 a.m. My father and I agreed to meet at the train and, as usual, I had been the first to arrive and had stowed away my bag and procured seating. I tossed my coat on the window seat opposite and, letting down the window, searched the milling crowd on the platform for signs of my parent. The hands of the big clock in the station pointed to 10.55, and still there was no sign of him. If one misses a boat-train one also misses the boat, so the matter was serious. The guard was blowing his whistle and doors were being slammed when, with a small suitcase in his hand, my parent appeared.

'For goodness sake, Dad!' I cried. 'Where's the rest of your baggage ?'

'I haven't any. This is all I'll use on the journey. As for the rest, it will be cheaper to buy tropical clothes in Jamaica.' He sank into his seat. There was another shrill whistle, followed by a jolt, and we were off.

Mr Harrow, the Chief Steward of the S S *Montagua*, was in the office on the main deck to greet his new batch of charges. He was an old hand at the game and had an excellent crew under him. There is nothing more delightfully conventional than a chief steward of the British merchant marine. They have, after all, carried passengers to every corner of the globe since Britannia ruled the waves, and they have learned to instil assurance and a sense of total dependability. But the ship was only eight thousand tons and the Atlantic – well, everyone knows what it can be like! As soon as we were under way, a cabin boy came with a note which invited us to sit at the captain's table for meals. We were well out of the English Channel by the time the dinner gong rang and the fun began.

There was, of course, the usual games' committee, and on the third day we were asked to come to dinner dressed to represent a well-known book or favourite novel. But the weather deteriorated and we ran into a storm. The ship was tossed about a good bit and all portholes had to be closed. Towels and porthole curtains stood out perpendicular from the walls of our cabin. I confess my appetite suffered and when dinnertime came neither my parent nor I had thought about appearing as books. In desperation my father pinned the cabin passengers' list on to the lapel of his tuxedo, and when asked what book he represented he blandly replied, *These Charming People*, by Michael Arlen.

I recall many details of that trip. After we had passed out of the cold waters of the north Atlantic and into the smooth and smiling blue of the Sargasso Sea, the deck chairs were brought out and the canvas swimming-pool was rigged up and filled with seawater. Flying fish skipped over the surface of the ocean and now and then the glassy plane was broken as a dolphin or grampus surfaced, causing a thrill of excitement on board the ship. On the fourteenth day we sighted Turks Island and entered the Caribbean Sea.

A friend of some friends of mine had been invoked to find us conveyance from Kingston to Mandeville, and while we were still battling with the port authorities Joseph made himself known. He was a simple country black boy in a rather shabby straw hat, and his car was even shabbier. We drove with him through Spanish Town and past the old parish of Clarendon, and so to Clifton, the home of the Misses Fisher near Mandeville. The car ride was not without its hazards, for Joseph had been indulging in some way that made it hard for him to keep awake, and more than once he fell asleep at the wheel, so much so that I was obliged to take over the driving.

Arriving at our destination, I was overwhelmed by the charm of our surroundings. On all sides palms, palmettos and bamboo trees lent majesty to the scene. Here was a wealth of tropical vegetation new to me. The house, the veranda and the adjacent buildings were covered with bougainvillaea, hibiscus or tacoma bush and the like, of every scent and hue. Joseph took his fare, reckoned at sixpence a mile, and departed. We carried our baggage through the garden to the front veranda, but found the door locked and the house deserted. It came on to rain, and for a time the two travellers sitting on their bags outside an empty house made a pathetic scene. The rain turned into a tropical downpour, scenting the night air, while millions of frogs struck up a chorus.

It had long been dark when a buggy, drawn by two fat horses, drove into the compound. Two elderly and extremely thin ladies descended. They were rather tall, and as flat in front as they were behind. Their sunken eyes, their toothless smiles, betokened hardship and poverty.

They said they had not expected us for another day or two and so had gone to a tea party. There being nothing to eat in the house, we went to a nearby hotel for supper. We dined well and returned to Clifton on foot, lighted and guided by a boy of sixteen, called James, and his lantern.

The Misses Fisher had done everything in their power to make our quarters comfortable. They had obviously seen better days but had managed to survive in spite of extreme poverty. The rooms were small, the heavy mahogany beds hard, and the general appearance of the house shabby. The crockery was cracked and the windows not too well cleaned. And, what was worse, there were no fly screens. But with all these drawbacks, there was an atmosphere of harmony and good-will, which overruled all signs of decline. And as I considered the staunch and resolute attitude of these two old ladies in the face of difficult circumstances, I saw them no longer as the Misses Fisher of Mahogany Hall but as the victors of a rearguard action into glory.

Next morning the sun shone brilliantly and we could see the grounds well stocked with flowers and fruits of many varieties, but on all sides banana groves dominated the scene. Amaline and Mrs Brown the cook served breakfast. The dishes were cracked and the brown sugar full of ants. Two old dogs scratched at their fleas in a patch of sunlight

on the floor, and a bare-necked rooster stumped in on the off-chance of a handout. But the breakfast was plentiful and the quality excellent.

The arrival of James, our guide of the night before, caused my father to ask what was happening in the village. Market day, he was told. This immediately aroused a latent mania for bargaining. He hired James as guide and bearer and we soon left for the town. Our progress to the marketplace was a halting one, for at every step my parent stopped to identify a species of flower or plant, shrub or tree, which were as profuse as they were varied. On this day the focal point of Mandeville was its marketplace, and we now found ourselves making a beeline for the heart of a concourse of shoving and screeching natives. My father's enthusiasm was only matched by the vigour with which he entered into the fray. To him it was like a pond to a thirsting duck, and he took to it with as much alacrity. His first purchase was a four-penny basket, as big as a clothesbasket, which he turned over to James to carry. He then proceeded to fill it with every conceivable fruit and vegetable – okra, custard apple, soursop, akki, sweet corn, and finally, a large lobster which had been carried up eighteen miles from the coast. The cost of the entire purchase was about the equivalent of fifty cents U.S.A.

And so our days were filled with interest, until Christmas was upon us. They were days blessed with a special companionship in the delightful and sometimes eccentric company of my father, days of harmony of spectrum and of octave: I did a few oil paintings, including one of Mrs Brown the cook. And music was provided by some classical records I had brought with me. Moreover, the high-pitched murmer of bees among the bougainvillaea and the tiny hum of birds as they darted from flower to flower were our constant music.

There were minnows in the water tank replenished by the rain. Why minnows? Because they ate the mosquito larvae. One morning while Miss Violet, the elder sister, was inspecting the tank, a donkey laden with vegetables came into the yard. This was a violation of the pet parrot's domain, and she flew into such a rage that Miss Violet had to pacify her. But in the bird's state of apoplexy she bit her mistress. Polly just couldn't stand donkeys.

'You naughty Polly,' said Miss Violet in a scolding voice, clutching her wounded finger.

'All right, all right,' replied the defiant bird, and she retreated into her cage.

I quickly got a bandage and, while I applied it, Miss Violet's tight little mouth softened for the first time and I saw no more the acidulated spinster but a very soft and gentle being.

Miss Violet was the right hand of the duo, Maybell the left. Like tenor and bass they had accompanied each other through every aspect of their seventy-year existence. I never heard them complain or criticise, or identify themselves emotionally with what is humanly called tragedy, their own or another's. Utterly guileless they were, and seemingly defenceless, yet towers of strength. Moreover, their generosity was exceptional; their charge for board and room was figured at the amazingly low rate of two pounds ten shillings a week each.

Christmas came. We dined around the big oil lamp on the dining-room table. The party was a great success. The roast duck provided the *piece de resistance*, couched in fried yams and apple sauce. My father and I provided a bottle of rum, but neither of the Miss Fishers would touch it. In fact, the bottle was still going strong on New Year's Day. They hoped we wouldn't be offended. They were frail to a point that aroused pity and so well-meaning that one couldn't help loving them.

I have met a good many landladies in my time. The Misses Fisher of Mahogany Hall stand out in my memory.

After this we moved to Montego Bay where an old coloured woman, with a Jamaican home nearby, rented me a room which I used as a studio. I settled down and did a lot of work. At noon, when it grew too hot for painting, my father and I would go down to the beach, purchase a sixpenny ticket from old Sarah and bathe. This very pleasant existence went on until the trade winds began to die down and the birds to nest. It was the time of the march of the land crabs and parties of natives with sacks and small oil lamps spent their nights hunting. It grew hotter and the sea became more inviting to us.

I had now collected sufficient canvasses for an exhibition in London. Among these were portraits of several of the better-known inhabitants of the island including one of the Harvard University astronomer, Professor Pickering, and also one of a wealthy rum merchant and manufacturer. The latter lived in real Jamaican style; his house, filled with old Spanish mahogany furniture, was very comfortable. I slept in a large four-poster bed and had a tray heaped with tropical fruit brought to me each morning for breakfast.

Outside, ox-drawn carts brought sugar cane to the mill. When not painting I would watch the process of making sugar and rum. The house was surrounded by an expanse of sugar-cane plantations in which gangs of blacks swinging machetes slashed their daily swath to keep the mill busy. To the south, the hills of the Cockpit country, to the north a deep blue sea. Never was I so loath to leave a place.

Life was as sweet as logwood honey. The Jamaican newspaper heard of my father's presence and there followed publicity through which I found myself also in demand. People wanted to meet my father, too, but he was reluctant to appear in public. I, on the other hand, gave several public lectures on modern art, sold a few pictures and was invited to judge at a couple of beauty contests in Kingston. In the physical sense beauty is a very relative thing and no set standards pertain to Jamaicans. Among the contestants were Spanish, Chinese and, of course, Negroid types as well as a very fair girl whose father was a German sailor and mother a black.

By the time I returned to pick up my father in Montego Bay, the heat was growing uncomfortable. I found my parent covered with newspapers rocking himself on the verandah. He even had a sheet like a roof over his head. 'The paraffin in the printer's ink,' he said, 'keeps away the mosquitoes.'

The tourists had almost all left; the beach was practically deserted. We had come to the time for our return to England. To catch our boat we would have to cross the island. My father and I left Montego Bay by car and, travelling via Falmouth and St Anne's, turned south over the mountains to Kingston where at the Myrtlebank Hotel we assembled our belongings and saw them safely on to the boat. Professor Cundall of the Jamaican Institute fetched us in his car and we drove back to his home for tea and a final talk before our departure.

Together we summarised our impressions of the island. The memory

we were taking away with us was a never-to-be-forgotton one, and my
father had benefited by the Milkriver baths, but he added, 'I shall be
glad to get back to civilisation – in Rome, where I have all the regenerative mental food I require; all cultural beauty necessary to feed
the intellect.'

But that did not quite satisfy me either and the question which had
lain unformulated for so long in my heart was not stilled by this itinerant
living and began to take conscious form: 'Why are we here? Why are
we on earth? Is it to seek out various forms of rendering our passage
more agreeable? Are we endlessly to seek acceptable means of escape
or distraction from life, because we regard it as a transient state, while
the real conditions of being come hereafter? What was the true meaning
of all this restlessness?' My father's regenerative mental food was no
doubt a pleasurable means of acquiring knowledge, but to what end
when he never left a record of it. And what value if he did? As soon
as it became a personal discharge one was drawing on a limited source
and one began to feel swept away.

These thoughts germinated in my mind as the ship carrying us
eastward was tossed about on the north Atlantic. 'How did man ever
become so deluded as to think he could live off his own strength and
intelligence?' I was moved by its absurdity, when my father entered
the cabin. He held tightly to the handrail. Every now and then the
ship lurched sickeningly and the porthole curtains swung inwards
from the wall. The delicate shades of green and white swept across
the ceiling as the ship cut its way through an unstable sea. He dropped
heavily into the armchair.

'I tried to get a sniff of fresh air on deck, but there is a seventy-five-
mile-an-hour gale up there and everything is battened down.'

We docked at Avonmouth a little behind schedule and continued
our journey together as far as Paris where we parted for a time, my
father going on to Rome.

I unpacked my canvasses and set them on view in my studio. I do
not think one should be too critical of one's work, nor should one be
so arrogant as to believe that one has succeeded. I spent the ensuing
summer preparing an exhibition of my paintings of Jamaica and
Maximillian Gauthier wrote the foreword to the catalogue. As a result
I sold a few paintings, but felt the exhibition was not a wild success.
Many socially prominent people came, made encouraging remarks
and then fluttered off to other engagements. Shortly thereafter the
thing was lost in the merry-go-round of social events.

Putting the frantic questionings aside, I drew. I drew simply because I loved to draw. It became to me like a caressingly recreative movement, giving form in subtle lines with all the best of my technical ability, in terms of planes and curves and other aspects and dimensions, to a subject seen in the light of its perfection. Not merely studies but portrayals, my drawings became to me a revelation in economical line of all the moods and subtleties of those eternally enchanting qualities in the subject. My art unfolded before me as a means of discovery and of sharing the truth as I found it revealed around me.

7

James Bond?

The Piazza San Marco in Venice was filled with colour and the whirling wings of pigeons in their tens of thousands as the figurines on the clock tower hammered out the hour. I went on to the Palace of the Doge for my rendezvous, the flurry of their wings almost deafening me and setting my heart to flutter. It was one of those occasions, recurring not infrequently in my life, appealing to my sense of drama in a setting of aesthetic and historical splendour. The exercise of higher powers of intellect and of a polished approach were called for.

Soon after the initial greeting in a domed vestibule, we walked through a marbled gallery, treading upon precious rugs which muffled the resonance of our movements, and so by some broad steps down to the colonnaded gloom of the water level. There we took our places in a waiting launch. Gliding slowly out from the vaulted darkness on to the sunlit water of a bright Venetian scene, the craft leapt forward with such speed that my hostess placed a hand upon my sleeve as if with apprehension. How expressive is a hand and how exquisitely revealing, which in one short gesture can make known so much. A dream imprisoned can break loose in one unrestricted instant and find fulfilment in a miraged hope. On her signet ring were the Royal Arms of Savoy.

What could I possibly offer to a troubled heart while my own was still in turmoil? The occasion was *de rigeur* enough so far as it went, for the restricting effect of an elderly lady-in-waiting prevented privacy, but we kept the conversation as sparkling as the sun upon the water and after lunch went on to the Island of Murano to see some glass. The moment passed and I recalled that my reason for being in Venice was Violet. Violet was an elderly novelist staying on the Dalmatian coast and a new Yugoslavian tourist bureau had supplied me with my ticket and itinerary. But, as I later found, their itinerary had little relationship to the actual boat and train services. I was told to leave Venice at such and such a time by train. On arrival at Trieste at mid-

107

night I was to board a Yugoslavian steamer. They had forgotten, however, to mention that it only sailed on certain days. On the midnight that I reached Trieste no such passenger steamer existed. However, a cargo boat of the same company said they would accept my ticket and I embarked with the assurance that they were bound for Dubrovnic. During the night in my dingy cabin I was devoured by fleas and mosquitoes. Exhausted, I finally fell asleep about dawn, only to be awakened by the unexpected rattle of the anchor chain. With expectation of relief, I looked out of the porthole, but to my dismay found myself gazing at a distant view of Venice. I decided to leave this dirty little ship and headed for the gangplank with my baggage, but the captain refused to surrender my ticket. He threatened to stop me by force, but in spite of his threats I gathered up my effects and took a gondola to the Piazza San Marco where I bought another ticket for Dubrovnic, as it is now called, and then, with another gondola, went out to an Italian ship riding at anchor. It was bound for the Dalmatian coast, sailing I was told at midnight. She was an old vessel but fairly clean. I awoke next morning to find myself back in Trieste! The steward pacified me with the assurance that the ship would eventually reach my destination. And so it did, where I met Violet and over a *schlibawitz* we traded our experiences.

It had been a picturesque journey calling at many ancient Venetian ports en route. In Dubrovnic I reaped a harvest of new impressions of national customs and costumes, of Croats, Serbs, Montenegrans, Turks, Jews and Bosnians. Violet was a sightseer and provided the stimulus which resulted in bus trips to many parts of that savage and mostly arid land. At one halt in the mountains we heard the wild strains of a Serbian 'goostler', a one-stringed wooden instrument upon the shank of which the head of an ibex had been carved. The virtuoso was playing strange romantic music, telling of love and war.

Then Violet became possessed of an overruling passion to buy the instrument and all attempts to dissuade her failed. She bargained with the man and right there and then in that rustic wayside inn got her way. Sitting on a wall with the bay of Hotor glistening in the noonday sun, I was irritated by this shortsighted act of possessiveness which seemed so senseless, and pictured her gazing at it as it hung inanimately on the wall of her small Paris apartment, a nostalgic reminder of the wild romantic music which it once emitted, for before he parted with it the young Serb serenaded us. He sang in a strong vibrant baritone voice.

'There were two flowers who had found a delightful nearness to
each other in a garden.' The theme was beautiful and the tune a happy
one. Then on a sadder note he told of a man who went to pick a pear
out of the orchard for his sweetheart and during his absence his friend
ran off with her. The girl then asks him to be best man at her wedding
and he tells of a night filled with doubt which ends in his decision to
go. His duty is to raise the bride's veil. While doing so he lightly
treads on her foot and whispers into her ear:

'Are you not sorry that you are not marrying me?'

The bus honked its horn, the serenade ended and Violet, clutching
her prize, returned to her seat.

I made many such trips during this period, going to Corsica and
Majorca, walking, climbing and sketching. I also made frequent visits
to my father in Rome. Rome blended with the pagan in my nature
and called forth memories of my childhood. A sensual mystical city
which claims eternity, it is at one time both deep and shallow.

On one such occasion I met Maud, a Swedish girl who was to
become my wife. I had dropped in on some friends for a drink after
a polo match and was attracted to her as she sat poised by the window.
I invited her to go with me to the Villa Guilia. My father, noticing
the attachment, raised his eyebrows in that quizzical manner I knew
so well. But the duchesses of Rome, making their investigations,
nodded their approval and agreed that she was impeccable. I was
thirty-seven years of age and felt the time had come for marriage. I
took Maud to Tivoli and there by the fountains of the famous Villa
D'Este proposed to her. She accepted me lightheartedly and, having
thus been confronted by a crisis, hurried home to Sweden. There
she told her mother she was sure her English friend would not follow
her, for she had given him no encouragement to do so. But he did
follow her and we were subsequently married in a registry office in
Paris.

My friend, Paul de la Tour, was present and if our mixed faiths
put a strain on the friendship he was too kind to show it. It saddened
my father, too, that I should have married in this manner. He did
not really take canon law too seriously, but accepted religious discipline
as an ingredient of his way of life, especially for his children. Had I
been wiser I would have recognised that emotionally I was quite
unfitted for marriage to anyone at that time and as for Maud she, too,
was emotionally immature. The marriage, though it proved ultimately
a failure, was by no means a dead loss. We had our happy moments,

but they were mostly overshadowed by ego storms. In fact we both had hard lessons to learn.

Soon after our marriage I took my Swedish bride to the Aldershot Tattoo near London, a military spectacle which causes the heart of every Briton to swell with pride, for surely we dearly love pageantry. I watched Maud closely, partly to see what her reactions were to this martial display, but also to make sure she did the conventionally right thing. Towards the end of the performance it grew chilly and we wrapped travelling rugs around our legs, but when the national anthem struck up on the public-address system I motioned to Maud to stand up. Of course, I stood very erect – fitting, as I thought, to the occasion. But my wife kept gesticulating to me. I hushed her crossly several times but in vain. When the final chords had died down, I asked what she had been saying.

'I was telling you,' she said, 'to take your hat off!'

During our honeymoon in London we purchased an old Morris convertible from a country squire, who was giving his son a better car for his twenty-first birthday. We paid £25 cash and as part of the deal the car was delivered to London. On the day before our departure for Austria the squire's chauffeur arrived with the Morris which was really an antique but, like every car of that period, mechanically sound. Nevertheless, as we left, all our well-wishers warned that it was a hazardous undertaking, for we would be crossing the Arlberg Pass in December. The dickey seat was crammed full of our baggage and more than once Maud, who had not learned to drive, had to push us through the snow. Traffic in the western provinces of Austria – Vorarlberg, north Tyrol and Saltzkammergut – kept to the right while to the east all traffic kept to the left, a fact which bore remembering.

We arrived in Vienna and found rooms at Frau Keller's *pension* not far from the Rathus. Other inmates included two young Englishmen, Maurice Bowra and his friend Martin, both young intellectuals of whom I was a bit shy and cautious.

The Vienna of Mozart, Schubert and Strauss still had a glimmer of imperial glamour and gaiety and, of course, all the post-war cliches, the cafes, Opera, Sacher's Bar and the Femina were crowded, but in the less fashionable quarters there was a hint of violence and resentment. Poverty and real hunger existed among the dispossessed. Vice of every description existed along the banks of the Danube, a drab flow of brown water romantically called blue, as it flowed on remorselessly through the capital to Budapest.

One is not inclined to eat a big breakfast in Vienna – coffee, two rolls and jam were the usual fare. Maud and I often saved a roll each which we would leave in the waste-baskets attached to lamp-posts in the streets. Soon a shadowy figure in shabbily respectable clothing would rummage them out and slink off again. Besides these destitute members of the upper classes there were the professional beggars, many of whom we got to know by sight.

The buildings even in Vienna's famous Ring were drab and the streets laced with tram wires gave them a strange feeling: weird and sinister and down at the heel. The wet cobblestones, the ill-dressed hustling crowd bundled up against the cold rain was like a back drop for a Dostoevsky novel or a spy romance, all of which was not lost on me. I could easily picture a body lying in some dark alley beaten up or drunk and face covered with blood. It was a city of incidents without a plot in an altogether tragic context. But Vienna seemed to be able to shrug it all off. It was a last post for diplomats, a run for the business jackals, the final ditch for the unemployable, where labour was cheap yet unobtainable. Elevators everywhere were adorned with 'out of order' signs, yet the Viennese would gaily whistle as they walked up to the sixth floor. When a new cask of Sud Tiroler was opened they would come in from every quarter to sing and joke and make love until the dawn. A pregnant woman could be trampled as she boarded the bus, but would be sure of being given a seat once she got inside. Unbusinesslike and romantically impractical in all regards. I ordered some flowers at the best flower shop for someone who had invited us to dinner. They were delivered to the wrong address and when I asked the manager of the shop why they had not been received, he was insulted.

'The *Genedig* Herr slanders me by thinking we take his money and do not deliver the goods.'

The fact that the flowers had not reached their proper destination seemed irrelevant.

The great palace of Schoenbrunn reminded me of the stories my father had told me of Franz Josef's lady friend, the actress Frau Schratt and how he used to see her entering the palace grounds by a side-gate each day. Silerns house, where my father had stayed, looked out on this gateway to royal romance.

It was 1933 and the fate of Austria was once more in the balance. The Austrian Chancellor, Dr Englebert Dollfus, was still in power, but was assassinated on 25 July 1934, twenty-four hours after his death had been officially announced. He was succeeded by Kurt von Schuschnigg. Following the advice of Baron von Oppernheim, I had been recording and watching the growth of Nazi power throughout the period of my movements on the continent and had discerned the nature of the man Hitler, who had aided and abetted it all, though, as head of state, he disclaimed knowledge. I was becoming well informed and knew also of the Nazi party's illegal meetings in Austria, their small arms caches obtained from Germany, while orders in the Reich were published simultaneously discouraging disturbances in Austria.

I had in fact, in conjunction with my early married life in Vienna, a desire to establish what contacts I could as sources of reliable information. I spent much time with a Dr Kamman to see what I could organise by way of a tourist business centred in Kitzbühel as it seemed that legitimate business opportunities could open the way for further flexibility in my movements. To this end I wished to form an association of the proprietors of small hotels and *Gasthausen* in the lesser-known parts of the Austrian Tyrol, the idea being to regulate the prices from the business standpoint but, also, to give me a network of places in which my appearance would largely be taken for granted. I sought the assistance of the Volksburo and the Credit Anstalt through the advice of Dr Kamman.

My task eventually accomplished I called my company Tyrolese Tours. Since Hitler had forbidden German tourists to leave the fatherland, I had the Austrian field very much to myself. A favourable exchange rate in Austrian shillings against the pound stirling was at that time available and I was able to offer a return trip, London to London with two weeks all found, in the Austrian Tyrol at fourteen pounds, fourteen shillings. Of course, the pickings were not great, but it offered a legitimate opportunity for touring about in the Innsbruck-Salzburg area and a portion of Bavaria north of that line. This included Munich, Reichenhal and Berchtesgaden where Hitler had his famous mountain hideout, Berghof.

I was walking up the Khertner Ring past the Opera to Joseph Platz when I ran into Dr Kamman, who had spoken to me at a legation dinner of the destructive policies of National Socialism. He talked very slowly and I was afraid he would never get to the point before the end of our walk. It was, moreover, cold with a promise of snow. For ten o'clock in the morning it was dark and the shops were turning on their lights. A powder snow drifted along the frozen streets as we turned into a doorway and up some dark stairs to the office of Dr Buchmayer. Initially there were only the three of us present and I was able to talk freely of the ways and means of achieving my aims in respect to my tourist activities, but, as it turned out, not only was Dr Buchmayer an ally but I found him also eager to discuss the political situation. Vienna was full of spies and intrigue and subterfuge. It took little to trigger a political discussion. Spies met, as a rule, in a cafe or in the foyer of the Opera, where their conversations would be safely drowned by the strains of *Die Fledermaus* or *Die Meistersinger* or, perhaps, the fate of some luckless Bohemian agent was plotted under the overtones of Johann Strauss.

Vienna was looked upon by some as forming part of the Sudeten-land because it was now the largest of all Sudeten population centres. The Sudeten Germans are a tough lot, raised in an atmosphere of constant border quarrels. Yet they are brave, industrious and highly gifted. Their role in Austria, especially Vienna, cannot be discounted. Dr Buchmayer was a Sudeten and a civil servant.

The leading circles of the political parties, especially the extreme left and extreme right, largely consisted of Sudeten Germans; likewise in the Catholic and anti-Catholic hierarchies. The National Socialist element was almost entirely under the direction and inspiration of Sudeten Germans. There was also a party connected with Czecho-slovakia which had its influence in Austria. The German Jews of Moravian origin were more or less in control of commerce, industry, journalism and the arts including, of course, the law.

'A Viennese born in Bruno or Iglau is either a Nazi or a Jew.' Dr Kamman was speaking in slow motion. 'And in either case very notice-ably so.'

'This is not surprising,' added Dr Buchmayer, 'because Moravia has been Vienna's strongest hinterland. These national trends have homogenised under the Imperial Rule and are now hard to separate.'

The picture was beginning to unfold.

Not only was I beginning to get the hang of the political kaleido-scope, but I was seeking a way to providing a means of circulating in the southern area of the expanding realm of the Führer.

In the initial steps of intrigue Maud, who I had not wanted to get involved in my research, began to feel excluded without knowing from what and partly in retaliation started a flirtation with the young musicologist who was staying in our *pension*. Harmless as this doubtless was, it caused me extra concern because it was all done in secret. She felt, no doubt, that if I could be secret then she would jolly well be secret too. Actually it was not my idea to keep her in the dark but S.M. thought women, as a whole, more vulnerable than men especially if their emotions became involved; and in this particular case the Swedes, though officially neutral, had during the First World War proved to have German leanings. But then he added with a wink, 'They have sporting instincts, you know, they like to back the winner.'

Maud's clandestine meetings with Martin were more amusing because they were secret. She was like a dog with a bone who, having no appetite for it, proceeds to bury it. The fun lay more in the subterfuge than in the bone. The weaving of a complicated net of deceit had for her a certain romantic thrill and, for his part, Martin was also in a powerful stream, being swept along on the waters of chivalrous romance, with the possibility of having to shoot the rapids eventually. It would have been funnier had I not been a little too possessive over Maud. A secret agent must be cool and uninvolved during danger and while in the most provoking and complicated situations. I too might have to shoot rapids but of a much more serious kind. It was ironical in a way that we were both engaged in secrecy one from the other but with different motives.

In the process of organising Tyrolese Tours as my cover, I was obliged to invoke the approval and support of the National Tourist Board who had agencies across the continent. The area I had particular interest in between Innsbruck and Salzburg took a great deal of time and effort to explore for it necessitated testing various resorts along the way and *Gasthaus* accommodation for their recreational amenities in summer and winter. Many wayside inns along this road were romantically attractive. Frescos adorned the exterior and the *Weinstube*'s panelled walls and vaulted ceilings, with carved or painted furniture in the neat and clean bedrooms. Sometimes, however, there would be no indoor plumbing. In one mountain inn I asked the *Wirt* if there was running water. He assured me that there was and promptly took me to a mountain stream at the back of the house. But prices were reasonable; a bedroom and two meals for six Austrian shillings was then roughly a dollar. The extensive desk work of Tyrolese Tours was taken care of by a Mrs Sylvester, an English resident of Kitzbuhel. I don't believe she had the slightest idea of what I was doing besides acting as a guide to the increasing tide of young tourists that came from England.

Maud and I based ourselves now in Kitzbühel, from where we

could conveniently operate a tourist business in a triangle, with its base on the line from Innsbruck to Salzburg and its apex to the north at Munich, and eventually another triangle with the same base but with the apex to the south at Bolzano or, perhaps, eventually even Venice. Kitzbühel was an ideal place to live as it was still unspoiled and naturally charming.

In a sunny corner of the Tiefenbrunner cafe some friends were having coffee. Peter Fleming and his wife Celia Johnson, the actress, shared a table with Arthur Waley and Ella Maillart. Ian Fleming, a little aloof, was reading a spy novel of Buchan's when I arrived with Maud and Margarita Brambeck, a house guest, just nineteen and a dazzlingly beautiful girl. Ian sat up and closed his book and we all joined in the general badinage. It was good to associate oneself with adults while the world was playing at soldiers. It was the popular hour of the aperitif and Maud suddenly announced that it was time to leave for lunch. Surprisingly, Ian stood up and asked, 'Can I come too?'

'Of course, of course,' Maud replied, delightedly, though a little taken aback. 'I hope you will not accept too much?' she said.

'I shall accept all that I am offered,' Ian returned, laughing, evidently amused at her confusion of words. Thus began a series of sometimes near compromising contacts with Ian.

The two Fleming boys were vastly different in character; unlike Rollo and myself, Ian was jealous of the successes of his elder brother and felt eclipsed, frustrated and defeated by Peter's ability to excel at whatever he did. And yet, funnily enough, when one reads the two books written by Peter and Ella, each describing their joint journey across the inner and outer Mongolian deserts, it was Ella who was the dominant personality.

These two were sons of Valentine Fleming, killed in the First World War, and grandsons of Robert Fleming, a wealthy banker in the city of London. In the presence of a husband, a mother can exercise her natural protective care and be generous with her tenderness and affection. But the responsibilities of both parents falling solely on her, she adopts a disciplinary attitude foreign to her role as a mother and very unpopular with boys. Ian's mother's anxiety over his success was evident when I lunched with her at her home in Oxfordshire in 1944. She meant him to be a credit to his family and his failure both at Eton and Sandhurst had been a personal affront to her.

The Flemings were a family of means, accustomed to leisure and being leaders in a leisured society. Yet Ian had a definite restlessness and resentfulness about him and seemed not to know how to handle it. He was ruthless with his girl acquaintances as if, by taking it out on them, he could fulfil himself. A Casanova depends upon conquest after conquest to convince himself that he believes in his true manliness. Sex, of course, can be an addiction or a means to prove something in oneself, but it is seldom done for the purpose of accepting responsibility for another. It is almost an indulgence which a witty Frenchman once described as '*l'egoism a deux*'. Nipping in and out of beds with girls is fun while it lasts, but it must never become a purpose in itself. It is rather like the hire-purchase system without the ability to conclude the deal.

That Ian was glamourous is certain. He was also nonchalant, restless, spoiled, more cynical than funny, strong willed and ambitious, and a first-class athlete. He was very much at home in Kitzbühel, having first come there in 1924 to the Forbes-Dennis's establishment at Tennerhof. Following his problems at both Eton and Sandhurst it was hoped that the Forbes-Dennis could help him to find himself. The blessing of this interlude was not lost on Ian and he was deeply grateful to this kindly and understanding couple.

At our time of meeting he was still employed by Sir Robert Jones as a Reuters correspondent and had recently returned from the Soviet Union where he had covered the then famous Metropolitan Vickers trial where two British employees were facing charges of espionage.

From now on Ian was a frequent visitor to Haus St Franciskus and I often ran into him in the town. We met at the houses of our mutual friends, at bars, or on the mountain. Kitzbühel had a few excellent ski runs and in summer there were endless excursions and, of course, the famous warm-water lake, the Shwartz Zee.

I was sunning myself there one afternoon after a swim and, as was my habit, I had changed into a pair of dry trunks. But these particular trunks had no belt. Surrounded by the rank and fashion of society, I was enjoying the interlude, when I saw Ian on the diving board. He did an exhibition dive and I thought to myself, I can do better than that. So, forgetting that my trunks had no belt, I went to the top of the diving board and executed my best swallow dive. On contact with the water my trunks came off, leaving me to swim in complete nudity. I remember how I prayed that the bloody things would float to the surface which they eventually did, but not before I had suffered some hideous moments of embarrassment.

Among the regular visitors and residents of Kitzbühel were Frau

Poland, Graf Schlick, Graf Rudi Lambert, the Brackens, Captain 'Pop' Stokes, RN, the Hadows, Count de Renville, Graf 'Chappy' Silern, Prince Tassilo Furstenburg, Prince Ferdinand Liechenstein and my intimate confidant, Baron Rudolfo von Gerlach. Of all those who came and went during the six-and-a-half years I made Kitzbühel my home, my association with Rudolfo was most fruitful.

Ian and many others were often to be found at Reisch's Bar. Once Rudolfo and I came in and joined a party of young people, including Ian, who sat next to a German whose name was Markwert. We sat together for some time. Ian expostulated his belief that financial security was all that mattered. I was a little doubtful of his sincerity, coming from one who was a complete romantic about money. To Ian it was more a medium of freedom from the material grind. A very complicated, imaginative and subtle character was Ian, who lacked stability and staying power and yet was most intolerant of failure in others. The realities of business bored him. There had to be movement, excitement and glamour. And so it was that Ian never stayed long with any undertaking.

We moved on to the topic of books, an interest he shared with Markwert, who spoke fluent English, and they swapped names of rare editions. It was all far above my head and the subject was soon changed to women. There was intrigue in discovering the various viewpoints of others. It became obvious that Ian's interest in girls was mostly carnal, a fact he made known to them sometimes within minutes of becoming acquainted. He was something between a wolf and a rake, equipped with good looks and money, a combination fatal for the average young female.

Rudolfo and I walked home together. His only observation about Ian was '*sehr Empfindlich*' (very touchy). Of Markwert he warned me, 'Watch him, I believe he is Gestapo.'

After the rape of Austria in 1938 Ian left Reuters and went to his spiritual home, the city of London, where he joined a well-known firm of stockbrokers. This, after all, was the milieu he felt at ease in. Latent in his character, deep in his subconscious, was the billycock hat and an umbrella of city life.

I had, meanwhile, been called to London and on my return I learned with some misgivings that Ian had introduced Maud to Markwert and that this German had taken my wife out to dinner, evidently for the purpose of finding out something of my activities.

'What can a man like Conrad possibly be doing in this sleepy old town ? Surely he is too active for retirement and too well connected ?'

Sensing this was dangerous ground, Maud refrained from comment. Then, with less subtlety, he came to the point, pouring her another glass of wine and leaning a little closer. He asked her if I was with British Intelligence. Maud froze, gave a nervous giggle and replied,

'Conrad, a secret agent ? Oh, no, he's much too stupid.'

This seemed to have satisfied her interrogator, but it gave Maud a shock. She knew little of what I was doing and this jolted her own curiosity.

Ian and I had, on occasion, discussed the subject of international politics. He was, after all, a member of Reuters news agency and kept abreast of the general trend; the Berlin axis was becoming an ever-increasing threat to the peace of Europe. But I had direct and indirect connections with the upper brackets of the governing classes in Europe, many of whom were contacts of Rudolfo's. These sources of information were vastly superior to those of any of the news agencies of the time. Certain items of public interest in my dispatches would, in due course, be released by London and so find their way into the press and broad-casting systems. But they had come to me straight from the source. Rudolfo was a wizard for smelling out a new political trend, a change of tactics, a scheme in the plotting stage, a shift in the ranks of government or army – and kept me informed. Compared with my more direct methods of approach, he was a genius at subtlety, logic, intrigue and political surmise. Besides him, I had other sub-agents who kept an eye on troop movements, installations and innovations, especially in the electronic fields.

In a way, Ian was a more blatant and irascible me, and I was inclined to be more open with him than I should. But after the affair with Markwert I drew in my horns, realising how utterly alone a secret agent can be. In the good old days when I was in Stockholm or Helsing-fors, I rejoiced in the wonderful companionship of Major Scale and his family. In fact, under his leadership the whole office became a family. But times had changed. British Intelligence was now run on a shoe-string budget and on my first day Claude Dansey, as new chief, had insulted me by slipping me a fiver as if he were hooking a common informer.

It was ironic that during my six years of Hitler-watching over a large area of southern Germany, with many sub-agents working under me, I was receiving less pay than a window cleaner. At times when I would meet C.D. at the Carlton Hotel off Haymarket, after coming from Kitzbühel at his request, there would be quibbles over my travel expenses. On another occasion in Paris, a most compromising situation developed over a lost questionnaire. We had met at a club on the Champs Elysee, when he drew me aside to one of the windows to read me this document. He never gave it into my hands at any time, yet later insisted that I had lost it. This and the fact that I discovered that my dispatches were being forwarded to their appropriate destination by him, but without giving credit to their source, accentuated that sense of being alone and embattled. It may sound as if I was being sorry for myself – I was, let us say, disillusioned.

On 7 February 1934, having established ourselves at the Pension Holzel we made an excursion, Maud and I, towards the border town of Kufstein. We stayed a night at Kossen at a *Gasthaus* for a mere five shillings a head for bed and breakfast, and set off next morning to cover the remaining 27 kilometres to Kufstein with some difficulty. The road which had been a sheet of ice was now deep slush, but the country on all sides was beautiful, far exceeding our expectations: deep pine woods with mountains in the distance and about halfway to our destination a partly thawed lake beneath the towering crags of the Kaiser Mountains. Then, on our way down into the valley of the inn, the Morris got into some soft snow on the shoulder of the road and skidded into the ditch. Fortunately, six stalwart men were tramping nearby and they bodily lifted our car back on to the road.

Shafts of sunlight from a rend in the smudge of cloud slanted on to the town of Kufstein with its ancient castle. By twilight we had checked into the Gasthaus zum Auracher Lochl and the car into the local garage, there to receive all the care it had needed for so long.

In the *Weinstübe* a harpist was entertaining a few peasants, while good wine and Tyrolese fare was being served by waitresses dressed in local costume. Next day after breakfast of warm rolls and thick honey, I turned Maud loose on the town. She was an inexhaustible sightseer. I went on with my letter of recommendation to interview the director of the local government tourist bureau regarding transportation, for I would need chartered buses for my clients.

The upshot was a meeting with one of the garage owners who would himself drive the bus. We quickly put our heads together and, since the man had also been a tourist guide for many years, he not only knew the area on both sides of the border perfectly but had, I found, managed to develop very decided political views in favour of an independent Austria. Through him I met a member of the *Vater-*

landische front and together we walked to the Castle of Griefenstein in the tower of which had been installed a very beautiful commemorative organ. At noon each day classical music would be played which could be heard for miles around. We ended up, our conversation developing warmly, with a jug of Sud Tiroler and by the time the organ had finished a Bach Cantata we were all in firm agreement that we were united against Hitler.

Meanwhile my noble father's condition had deteriorated and in November I was called to his bedside. He died that winter and in the following autumn, marital strains having overwhelmed our relationship, Maud and I agreed to separate. These years seemed to me then as the autumn of the world, presaging winter.

One of those Indian summers with day upon day of calm sunny weather, yet with an inevitable sense of the sinking year, was upon us. The peaceful south Tyrolean villages were scented with drying plums and sweet chestnuts. Together three of us, Maud, myself and a mutual friend, climbed in the Sella group, sitting among rocky summits which overlooked the Lombardy Plain. Above all, there was that sense of release mingled with regret and a desire to make amends. A final mingling, a belated embrace and on 28 October at a frontier station a train left for Vienna and parted two immature persons who had not yet learned to know themselves or each other. Little did we know that a daughter, Christina, had been conceived.

The train steamed out into the night and I watched the red light of its last carriage disappear from view. I shuddered a little, for the autumn frosts had come. Inwardly I was feeling emptier than when the train had left me alone on the Canadian prairies. Was this the completion of another life-cycle? Was this the way things should end? I was plagued with questions.

On reaching Vienna, exhausted after a tearful journey, she wrote in her broken English of the love that she felt for me, yet had never been able to show during our union. She was not made for marriage, she said, as indeed she did not think I was either.

8

Black Ore for Death

I passed the winter a little morosely, buried in my work and organising my tourist bureau. Spring came, followed by an early summer. It was now the middle of June and, having exhausted the possibilities of skiing in Switzerland, I decided to move, for a time, to Lapland. Urged by my idiosyncrasy for southern aspects, I wrote to the management of a small hotel at Riksgrenzen to give me a sunny room. This was done with a vengeance for I got a room in the north of the house.

'In this room,' explained the manageress, 'you will get the sun from nine o'clock at night until nine o'clock in the morning.'

I borrowed blackout material and pinned it over my window, but though it shut out the light it could not dispel the northlands awakening to life. The whole world outside seemed astir and it infected me. It pulsated like the rhythmic spasms of a woman in labour. It was springtime in the Arctic and the world was bursting into life.

In many parts of the world man craves the sun and in others he shuns it, but here the call to life after the darkness of winter is so compelling that every part of one – every cell and organ – responds to it. The gentle but endless slopes of these northern fjelds and the sun that never sets, the nomad Lapps and their herds of reindeer, provided an added attraction for cross-country skiing. But I found other interests as well, quite inadvertently.

The hotel was close to the railway. Sitting one morning by the hotel entrance waxing my skis, I noticed that increasingly frequent trains laden with iron ore from the Kiruna mines were following each other closely, travelling towards the Norwegian coast and seaport of Narvik. Impulsively, I pocketed my passport and hopped one of these trains riding down to the sea past cavernous fjords and enveloping mists to its destination. There I found trainload upon trainload of ore pouring into the holds of German and Dutch ships. I spoke to a Dutch sailor and asked where it was all going. The Rhineland, I was told, either to the Krupps munition factory or to the Saar.

'How long has this been going on?' I enquired.

'Not very long,' was the reply. 'Hitler has just begun to rearm.'

This was news indeed! But it was not all, for I found that Germany was buying iron ore from every mine in Sweden, many of which had never before exported it.

Leaving quickly for Stockholm, where Maud was expecting the baby, I searched out the British Minister and the Consul-General, the Commercial and Military Attaches, enquiring of all if they knew of this massive flow of resources. They did not. I wrote immediately to S.M., now Director of British Intelligence, who upon receiving my letter called me by phone at the British Legation, where I was staying. After warm congratulations he said I should report to London without delay.

'I can't do that,' I replied, 'I'm expecting a baby any day now.'

There was a pause, then he said, 'Come as soon as you can,' and rang off.

Luckily the baby was not long in coming, and we called her Christina.

It was 9 July 1935 and Gustav von Rosen and I had been out riding. I made a special effort to return by 1.30, for the Palarets with whom I was staying were having a few people in for lunch. Apart from Rebecca West, who like myself was a house guest, they expected the Belgian and Italian ministers and their wives, a Marchesa di Paterno and an Austrian baroness who was engaged in writing a book on Charles XII. The Italians had been in charge of a diplomatic mission to the court of Haile Selassie and so the inevitable subject of Mussolini's war on Abyssinia was brought up. 'A war,' whispered Rebecca, 'of white men in black shirts against black men in white shirts.'

I was hungry after the vigorous exercise of the morning and noted that the entree was breaded lamb chops adorned in paper frills. A footman whispered in my ear that I was wanted on the phone so, making my apologies, I hurried to the library. Maud's voice sounded urgent, 'My hour has come!' Getting a taxi I quickly picked her up at her mother's flat and took her to the hospital where, refusing to use the elevator, she tramped up to the maternity ward on the fourteenth floor. The concept that prospective fathers should be present in the delivery room was not current in this hospital, so I took up my vigil in a small waiting room where I was eventually informed by a large white nurse that I had become the father of a daughter.

The baby was very healthy and put on weight and I felt I should go to London to see S.M., but there was more information needed

in corroboration of my first report. I bought an English sports car
and set out in search of the smaller mines. I thus discovered that
most of them, with outputs ranging from 300 to 500 tons a day (some
with 50 per cent pure iron) were exporting to Germany for the first
time. While doing this I based myself near Ludivika where my mother-
in-law had a charming old country home. Here, when not with my
wife and child, I tramped or canoed around the district with Leica and
binoculars in search of wild birds which in summer throng the Swedish
lakes and forests. I frequently bathed too in the midst of that glorious
scenery. There were other sports as well and I received a letter from
S.M. that a 'friend' of his was coming to do some fishing for whom
a room had been booked at an hotel in Grangard. So I drove over
there but found no one answering to his description. But I met two
young Englishmen working at A.S.E.A. – we sat over coffee and
discussed the situation in Ethiopia. The League of Nations was shaking
its finger at *Il Duce* and at France's Laval who was applauding him.
Ramsey McDonald, too, had uttered a lot of restraining phrases and
Anthony Eden threatened economic sanctions. Yet the conclusion of
the explosive situation was not far off.

A glance at the world situation was both exciting and disturbing,
filling one with doubts for the future. Patterns of power were again
shifting. It did not take much imagination to see the fissures which
were appearing in Western European politics. Yet there was a wilful
blindness. Smug little islands were isolating themselves from the
headlong race that was developing for world domination. An ability
to break from tradition or, better still, having none to cling to, was
an advantage. It is the countries that 'have' which find that 'having'
hampers their development. But of all examples of reactionary con-
servatism, we Irish are among the worse. We love tradition, custom
and deep-rooted usages. Whenever we have a grievance we enjoy
meeting a fellow griever with whom we can commiserate and soon
get down to all the gruesome details and dreadful aspects of the situation. We derive, it seems, satisfaction from re-fighting wars or reliving experiences when none of the rancour escapes us and where
there is no present reality of danger.

While in Finland as Military Attaché, I had striven to help my
relation Kathleen ffrench and I had managed to get her out of Soviet
Russia, only to find that her real bondage was self-imposed in her
attachment to her worldly possessions. Idealistically, I hoped that
my assignment would now enable me to continue to help others, this

time out of Germany. Such are the dreams of the perfectionist who
desires to eliminate the evils from the world. It is said that the error
of the extreme idealist is in endeavouring to realise the absolute without
the relative, and of the extreme materialist in endeavouring to realise
the relative without the absolute. The world scene drifted inevitably
in all its facets toward disintegration and conflagration but I, strangely,
felt within myself some peculiar sense of growing confidence which
affirmed, nevertheless, that all was going as it should. To my outward
vision there certainly seemed no justification for such an attitude of
integration and it puzzled me. But I quietened myself with the realisation that the heart often has its reasons the mind knows nothing of.

The old ways were passing, but I nourished an urge to look in on
Monivea to see Rozzie ffrench after my interview with S.M. She
remained in residence at our old seat and, feeling her age, seldom left
it for any reason. The attraction of better wages elsewhere had drawn
away her few servants. Money was not coming through from Kathleen,
indeed, she had none to send and the estate was becoming dilapidated.
I detected a note of apathy mingled with resentment in Rozzie's
attitude; there was no one to cut and haul turf, and a piece of masonry
had fallen and blocked the hall chimney so that the fire that had
welcomed the arriving guest was extinguished forever. She now lived
in the study which her father had occupied during his lifetime, surrounded by thousands of knick-knacks commemorating the past.
Her welcome was cold; I would do better, she said, to go to Ballyglunin
to my cousin's where John Blake could offer me greater comfort.

John still lived in the old style of an Irish country gentleman. The
Blakes had always been men of property and hospitable to a fault. They
still had maids, were waited on at meals and celebrated my visit by
opening a bottle of Veuve Cliquot. I borrowed John's gun and went
out after snipe. There were golden plover, too, and tawny woodcock
on the edges of the woods. We went to Galway city in the family car,
tramping the wet pavement there as we did the weekly shopping. We
lunched together, John and I, at the County club where there were
still signs of prosperity thanks, in part at least, to John's generous purse.

Some of the country gentlemen, rather frayed at the cuffs, were
dozing in leather-bound chairs comfortably ensconced behind their
newspapers. Others argued briskly over local matters. They spoke
of the future of Monivea and shook their heads pessimistically. The
climate, like the lunch, was plain, warm and friendly. At Ballyglunin
I had felt the straight-jacket of religious discipline, for after meals

we would repair to the frigid atmosphere of an unheated oratory in the tower and recite the rosary, the Hail Marys tumbling out of our mouths like Irish mist. A hard frost had descended on the country, but when the thaw returned we went shooting by Loch Corib where a Canadian senator, Colonel Lynch Staunton, and other members of the Galway families had a shooting syndicate. The salty breezes of the Atlantic swept the land. It was good woodcock weather, stirring the blood. Yet blood and spirit were in conflict. It was 'land of my fathers' with its age-old traditions and prejudices versus freedom of thought and expansion.

There were fifteen brace of woodcock by the end of the day, two brace of pigeons and a golden plover. The senator invited the guns into his house and the beaters were taken care of elsewhere. The wind increased and roared through the naked trees. The guests were warmed with whisky before they departed and as they left the game-keeper touched his cap and took his tips. The cars moved off to their various destinations in the dark. I felt that there was a great gap in this society. There were the gentry and peasants, each caught fast in the grip of their own traditions. And then there was the middle class, provincial to the core and the backbone of Ireland.

John's driving was somewhat erratic as we sped past the stone walls. He took off his cap whenever passing a church, a priest, or a cemetery, but nearing home he got tired and only touched the peak of his cap respectfully. There was very little freedom in this sort of approach to living.

'The people of Ireland,' said John, 'are now less downtrodden and servile with the passing of English rule. They have more self-assurance but have grown arrogant and interested in nothing that does not bring them gain.'

These familiar words were not peculiar to Ireland, of course; everybody was saying them all over the world, for in all social grades the lower stratas were rising to the surface like layers of skin. The world, more than ever a victim of economic determinism, was sinking into chaos. The spirit of Communism was making itself felt.

'In all this,' I asked John, 'have they forgotten how to smile?' Ireland without a smile was destitute indeed!

'We still have a certain sense of security and that is what raises the smile, though God knows it is not a material one!'

I wanted to corner John about Monivea. He was a close friend of Rozzie and knew what was going on. People often suspect plotting and scheming when in reality it is they themselves who are doing it, and in this case Rozzie probably was innocently allowing things to drift. Yes, she was feeling her age alright and suffered a good deal from rheumatism. Having guests became more of a chore, especially as she now clung to the impractical traditions of entertainment even more firmly, simply because they had been in vogue in 'the good old days'. But John was not to be drawn. He knew well enough how quick any remark could be spread around and distorted. As we drove away from the castle one afternoon, opening the white paddock gates and passing through the beech woods towards the West Lodge, he hazarded the remark that 'unless money could be got from somewhere, the place would go to ruin'.

Through the wrought-iron lodge gates, the village green opened out before us bordered on either side by white cottages. It was always populated by geese and the odd donkey and after school hours it was a playground for children or a lounging place for stalwart policemen in their dark green uniforms. The limestone road, like a white ribbon in the sunlight, stretched through the village to the top of the hill where stood the ruin of a flax mill.

'Your great-grandfather,' pointed John, 'built that during the potato famine to give the people employment. Today they are waiting for the signal to pounce and grab what land they can from their bene-factors."

'You mean the park?' I asked, somewhat horrified.

'Yes, the whole place. They will break it up into small holdings and tear down Monivea if they get the chance. The authorities in Ireland today work against the county families and all is done to level down the classes and break up wealth and possession in order that the peasants should profit.'

On another occasion as we drove through Galway, John pointed to Abbeygate Street, the Faubourg St Honore of the city, where houses that were once of great elegance now stood gaunt and roofless.

'Most of these mansions once belonged to me,' he said, 'but the government has obliged me to sell them, or pull them down.'

Ireland was taking its liberty and progression literally, if not tragi-cally, and a people with no natural taste for materialism were being forced into industry for which they had neither aptitude nor appetite. It was a grey day and the lapwings flew over the stone walls and sodden fields.

At Ballyglunin over a whisky, before the turf fire in John's study, I asked him point blank what the situation was with Monivea.

'The agent is over a thousand pounds out of pocket. The stables are rented, but the kitchen garden is not worked. I suggested Rozzie should take paying guests but she doesn't like the idea. Plenty of saleable wood on the property, but Kathleen refused to allow it to be sold. She will not answer letters and, although she is attached to the place, she seems wilfully to let it fall to ruin.'

The situation seemed critical and the key to its solution rested I thought with Kathleen. Somehow or other she must be reached. Then, as if by magic, I received a New Year greeting from her in Harbin. I cabled a reply: 'Hope you are being properly cared for, wire if need me.' I followed this up with a letter describing the plight of Monivea – that I would gladly work the property with my own hands, care for Rozzie in her old age and only waited her blessing and sanction to the scheme. I sent a copy of this letter to Rozzie. It was a risky thing to do and it did not pay off. From that day on Rozzie regarded me with suspicion. There was now little point in lingering on and, having completed my business with S.M., I returned to Austria.

I had reorganised my life in Kitzbühel. A competent Hungarian lady had undertaken to run my home for a stipend. To offset this expense I took on paying guests. The arrangement left me free to make further contacts in Austro-German frontier towns and with them I would meet from time to time to discuss the situation.

The upsurge of national socialism in Germany had produced a violent reaction among its neighbouring states. I found no difficulty in picking up anti-Nazi associates. At my request they would write, telephone or, in other ways, send me interesting bits of news. Of course, I ran the risk of being looked upon as a secret service agent, but 'espionage' was a loose term with the Fascists and Communists applying it to all opponents. It no longer seemed to carry a stigma.

To all outer appearances I was a playboy. There were, after all, plenty of retired middle-aged men who were living the life of dilet-tantes on the continent and my pursuits veered from the studious and meditative to an unostentatious life of pleasure and danger. Perhaps I was trying to overcome a serious lack in myself, yet I had never been able to put my finger on its actual nature. Whatever I did, I preferred to do alone. My mountaineering was done on the spur of the moment when conditions converged to make the time propitious, yet which, to the average individual, would seem to be out of season.

I had an inquisitiveness about what lay beyond, around or behind me. Beyond a ridge or behind an exterior I was interested in the cause of all appearances. I saw the Nazi cause as evil, although it had plausible, even most convincing, reasoning. This thing that would rationalise man's soul, usurp the principles of Being and rule the world, did it understand itself? Did it not argue like Job's miserable comforters, darkening counsel without knowledge? The more I found out about it, the more I was convinced that my mission was to refute it wherever possible. I ran great risks and became identified with a subversive war against a malignant type of human nature which, by whatever name you call it, was international in scope, emerging more as a focus of something in the human heart than constrained to one region and one people. True, it found a focus in Nazi doctrine in Germany, but its roots were deeper than that.

From time to time and by arbitrary means, these lower instincts are kept in check by codes of ethics or international law enforcement, but they exist and go on the rampage when man departs from his codes. Slowly I was awakening to the fact that, of himself, man had no authority to make laws. And all that he could do in that way was to surrogate arbitrarily. The thought was very disturbing and caused me to find myself being driven by an almost frenetic energy. I flung myself into the arms of mother nature for the sake of its soothing influence, its sense of permanence in the midst of change. Once again I took to the hills.

The strengthening sun was causing avalanches but I was restless beyond measure and would not be dissuaded from climbing the Gross Venediger. I was lucky enough to get a muleteer to carry my skis and rucksack from Neukirchen to Post Alm. School children were collecting for their morning lessons around the village fountain. The church bell rang for matins. I emerged from the inn refreshed, yet what I had heard in the *Weinstübe* caused my cautious side to reassert itself. The proprietress had recently lost her husband, he and his companions having been overwhelmed by an avalanche. But this did not apply to me, I shrugged, as I started off on the seven-and-a-half-hour walk that lay before me. At the Post Alm, I picked up my skis and, opening my rucksack, sat down to eat. It was high noon and the burning sun suggested an afternoon storm.

The packer's wife brought tea and a farrow of piglets, smelling food, determined to get some. But the only things in reach were my legs. I didn't feel like chasing them so climbed on to a trestle to avoid their attack; but the rucksack lay on the ground and, had I not sprung to its rescue, it would have been torn to shreds. While I was saving

my belongings, another pig caught the tablecloth and swept it off the table with a crash of crockery which so frightened the farrow that they capered off with a volley of grunts to a safer distance. The poor woman ran out and picked up her broken cups. She hoped the *Herr* had not been *belestiged*. The loss had been her's and she wondered if I had been disturbed! There was another chorus of grunts as I again took the path up to the moraine towards the glacier.

There were footprints only a few hours old. I followed them up, but my feet sunk deeply into the melting snow. My aim was to reach an Alpine hut at the base of the peak. The tracks disappeared and soon I was forced to use my mountaincraft to find a way up. There was an obvious route, but an avalanche had swept down over it making it impassable. The way opened out – I could see moraine, glacier and snow extending for miles towards the towering peaks where the Gross Venediger rose majestically. I then found ski tracks, but they were old and led over countless gaping crevasses.

I wandered on the moraine for a while, but it was very loose and treacherous. A thunderstorm was approaching; the sun was hot and the west was dark and angry, throwing the sharp white summit of the mountain into dramatic relief. Looking up at a rocky face I saw some handrails and decided to climb up to them, for that surely must be a way to the hut. My rubber-soled skiboots were good on snow and rock as long as the rock was dry. But to my surprise, there were no footprints to be seen. It was a man-made path and marked so it could not be wrong, I thought, but it led me into one of the most treacherous places I had ever been in. The whole mountainside was little better than a precipitous moraine and it had fallen away in a landslide. It

was, in fact, still sliding and hurling stones and debris down its course. I found a few remaining signs of handrail and a pitoned cable twisted and mingled with debris, but the rest was far below on the glacier where it had been hurled by the landslide. Above this, an avalanche had piled itself up to the top of the precipice. I now had no alternative but to traverse it and the experience was terrifying. I would have given a lot for a couple of companions and a rope. At one point some handrails were suspended 1000 feet over space, the ground having disappeared from beneath them. I chose my path carefully across the avalanche and, in spite of the heat of the afternoon, it held. After that the way was easy though the snow was deep. On arrival at the hut, I found Sepp, the caretaker, peacefully sitting on a bench. He took his peasant pipe out of his mouth and said: '*Gruss Gott*,' and in a casual manner added that I was lucky to have got there at all. Three had been killed in an avalanche the other day, including the *Wirt* from Neu-kirchen. We ate our meal in silence and went to our bunkbeds early, while the thunder storm gathered, shaking the rafters of the hut. But the morning was clear and hopeful; snow had fallen on the glacier and upon the peak it was well over a foot deep.

By 5 a.m. there was sufficient daylight to make a start. Shouldering our skis we crunched up over the smooth crystals. Close to the hut we saw a fox, a hare, some ptarmigan and an ermine. As we climbed up, hour after hour, it grew steeper and the surface became hard as marble. To relieve the monotony, Sepp treated me to reminiscences of the Ober Sulzberger Glacier, reliving countless tragedies in which he had played, to whatever degree possible, a beneficent part. He grew very jumpy about the thinness of the snow-bridges; there were myriads of crevasses which ran criss-cross as the ice wall grew steeper. Towards the north col he spared me no details.

'About under you now lies a Berliner,' or, 'Somewhere about there is a Krimmel guide who made a trackless disappearance.'

Nussbaumer, a guide, had broken through the cornice on the peak of the Gross Venediger and had fallen 800 feet without harm.

'Eh,' he sighed, 'poor man, he had left his new iceaxe and two ladies up on the peak and had to go back up and get them.'

In the icy shadow of the peak I lost all interest in Sepp beyond keeping a pretty tight rope. The snow-bridges sounded like drumheads as they resounded to our footsteps, echoing with a deep and hollow sound. Once or twice Sepp said a bridge quavered, but we reached the peak by nine o'clock. From there we got a magnificent view and saw into Germany, Italy, Switzerland, and Yugoslavia. A mass of low clouds menaced some of the peaks to the west. From somewhere below us a detonation sounded. Sepp jumped as he said, 'That was the birth of a new crevasse.' His stories about crevasses, cornices, avalanches and *steinslags*, seemed endless and had he paid more attention to his skiing and less to reminiscence, the downward trip roped together would have been more fun. He sideslipped and

kick-turned to where the glacier flattened out, but below the icefall he liberated me and the remainder of the way to the hut was a series of heavenly *schusses*.

I later learned that Sepp had himself spent a night in a crevasse – an experience few men have survived. The sky was cold and grey and the peaks of the Hohe Tauern were glowing in sunlight as we reached the hut. Down in the valley I bought a newspaper. There had been strikes in Jerusalem and France. The new *Queen Mary* had crossed the Atlantic on her maiden voyage and the Emperor of Abyssinia had fled to London. There were letters awaiting me at the post office – my friends in Intelligence wanted me to confer with them again in London.

Before long I was lunching with my chief, S.M., at White's. We discussed the general situation in Germany and Italy and, strange as it may seem, the immediate course of action suggested was a journey to Harbin in Manchuria, utilising the cover of family affairs relating to Kathleen. I had a general idea of what the journey entailed and also the conditions of the country itself, for I had shared many hours with Peter Fleming, William Teiling and others. From London I went directly to Kitzbühel, picked up some clothes, and set off for Berlin to board the Manchuria Express.

9

Trans-Siberia

The train left at midnight for Warsaw and Stolpsce and the Polish-Russian border at Nigorellye where passengers for Moscow and the Far East changed into a Russian train, the Trans-Siberian Express. All this while I had been taking stock of my fellow passengers and found that only a few of those who had boarded the train at Berlin were travelling right through. Of these, a German courier accompanied by a Gestapo agent, some Japanese and a young English girl of nineteen on her way to a job in Shanghai caught my interest.

Class distinction having been eliminated by the Soviets, they renamed the categories of travel 'hard' and 'soft'. It was my good fortune to travel 'soft', and I found myself having to share a sleeping compartment with a Japanese. There were two Japanese gentlemen in this category; the other was allocated to a berth in the English girl's compartment to which she was strongly objecting. I had my own good reasons for not liking these allocations and was much relieved therefore when the English girl asked to be transferred to my compartment.

At Moscow those travelling to Manchuria toured the city in an open car under the guidance of a Caucasian Intourist agent. Our tour was naturally to places which did credit to the regime and included their new metro, Red Square and Lenin's grave; the day was fine and warm and the squalid parts of Moscow were avoided. We sped by the stadium, the aerodrome and workmen's quarters and before the end of the day our eyes and clothes were so filled with dust that it took the remainder of our three-hours halt in Moscow to get cleaned up.

Then began the lengthy journey across Siberia with Betty, the English girl, as my companion. The train took a northern route. Many of the towns through which we passed had been renamed. The sleeping car, an oversized *wagon-lit* type, was thirty years old and full of red plush and brass fittings in a style sometimes referred to as Yugent. There was a small washroom which we shared with our next-door neighbours, the Japanese. The *provodnic* (attendant) was a member of the secret police, the O.G.P.U. Realising this I took special care not to leave things around. The Russians seemed to suspect everyone at that time including themselves and so strong was the feeling of subter-fuge that I felt like playing up to it just to enter into the spirit of secrecy! In my case, however, it might have proved fatal because of the actual realities. Russians have a peculiar sense of humour and I decided not to put it to such a test. The train stopped for twenty minutes twice a day. At such times, as likely as not, there would be freight trains blocking the view on either side. In any case, as Betty said somewhat peevishly, 'The Siberian landscape isn't worth seeing anyway.'

The popular concept is that during these crossings one sees just thousands upon thousands of miles of empty space. Actually, one is seldom out of sight of habitation, cultivation and interest. At some stations the local inhabitants brought vegetables and fruit, displaying them on counters ranged alongside the platforms. Emaciated children begged bread from the sleeping-car windows on the track side of the train. I managed to throw them a few copeks before the *provodnic* shooed them off. The windows of the sleeper were supposed to be kept closed to prevent dust and cinders entering the compartments but since the coaches had no air conditioning and the plush upholstering was already full of dust, the fustiness and heat inside became unbearable.

The track was a single one, becoming double only where there were bridges. Some large rivers were crossed – the Lena, Ob, Yenitsie and Kama – all of which flowed northward. I was reminded of my old friend Logwinoff's song about Lake Baikal – 'Beautiful Lake, Eternal Baikal.'

We skirted the southern extremity of the lake and the breeze from the north of that bottomless expanse of water cooled the train down. On the sixth day out from Moscow we passed the wreck of a train, its material and debris strewn along the track where nothing seemed to have been done to clear it away. The return to order after the revolution was still in its early stages and inessentials had to wait. Life had to go on.

The further east we travelled the greater the evidence of military defence and as we approached Manchuria the country began to grow more desolate. At Erkutsk we passed trainloads of human cargoes guarded according to the category of their status as political prisoners. As a general rule they were herded together in cattle trucks. This was enforced labour on its way to northern Siberia.

The fine weather returned and the open tundra with its Mongolian

inhabitants provided a freer landscape. The train was operated on
Moscow time and the restaurant car served its meals without respect
to the rising and setting of the sun. Natural cycles were merely an
inconvenience to this regularity. Thus by the time we reached the
Manchurian border, breakfast was being served at 3 p.m., lunch at
8 p.m., and dinner at 2 a.m., local time. The train was eleven hours
late getting in at the frontier town of Munchuli, so it was all very
confusing.

Betty, the English girl, had been born with a constitutional preference
for Europeans, but she had no political bias in the choice of her male
companions. She took up with a German youth in the S.S. who was
travelling 'hard' and, taking compassion on him, brought him and
his accordion into our 'soft' compartment. Unlike modern American
trains, passengers on the Trans-Siberian had no place to go other than
their own compartment unless, of course, the restaurant car happened
to be open. And so Hans and his accordion soon became a nuisance.
I put up with this for some days and then firmly told Hans that though
he was welcome his accordion was not.

At Munchuli, the passengers for Manchuria got out and after a few
hours of intensive red-tape we continued our journey in a much more
comfortable train run by Japanese but staffed by White Russians. The
landscape continued much as before, being open plain with distant
hills, but every station which we now passed was burned out and
roofless, for the country was infested with bandits who plundered and
pillaged wherever they could. At Halear our military escort blacked
out the train by drawing blinds. We passed through a highly fortified
zone, but the windows being open the blinds bellied like sails and I
was able to see out most of the time.

In the early hours of the next morning all the passengers were
thrown rudely out of their bunks by a terriffic jolt. First I got the
impression that our sleeper was travelling sideways and threatening
to overturn, then chaos, followed by an ominous but brief silence. This
was followed by cries from injured passengers and orders shouted by
excited Japanese. My first thought was that we had been derailed and
ambushed by bandits, but in actual fact it was only a derailment with
no loss to life. The first-class portion of the train was wrecked, the
sleepers and restaurant car were slightly telescoped and unable to
continue. After some delay the passengers were packed together into
the third-class cars and the diminished train continued on its journey
to Harbin.

Of all evil cities, Harbin was said to be the worst, consisting of a mushroom growth of 200,000 Asiatics and 65,000 Europeans under a tyrannous Japanese rule. It had been a simple Chinese village until the Russians had built their immense bridge over the Sungari River. Since that time a large portion of the Russians had moved out. The Red element returned to the U.S.S.R., the Whites to Shanghi or elsewhere. But owing to the comparative order, suppression of banditry and so on, a large Chinese immigration was going on.

I established myself at the Hotel Modern and then made contact with the British government representative from whom I got some useful information about the local conditions. Together we went up the Sungari in a launch where we could talk without being overheard. The limit of safety was six miles upstream, beyond which one might run into bandits. We passed close to the bank of the west side of the city and there saw a Japanese officer beheading a malefactor with his sword. The execution was as swift as the waters of the great riverwhich in an instant had swept us past, leaving only a gruesome memory of ruthlessness and a despotism which, without either trial or burial, ended in the river.

'To extract information from prisoners,' said my companion, 'the Japanese tube water into their stomachs through the nose, and then, when their intestines are fully distended, jump upon them until they confess.'

'The Chinese of Harbin are either merchants or coolie types. In the latter instance they live in great squalor. The local Russian inhabitants, indolent and naive, live an existence of beggarly ease wasting time with sad stories of past glories. The Japanese are fit, hardworking, thrifty and aggressive; their role, one of grabbing and monopolising wherever their efficiency permits.'

The British Consul had already informed Kathleen of my arrival and now he explained to me how to find her. I was soon in a taxi dodging through the dusty streets filled with Orientals of every description. At 16 Bolshoi Prospect one of Kathleen's friends, a Princess Uhtomski, opened the door to me. She was a plump woman with a sallow skin and melancholy eyes, who had appointed herself lady companion to her one-time neighbour in Russia. She found it impossible to believe that a British subject could ever have her total wealth confiscated by the Soviets. She even encouraged Kathleen in that belief, a delusion they both enjoyed to the end. There were many so-called White Russians who kept up that pipe-dream until the cruel

facts caught up with them. Even after that they kept up the pretence
by dwelling in the good old days.

The Princess showed me into a conservatory filled with flowers
and wicker furniture. I found Kathleen reclining on a chaise-longue.
She looked up and smiled, but quickly closed her eyes as if in pain.
She was fatter, and older now and her gums were toothless. Her hair
hung in loose grey wisps about her face, as pallid as the pillows which
supported her, while on her counterpane rested hands, the nails of
which had been allowed to grow as long as a Chinese mandarin's.
After our preliminary greeting, I listened patiently to her troubles and
ailments and realised that whatever else she had lost, her memory
and her wit were still unimpaired. She could talk fluidly and lucidly
on every imaginable subject in most European languages, but her
interest in politics overruled all others and filled her with mistrust
for the overlords of Manchuria. She expressed a desire to return to
Monivea to die, although she had nothing but bitterness for Rozzie.
That evening the Uhtomskis, myself and one of the many doctors in
attendance dined there, while Kathleen rested in her conservatory.

Dinner, which was not announced until eleven o'clock, was elabor-
ately served by a Chinese servant. My body had not become adjusted
to the change of times and customs and by two o'clock in the morning
I found it hard to keep awake. Russian was the medium of conversation
and I was delighted to find myself able to move easily in it. After
dinner, Kathleen, revived by her nap, monopolised the conversation
and held forth in a reminiscent vein until three in the morning. No
vital subjects seemed to be touched upon. She took us back with her
into the past and described it all in minute detail so that I was trans-
ported and enthralled. But of Monivea she said nothing. Tired and
discouraged and learning that the cook was also a taxi driver, I got
him to drive me back to my hotel.

After this I was frequently at Kathleen's. The villa which she lived
in was only partially rented to her by a Russian abbess. This princess
of the Russian Orthodox Church, preferring a life of complete retirement, was only occasionally seen and then only when she appeared
at a window. On such occasions she was said to be wearing her habit
as well as a crozier, which caused Kathleen to comment that she ranked
as an Archbishop. It struck me at once that all these poor people were
living in an illusionary past.

Usually I remained for supper. Generally the British, French and
Italian Consuls would also drop in and it soon became obvious that

this had become a focal point for political discussion if not intrigue in Harbin, and accordingly I kept my eyes open for informers.

Kathleen had continued to entertain lavishly; she had not been able to adjust herself to the facts of her financial circumstances. She hardly ever left her chaise-longue and as the conservatory adjoined the dining room, she was able to direct operations from it through open glass doors until she fell asleep, which was often. The evening meals seemed not to vary. There were three sorts of wines, including champagne, besides beer and mineral waters. The menus consisted of Zakoushka, including the very best caviar, borsch soup with perusehki, fish, a tournedo of beef and a whole half-grown chicken to each guest followed by dessert, cheese, fruit and coffee. This should not have taken two hours to serve, but somehow long and dreary delays took place while the Chinese servant and the Russian taxi-chef argued in the back premises. After the meal, the guests were shown into a little darkened sitting room there to doze and digest their meal until their hostess woke up and called them to join her.

I mentioned that I would prefer avoiding such late nights and Kathleen suggested six o'clock in the evening for *butterbrods* (snacks) as an alternative hour. But when I called at the villa at that time I found everything closed, blinds drawn, the garden gate padlocked and no means of attracting attention. Having dismissed my taxi I was determined not to be defeated and so, leaping the gate, I walked up the path. On reaching the verandah I was stopped by two Chinese servants who told me 'Mees ffrench' was sleeping and I was to return in an hour.

I was at a loss to know what to do with myself out there among those rows of little villas and decided to go for a walk towards the outskirts of the city. I was not dressed for an hour's hike, moreover it was very hot. Beyond the Russian residential quarter, I became aware of an evil smell and, looking into the ditch, found it filled with corpses of Chinese who had been shot in a bandit raid. I turned back and, as luck would have it, ran into Princess Uhtomski who said that Kathleen had just sent for her. It was not altogether convenient but she would go in spite of it being the anniversary of the death of her grandmother. On returning to Kathleen I found them together and quickly realised that Kathleen was using her as a hedge, lest I should try to approach her on the subject of Monivea. Others then dropped in including a Latvian and the wife of the Belgian Consul.

Now at last there was movement. The Latvian had just returned from the country along the Amur River in northern Manchuria and was in possession of a great deal of valuable information about that northern frontier on both sides of the river.

'The Japs,' he said, 'dislike the Vladivostok salient which they consider a threat to them, being within flying distance of Tokyo.'

I arranged to meet him at his house at a later date where I subsequently obtained many important details, maps and dispositions.

In between my visits to Kathleen I found time for other interests. I tried my best to locate my old friend Logwinoff, whom I had heard of in Shanghai. I learned that he was now in Darien and was ill with an injured back; I meant to go there to see him. But as I was planning this I found out that it was another man of the same name.

Through the Latvian I got in touch with Ivan, a Russian officer employed at the Japanese military headquarters in Harbin, and from him obtained a detailed disposition of all Japanese military units in Manchukuo. With this scoop I was ready to go home. I only needed something definite about Kathleen's plans for Monivea to round off a very successful trip. But Kathleen was like a clam. She was altogether too sentimental and would not face facts and, accordingly, was unable to commit herself.

She had experienced the total loss of all her vast Russian possessions. Small wonder, therefore, that what little she retained she intended to conserve. She was a borderline Catholic and Russian Orthodox. In religious matters she suffered double vision. Being doubtful and perplexed as is inevitably the case in such instances, she made what use she could of her mind. The result was confusion. The certain way to make a mess of things is to try to rationalise emotion. She had tried to escape the onus of feudalism by hiding her head in the sands of culture. She had lost her possessions and now found refinement and sentimentality of little help in facing hardship. She was, in other words, utterly impractical.

When her relative, the Duc de Stackpole, who was acting as her agent in Ireland, had stressed the need to sell timber off her land while it fetched good prices, she had wired from her Manchurian hideout, 'Not a stick or stone of my dear old home must be removed.'

I found further proof of her conservation mania when one day she asked me to fetch some photographs from a spare room in her villa, the room which was bare of furniture but filled with every conceivable kind of memorabilia. Nothing had been thrown away. All letters, papers, books and other objects that had passed through her hands had been carefully tied into bundles and made into piles. She knew where everything was and had a meticulous indexing mind which objected strongly to anyone else entering the room and tampering with her momentoes. There were a few objects of value, no doubt, but for the rest it was to anyone else a collection of rubbish.

On this particular occasion she had asked me to fetch photographs taken of her during her trip through inner and outer Mongolia to the hills south of Sludyanka where she had hoped for news of Orloff. Part of this journey had been made in the company of a Swedish lady in a Dodge car – as far as the Tanny-Tova Republic, ostensibly to find some mineral springs, for Kathleen had much faith in natural remedies. But after that she continued alone with a cossack horseman and rode to a point where she transferred to a dromedary and finally on foot until she had reached a spot where she met with evidence which convinced her of Orloff's death during the affray on the station platform. Broken-hearted, she retraced her steps to Harbin where she became increasingly bed-ridden.

The filth and evil smells of the Chinese quarter of Harbin surpassed anything describable and was almost equalled by the noise. On one or two occasions during my visit I walked about with my camera photographing typical scenes. I recorded the removal of a corpse which could not afford a proper burial. It hung limp and inanimate from a bamboo pole, with nothing but matting wrapped around it; the head lolled down at one end of the parcel while from the other end the feet dragged in the dust. Carrying the bamboo pole on their shoulders two coolies bore the gruesome thing away.

On another occasion a cart drawn by an ox and a pony had sunk and almost disappeared into a mudhole in the street, not three feet from the pavement and the shops. I saw a hideous hell of cruelty committed to man and beast alike. A pony, whose cart had been abandoned by the roadside, lay dead in the ditch.

In another place a dead Chinaman lay in front of the Hong Kong and Shanghai Bank because no one seemed willing to accept the responsibility for removing his remains. Death and life, filth and gaudiness living cheek by jowl in the dusty heat of a late Manchurian summer. Better-class Russian girls, finding no other form of livelihood, became dancing girls and prostitutes and, being stateless, had no one to turn to for relief and protection. It was not unusual for the night porter of an hotel to open a single man's bedroom door with his pass key and push in one of these charmers. Being a light sleeper the rattle of the key in the lock awoke me and my security-mindedness prompted me to tell the intruders to go to the devil. 'That's just what I thought I was doing,' said the girl brazenly in purest English as she approached my bed. This greatly enriched the dramatic situation for both of us and before she left I had learned a great deal about the plot against western ethics and morality.

Below my window at the hotel cyclists by the score endlessly sounded their bells, the idea being that bells and horns alike should be sounded while the vehicle was in motion whether there was other traffic or not. The Kitayskaya was a noisy street and, since my bedroom windows overlooked it, I found it hard to relax. It was too hot with my window closed, and there was too much noise and too many street diversions to make relaxation possible with it open. Either there were street arguments or cries of vendors, or a troupe of Oriental musicians in rickshaws playing Russian airs with Chinese rhythm and cymbals. These were usually so strung out that the musicians at the rear of the rickshaw-cade were quite out of hearing, time and tune with those in front. There was always some commotion going on, some incident or accident that kept me jumping off my bed and rushing to the window. The flies, too, tormented me.

Perhaps the most spectacular incident of all, however, was the passing of a Chinese funeral. Compared to its European counterpart it was quite festive, being attended by uniformed musicians with long flowing robes and round black hats. Following the pall, which was an odd-shaped painted affair somewhat resembling a wheelbarrow, came a yellow paper cow which was later burned together with the corpse. Meanwhile the street was filled with Russian dope addicts clammering for money with which to acquire narcotics. There was little to distinguish them from the whimpering beggars except that they were being sold heroin by the authorities in the hope of getting rid of an unwanted element.

Once more I went to Kathleen's about six in the evening and found her on the verandah, but again Princess Uhtomski was with her. The evenings grow chill in Harbin and as the dampness of the air increased I set myself to out-sit the Uhtomski. In the end she was forced to leave, though unwillingly, and I had Kathleen to myself for the first time. But she took the initiative and from that moment on talked without ceasing until 1.30 in the morning.

Meanwhile a meal was served in the dark for me on a small wicker table by her bedside. I had been thwarted, but the process was not an unpleasant one. I found her easy to listen to and the hours passed pleasingly, for she never uttered a boring sentence. She described her properties in Simbirsk, her love for Orloff, her priceless treasures and her trip to the north over country hitherto untrodden by a European. She had had all that life could offer, she said, and now she asked for nothing better than the oblivion of death.

'I have made the Sign of the Cross,' she said dramatically, 'on all the beauty with which in a reign of thirty years I have succeeded in surrounding myself. I have put all behind me because I could not bear to think of it anymore.'

It was gone and lost forever. She compared her wealth and possessions, especially certain paintings by Van Dyke, rare books and gold plate, favourably with those owned by the Imperial family. In fact, as regards certain paintings and horses, she said that the Tsar had nothing to touch hers. A portion of her gold plate had been frequently borrowed by the local aristocracy without her suffering any inconvenience, leaving her enough to entertain a party of as many as 200 guests in the meanwhile.

She spoke of terraces in her gardens and of trees which surrounded the mansion, unequalled in size and layout. She also spoke of four or five other mansions which she possessed, dotted about throughout the eight counties of the province of Simbirsk and of the house in the town of that name which, occupying a block, was bounded by four great streets and was now turned into a museum containing her treasures, while objects of greater value had been sent to the Moscow museum. Her miniatures, worth a fortune in themselves, had all been stolen by the mob for the sake of the paltry gold rims on their ebony frames.

The country house near Simbirsk had been burned to the ground and her ornamental woods and forests destroyed. Forty million roubles worth of property and an annual income of four hundred thousand roubles were cut off in three ghastly days. On 18 August 1917 she had ceased to live.

'And yet,' she added, 'I look back upon the period that followed as a paradise compared to my time here in Harbin.'

I had not known the Kathleen of pre-revolution times. She must have been a very different person to the humbled, long-suffering, yet unrepentant materialist with whom I now spent my evenings. Somebody had dropped in from the servants' quarters and sat in the shadows playing Russian folk songs on his accordian, evoking dreamy thoughts as I sat beside her moonlit bed. But to Kathleen the music was but an accompaniment to her endless flow of reminiscences and accounts of current feuds with Japanese authorities over cutting down trees in her garden. 'Vandals' she called them, but the tree conflict kept alive her fighting spirit and she had even enlisted the reluctant abbess in her private war. The simple truth was that the trees were in the way of a new power line which was under construction and had to go.

I had now accomplished my mission in its broader sense. The time for my departure had come. I took one last meal with Kathleen which never got served before midnight and so dragged on almost interminably until three in the morning.

The practice of eating late had heavily disagreed with me, trying my patience, digestion and causing fatigue. Kathleen apologised for the long delays between courses, but she had no control over the servants. They were always leaving her. She had had 249 of them, she indicated, since coming to Harbin. When I finally took leave of her she kissed me affectionately and gave me a set of Russian gold spoons, decorated with enamel. I never saw her again.

Hardly had I dropped to sleep on my return to the hotel when the room was filled with morning noises. The perpetual ring of bicycle bells again, the wailing of dope fiends and the brain-piercing whistle of the street *samovars* mixed with the endless gabble of Chinese made an unrestful cacophony. Hastily I packed my bag, paid my bill and went out into the street. Beggars clung to me like leeches who had to be sloughed off. Their grimy clamour, their half imbecile expressions were horrifying and awoke memories of the beggars of Frascati. I drew my return ticket out of my pocket and looked at it affectionately. At least this would solve the immediate problem. Somebody touched me on the shoulder. I turned and found myself facing the Latvian.

'Your train does not leave until noon. How about a cup of coffee?' He drew me back into the hotel.

'Ivan has been arrested. The charge against him is espionage.'

I looked at my informer blankly and took another lump of sugar in my coffee.

'This coffee is awfully bitter,' I remarked.

'Perhaps the Russian coffee is bitter too, and the German coffee as well,' said the Latvian significantly.

'Yes,' I sighed, 'Cafe au lait is best.'

On the homeward journey I shared a compartment with a Scotsman in the Royal Marines returning from the Far East. On our way to the Russian frontier we were delayed by our locomotive breaking down. We walked up the track and saw that water was pouring out of the boiler. In the course of time a relief engine arrived and we set off again.

After the usual formalities at Manchuli, I took stock of my travelling companions. In the compartment next to mine were two more Scotsmen, Donald and Colin – the first, an employee in the Hong Kong and Shanghai Bank and the second the chief engineer of a ship. The other passengers consisted of a lot of Germans, a Rumanian woman, a Franco-Russian Jew and some members of a crew of a British freighter, now sold to the Chinese. There was also a girl, Irene, whose English father had married a Russian woman. He had fought against the Reds and had eventually died in a Soviet prison camp. His wife and child had escaped to Harbin. Irene was on her way to England to claim her citizenship, but she spoke only Russian and from a Soviet point of view was a White Russian. Her chances of getting across to Poland were doubtful, added to which she was travelling with far too much luggage, most of it being cheap Chinese trunks whose flimsy locks and hinges were already bursting open.

The steppes, broad and flat, stretched out like a solid ocean. Grey crows and an occasional hawk were the only signs of wild life. Clumps of birch, a lonely mud or log cabin and a *mushik* trekking wearily along with his pony and cart. Every now and then the monotony of the scene would be relieved by a small lake.

The effects of travel and readjustment gave me no appetite. Climatic changes and, above all, the food supplied, were upsetting most of the passengers. The temperature dropped as the train toiled across the high prairie lands, but it remained sunny until we reached the Ural Mountains, beautiful, but not spectacular. At Perm, one of the Scotsmen said we were back in Europe.

I was lucky with my travelling companions but Colin, the chief engineer, was having trouble with Don whom he described as 'seemingly pious and thoroughly self-centred'. He said he had tinned foods as an alternative to the fare offered by the restaurant car and these, with the aid of his tin-opener, he endlessly opened and closed as the mood took him. He prepared meals, washed up after them and stowed the things away again. Some people take up more space than others, turning their presence into an invasion as they spread themselves out. Such people became a nuisance to others and no less Don, as in a sanctimonious manner he littered all available space with paper bags

and refuse. His travelling companion complained that he had been
left no room in the compartment what with Don's jars, tins, boxes and
prayer books.

'Don spends his time reading the Bible and has permanently monopolised the window seat for that purpose.'

Things nearly came to a head when Don upset liquid cascara all
over the table as well as on Colin's bed. Then the bottom fell out of
his tooth-powder container and covered the floor with medicated
chalk. Once he turned the whole compartment upside down looking
for his gold cross which he eventually found under his pillow. Poor
Colin, who had a bad cold, spent many unhappy hours in the corridor
or in our compartment. The climax came when Don, deprived of his
cascara, asked Colin to administer an enema!

In the 'hard' category of the train the Intourist agent Dimitri –
the voice of the secret police – went to work on the British mariners
with his parrot-like propaganda. But like any truly indoctrinated
subject he was unable to see himself objectively, and was unconscious
of the leg-pulling that the seamen were enjoying at his expense; it
was ages before he found out that he was getting nowhere with them.
He was smart enough, however, to draw the line when they turned
the tide and began to play on him for free cigarettes, stamps or illus-
trated magazines. At one of the stops a British stoker dropped a cigarette butt on the platform. In the dirt and squalor of the place one
would not think such a thing would have been noticed, but he was
sharply reprimanded by Dimitri who said: 'In our country we put
cigarette ends in the ashtray.'

He also lost no opportunity to boost the Red way of living.

At Moscow a delegation of international brass who had been invited
to witness the flight of the Soviet's giant aircraft ANT 25 were being
seen off by top-ranking U.S.S.R. officials. A British Air Vice-Marshal
recognised me, for we had skiied together in Austria. He joined me
and my fellow travellers who were all chatting and joking on the
platform. Then we noticed Irene being led off by some Soviet officials
which included Dimitri. Someone said:

'She looks as if she's under arrest.'

'Don't let's get mixed up in it,' said Don nervously. 'We'll only
get ourselves into trouble.'

I excused myself and hurried after her. She was expostulating in
her very limited English, most of which she had picked up on the
journey. I saw in a flash in what danger she was. Practically speaking,

Irene spoke only Russian, but her mother had told her not to let that be known. This was handicap number one. Then she had been given baggage, including a mink coat to be handed to her aunt, whom she was told would meet her at the station. Needless to say, the aunt was not there, for everyone living under the Soviet regime at that time knew that it was fatal to be caught making any sort of contact with White Russians, least of all accepting valuable mink coats and suchlike from them.

Luckily Irene's problem had not reached its crisis. Something could still be done. I went into the office where they had gathered and took over from there. Dimitri understood my English, Irene did not. There had been complaints about Irene's baggage – it had been cluttering up the whole compartment and the conductor could not get along the corridor because of her Chinese trunks. Irene had checked the rest of her stuff, but these other pieces of baggage she had retained so as to be able to hand them over to her aunt at Moscow.

'It is all a mistake,' I interjected emphatically to the Intourist agent. 'These things were supposed to have been checked at Harbin. Her mother asked me to have it done. It must be done immediately! Put seals on them, please, that they may go right through to Berlin!'

Irene's jaw dropped . . .'But . . . but . . .' she began.

Without a word I seized her by the arm and whisked her off.

'If you don't want to go to a Bolshevik prison and get your aunt shot, please shut up!' I hissed at her when we were out of hearing range of the others. 'Now go back in there and get your checks and please remember, not a word about your aunt! It is a matter of life and death!'

Meekly she obeyed. Dimitri, whose tour of duty ended in Moscow, was anxious to get home to his own bed and the incident was closed there and then. Then hurrying to the train which, after being shunted to the Little Russia station, was waiting, we continued on our journey.

That night as we sped from Moscow to the Polish frontier the new agent of the secret police and the chief of the train opened the door of my compartment and awakened me by flashing a torch on my face. They sprung a question on me in Russian. Caught off my guard, I answered them in the vernacular.

'Ho, Ho!' exclaimed the agent. 'So you do speak Russian!' And from that time on until I had safely crossed into Poland, I knew that I was under constant observation.

Once we were out of Russia, 'Biffy', as the Air Vice-Marshal was called, exchanged his views with me while we enjoyed a decent meal in the Polish restaurant car. I was anxious to hear his view on the Russian air force and in return told him of what I had seen on my trip, of the sordidness of Harbin, of the merely aesthetic value of the Russian cavalry division under canvas which I saw amid the foothills of Transbaikalia, and of the trainloads of human cargo.

From then, the remainder of the trip was uneventful all the way to London, which bothered me not in the least.

10

Rudolfo

It had been a fruitful but demanding time in Russia and now, back in Great Britain to report, I was glad to take an opportunity to rest in the comforts of a Scottish castle. I boarded the Flying Scotsman at Euston and by breakfast time on the following morning was already approaching my destination. A car met me at the station and as it drove up a wooded glen I saw the brown waters of the burn coming down from the hills and was filled with gratitude for the constant flow of life in myself. I thought of the gangs of prisoners I had seen in Russia and was grateful for my freedom.

At the lodge gates we drove up between lawns to the drawbridge of the castle. My kilted host came out to greet me and led me to where his other guests were sitting at breakfast – at a table well stocked with Scottish fare. A far cry indeed from the streets of Harbin.

Above the castle, magnificent trees almost hid both glen and mountains. I gazed out of the window. The talk at the table was of the Inverness Ball. The men in their tweeds were discussing politics – before long they would be in their butts with grouse being driven over their heads. The ladies would join them for lunch. For me there seemed no alternative between hard plodding or complete inactivity by the immense log fire, with an inviting library of books and charming companionship. I had no gun, so I compromised with a stroll up the glen. The leaves were yellowing and scattered by a breeze. Winter was not far off.

Looking down the valley I could see Moray Firth gleaming in the distance. The song of the whitethroat mingled with the sound of water in the rocky gorge. Otherwise it was all very silent.

In the near distance I heard the yap of a cairn terrier in pursuit of a rabbit, a noise in the underbush. My hostess was coming up the path. For a while we stood together.

After an absence of some years I felt I had the privilege of dispensing with formalities, yet now I felt a barrier between us that gave

149

me a twinge of loneliness. I felt inquisitive and would have probed
into her private life, as if our past relationship in that giddy life of
London in the 1920s gave me the right. An urge prompted me to
share with her some of my exciting and secret experiences, partly to
relieve the pressure or as a step towards regaining our mutual partici-
pation in something intimate. But it could not be. I was full of secrets
now, most of which were not for sharing. A secret agent could not
afford to indulge in any other love but for his work. It was a complicated sort of life in which I was hiding behind the facade of an international playboy. Others saw me only in this role and were inclined
to judge it.

On the distant mountain, men were scaring up grouse so that gentlemen could shoot at them. Occasionally a volley of shots could be heard.

'You should have brought your gun,' said my hostess in such flat
tones I knew she didn't really mean it. Nowadays I was accustomed to
carrying a small automatic pistol.

'No, well you see I came quite unexpectedly, didn't I? And one
mustn't forget that there are only the right number of guns for the
right number of butts. I like grouse, however, especially for dinner
with lots of breadcrumbs.' We laughed. 'It's the corruption of a
pleasurable instinct almost as primitive as making love and far more
destructive.'

Down in the hollow behind us we could see the turrets of the castle.
The ladies of the houseparty were indulging in sophisticated conversation. The King was ill. It was a serious matter. What kind of
problem would confront them if he died? But of course he would
recover! It was altogether too unpleasant a thought. Who was this
Mrs Simpson the Prince of Wales was running around with? They
were loyal, circumspect, but worried.

The time had come for me to report again to Headquarters. This
took place in a much more streamlined office than the attic labyrinth
of old. The office looked like millions of others in London which are
equipped with steel furniture and its unorthodox activities were run
on strictly business lines. There was nothing of that romantic infor-
mality which had appealed to me and I had to comfort myself with
the thought that I was serving and, perhaps, making up in some
measure for having been a prisoner-of-war. The pay was negligible
compared with the risks involved and I was frequently reminded that
times had changed.

As instructed I returned to Central Europe, travelling by car and passing through Belgium and southern Germany as a means of varying my route. Since it took me a couple of days to reach my destination I sometimes stopped with friends rather than stay in hotels. I still carry pictures in my mind of the grace and beauty of one of the places at which I stopped. This was Beloile not far from the city of Mons. Here lived Albert de Ligne and his beautiful wife and daughters whom I originally had met in the Hague. The place rather resembled a small Versailles and my friends, strange as it may seem, lived in the stables. These had been converted into a sumptuous residence with the ground floor, which was vaulted and pillared in stone and brick, now their dining room. There were rich carpets on the flagstones and valuable oil paintings where once iron hay racks hung on the walls.

A fellow guest, Count Baillie de la Tour, who had succeeded Albert to the post of Secretary-General and Chairman of the Olympic Games Committee, kept us all amused with stories.

'Japan,' he said, 'is going ahead with her preparations for holding Olympic Games in Tokyo, in spite of her war with China.'

He also told the company of his success in getting the anti-Jewish posters taken down in Berlin and Garmisch during the Olympic Games there, and how, when the Führer had become furious at such a monstrous suggestion, Baillie de la Tour, who was bald, had removed his hat saying:

'If His Excellency were to object to bald men, it would be tactless of him to write it upon the walls while I was visiting.'

Hitler had laughed and had the offensive notices removed. But when Mussolini had tried to use the Olympic Games as political propaganda, it was not so easy to manage him. But he did so, nevertheless, by merely shouting louder than *Il Duce*.

The city of Mons was only a short drive from the palace and, the next day being Sunday, my hosts and their daughters drove me over to see my regiment's war memorial and the field where I received my baptism by fire. And so, having added interest to my itinerary, I continued my journey into Germany.

The season changed to winter and the British Empire suffered the loss of King George V with the characteristic stiff upper lip. But the abdication of his successor, Edward VIII, hit them at a different level and shook their morale badly. The Duke of Windsor, as the ex-monarch was now styled, arrived in Austria and stayed for a while in Shloss Enzesfelt, but later moved to Corinthia. The dictates of his heart were at cross-purposes with the British Constitution. The subject is altogether threadbare and, in any case, by which standards could one judge?

When the Duke recognised me in Kitzbühel, he enquired whether I could give him some lessons in skiing. Being myself no professional, I suggested Billy Bracken, a British ski champion. I saw a good deal of His Royal Highness and Mrs Simpson at that time. Kitzbühel was brimful and overflowing with visitors and, as always, I found it hard to separate the social from the political.

There were many rumours abroad to which I listened with circumspect attention. Rumours of Germany's alliance with Russia; of a Hapsburg restoration backed by Mussolini and of a return to monarchy in France. Spain was an ideological laboratory from whence confused noises of gunfire were heard. The Duke of Alba was at St Moritz, also a Count de Sangro and a Count Wildczec. I kept myself pretty well informed and was right on hand when the chessmen on the European board were moved. En route for St Moritz I met a French diplomat who insisted that Stalin was a double-crosser, pressing for a military as well as an economic alliance with Germany; at least my informant said he was a Fascist. He also spoke of the Croix de Feu movement in France on which subject he was most revealing and proved to be absolutely right in his information. All these things were worth examining in case they together revealed an element of truth. Without getting my own vision befogged or warped I had to remember that S.M. expected to be told what was relevant to British and Allied interests. It could have been too confusing had I not begun to see that order is the eventual norm in any part of the universal design; it was order, not political manipulation that counted in the long run.

In this regard I cherished an acquaintance in Rudolfo – first of all his background was most intriguing. A Bavarian nobleman, jovial, intelligent and fluent in many languages, he had had a military career and had also worked for some time in a political department in the Vatican, in which job he so excelled that he was made a monsignor. But the Italians, believing him to be the cause of leakages of vital military information, demanded his immediate expulsion.

The defeat of the Italians at Caporetto in the First World War and the blowing up of some of their battleships in Leghorn were, they said, directly attributed to this gentleman's activities. He had been a close friend of Franz-Joseph and was still intimate with the ex-Kaiser Wilhelm II, Von Bulow, Betman Holbeck and others. Now, having married and cast off his priestly robes, he disported himself where sun and snow attracted the young in heart and the political intriguers. Rudolfo was determined that, by subtle means, the Nazis would not have it all their own way. And he was not the only one courageous enough to live up to such sentiments. It was believed that the keystone of the Nazi doctrine rested on the concept that the German people were racially superior to others, rather like the view held by the ancient Greeks that all who were not Greek were barbarians.

That spring in an Innsbruck café I met a German socialist who let loose such a tirade against the Nazis that I asked him his name. He turned out to be one of a very large number of Germans who were working underground against Hitler because, as he said, he was exploiting a national weakness for plausible premise without respect for truth. He hit the nail on the head when he said, 'One cannot rationalise the soul.' His dark flashing eyes devoured newspaper after newspaper. His character was undoubtedly that of a revolutionary, at least he was no ordinary man and if ever there was an anti-Nazi *putsch* in Germany I was sure he would be in the midst of it. Unfortunately, he was too outspoken and he and his wife both ended their days in a concentration camp. Meanwhile I managed to get together with him and one or two of his associates. These meetings threw a light on the Nazi movement which was interesting – and worth investigating. It showed how man can become the instrument of magic powers depending on his openness or responsiveness in a given direction. Hitler, they told me, was a medium, his evil genius Dietrich Eckardt from Bohemia – poet, playwright, journalist; and secondly Professor Obert, a friend of Dietrich; and thirdly Haushofer who had the greatest influence over the Führer; and, finally, Alfred Rosenberg whom he met in Wagner's house in Bayreuth.

Konrad Heiden in his *Adolph Hitler* states that Eckardt undertook the 'spiritual' development of Hitler, teaching him also to write and speak. He was one of the founding members of the National Socialist Party.

The Legend of Thule takes one to the roots of the Germanic race and was supposed to be an island that had sunk beneath the surface of the sea somewhere in the extreme north of Greenland or perhaps Labrador. Like Atlantis, Thule was supposed to be a magic centre of a vanished civilisation of which some history is still extant.

Being intermediate between man and other intelligent beings from outer space a fund of power became available to the intelligent initiates which could be tapped to enable Germany to dominate the world and thus become the cradle of a super-race resulting from mutations

of the human species. One day Germany would set out to annihilate
every human element that stood in the path of her spiritual destiny
on earth. Her leaders, omniscient, derived their wisdom and strength
from the primary source of energy, guided by the great ones of ancient
times. Such were the myths on which the Aryan doctrine of Eckardt
and Rosenberg was founded and which these prophets of a magical
form of socialism instilled into the receptive mind of Hitler.

Now all this could have fitted nicely into the pattern. I had once
been told of occultism and that it teaches that, after concluding a
pact with hidden forces, the members of the group cannot evoke
these powers except through the intermediary of a magician or high
priest who, in turn, can do nothing without the mediums. Hitler was
probably the medium of Haushofer the magician. Mediums are usually
ordinary, rather negative types who thus suddenly find themselves
with superhuman powers which set them apart from the rest of the
human race. It would seem that Hitler was possessed of forces outside
himself of which he was only a temporary vehicle. He was born at
Braunan am Inn, at no. 219 Salzburger Vorstadt, on 20 April 1889,
at 5.30 p.m. Braunan seems to have got a reputation for producing
mediums.

The swastika on an orange ground is the flag which the Cuna Indians
of Panama gave to their republic of Thule in 1925.

I was lucky in that my contacts were all good at procuring reliable
information without drawing attention to themselves, and in this
regard Rudolfo was my star performer. Being a prominent socialite
in Europe, and having an attractive personality, he was endowed with
a very sensitive nose for important facts and on top of all this he was
a personal friend of those in positions of authority – exceedingly
entertaining and very desirable company at all times. I gained a great
deal of information through him and his contacts in the Vatican with
their advanced knowledge of international affairs.

News reached me of Dr Otto von Hapsburg's refusal to return as
King until the vast majority of the Austrian people clamoured for him
and a plebiscite had been taken. But the National Socialist bug had
already infected the urban population of that country and unity under
a monarchy could no longer be established. Oh, that Hitlermania!
How vulnerable the Teuton seemed to be to it!

My tourist bureau, enabling me to travel across the Austro-German
border without difficulty, I soon became acquainted with the terrain
and its people and was able to keep a check on the rapidly growing

military installations around Munich, Rosenheim, Berchtesgaden and Reichenhal. Nevertheless, military strength, I argued, was not everything. The rearmament programme was not palatable to the finest brains in Germany and I knew that those in charge were there more by cunning than statesmanship and that blunders were accordingly very common.

Such people as Ritter von Elz refused to belong to the golden party and left the cabinet. There was insecurity, unreliability, lack of training and I concluded that they would not risk war for at least two years. London frequently sent for me in these days to discuss the situation. Everyone seemed worried about the arms race which the two dictators were forcing upon the world. Yet the only conceivable end was tenaciously repudiated.

Talk in England was veering towards socialism. A move was being made towards nationalisation of public services, transport, power and fuel and finally the roads. They spoke of this as an economical achievement and waved aside the objection of competition as adjustable by public vote. Perhaps, I thought, this would eliminate strikes. 'The English,' said a garrulous member of my club, 'would soon have a first-rate modern socialist state next to none in the world, and if the public saw any sign of deterioration due to lack of private enterprise, there would soon be an uproar.'

Luitpold of Bavaria and Ludovic Wilhelm had recently visited King Leopold of Belgium who had not minced words over Belgium's future attitude towards her neighbours. She would have no truck with them, especially France.

There appeared on my horizon a Colonel Wolf who, allegedly, had raised a small army in a few days during the *Freiheit's Kampf* and was, he said, invited by Hitler to join his government. On a lecture tour he was a friend of General Goering's and, likewise, a monarchist. But the difference was that the gallant Colonel claimed to be an out-and-out monarchist. He said he recognised that the stumbling blocks to world peace were Rosenberg, Ribbentrop, Goebbels, Wagner and Himmler. They must go; Generals Goering and Fritsch were agreed on that. He sighted a forthcoming crisis which England could make use of. The opponents in this internal conflict were the steel and armament industries on the one hand and the government on the other; the former refused further output unless paid in gold currency. The crisis originated in the lack of raw materials which had to be paid for in hard cash, while the arms were paid for with paper money.

Hitler had threatened to nationalise these industries including Krupps.
Goering, said the Colonel, spends his nights in tears and is getting
very neurotic about it. The monarchist anti-war party, he indicated,
was growing rapidly. Taking into account that the man was thinking
wishfully and flat broke, I listened with caution. I got Rudolfo to
revise all information from this source and it was soon decided that
Wolf, though well informed, was to be handled gingerly.

I was taken to lunch by Rudolfo to meet one of the richest land-
owners in Bavaria. Our host, though paralysed, was keenly interested
in world affairs and all conversations at his table were taken down in
shorthand by a staff of male stenographers. Aside, he confided ·to
Rudolfo that he had recently spoken personally with both Hitler and
Bruckner, who had told him of the existence of a secret pact between
Germany and Italy which provided Germany with Italy's permission
to step into Austria in the event of political or social unrest in that
country, on condition that they would not lay hands on the south
Tyrol. Other reciprocal arrangements were left open as, of course,
they were subject to adjustment to suit events as they happened.

There was also friction between the Vatican and the Reich over
interference with the freedom of Catholic practices in southern Germany. Goering's friendship with the Italian royal family through
Prince Philip of Hesse was the cause of many jokes, at his expense,
about being a pothunting snob. General Blomberg was a conservative,
but he worshipped Hitler. General Fritsch, also a conservative and
a royalist, was devoted to his army who in turn worshipped him. Von
Neurath was being driven crazy by the proteges of Goering and
Goebbels in whom they had confided all state secrets. Rosenberg,
scheming and plotting diabolical concoctions for the general unrest
of the world, was also poisoning the minds of the young.

The Germans had all the plans and details of the Maginot Line. I
discovered this and also how they intended to put the electric power
plants governing these underground installations out of commission.
They knew just where they were located and just how it could be done.
These and other vital secrets were known by them, necessitating
readjustment. It resembled a game of chess – one side made a move
with its cause in the past and its effect in the future. The other side,
foreseeing the intention, made counter-measures. It was all part of the
scheme of the war of nerves. Life, however, went on. Spring was some
way off yet, but the days were already lengthening.

About this time news reached me from Harbin that Kathleen had died.

In the early part of 1938 a Royal party came to Kitzbühel and rented Villa Erna, which was adjacent to my chalet. It comprised King Leopold of Belgium, Queen Elizabeth his mother and Countess Sophie Toerring, his aunt. And being presented to their Majesties by Ludovic Wilhelm, the Duke in Bavaria, a friendship soon sprang up between us. The Dowager Queen, who had a brilliance of spirit, was the life and soul of the party. The Duke, too, nicknamed 'Bubi', had a ready wit and many happy hours were spent in their company.

The Queen's wide range of interests and accomplishments made her an interesting companion. Unlike Kathleen, she had her feet firmly planted on the ground. She was an idealist, but she resorted to practical forms of ideology. She was a good linguist and interested in Egyptology, having spent much time with King Albert at Luxor during the excavations there. King Leopold was restless and moody; all sorts of problems, of a political and personal nature, were looming up on his horizon. He was much preoccupied. It was good for him to get out skiing.

The 'ermine moths' of Kitzbühel were, of course, in full flight and every kind of ruse was practised to entangle the Royal party in social engagements. But with equal dexterity, and without giving offence, their Majesties managed to preserve their incognito.

One night after I had dined at the Villa Erna and was returning to my chalet, I noticed that the jagged peaks of the Keiser Mountains were silhouetted against a blood-red sky. It was two o'clock of a winter's morning and I recognised the phenomenon as the Northern Lights. I went back to the Villa and drew the attention of the Queen to it and soon the whole party was out there witnessing the spectacle. Bubi, who knew the superstitions of the peasants, said that last time such a sight had been seen, they had foretold war. The red sky proved no empty warning. The account of the gathering of political clouds and the subsequent massing of troops which spread over the remaining fragments of the once glorious Hapsburg Empire was carefully recorded by my agents and myself.

II

The Passing of Monivea

Maud had returned to Sweden and Christina, now three years old, was with me and her nurse, Theresa. But for the reliability of Theresa, Christina might have hampered me seriously at this crucial time.

The gathering of German armoured divisions on the Austro-German frontier between Mittenwald and Kufstein, never really cleared the Berchtesgaden Dictates which only shortly preceded the *Anschluss* of the 11-12 March 1938; the so-called plebiscite of 10 April was merely their shadow spreading over the face of Central Europe.

Fifteen thousand troops performing a manoeuvre in the Tegernsee-Schtersee district kept themselves ready and on their toes while the browbeaten Chancellor, Schusschnigg, tried his hardest to wriggle out of his predicament. He had been pinned down to making certain distasteful concessions to the Nazis, whose sympathisers in Austria made very alarming demonstrations. The Hitler *Grüss* was allowed on all official occasions. Dr Seyss-Inquart, said to be a friend of Schusschnigg's and an ardent Catholic, was given the portfolio of Minister of the Interior, the key to the whole position. He raised a hand to stop the clamourous spread of Nazi agitators, but his raised hand was nothing but a Hitler salute. Schusschnigg's goose was cooked and he had known it from the moment the four generals of the German Southern Command met him at Berchtesgaden.

Desperately, however, he sought a way out. The generals showed him the plans and dispositions of the troops actually poised on his frontier. They had said: 'Either you obey our wishes to liberate our tormented brother Nazis in your country, or we march in.' It meant Nazi occupation in any case, sooner or later, but it struck them as better to release the so-called bonds on the Austrian Nazis by placing Seyss-Inquart in the Ministry of the Interior and then stepping in as mediators in the interest of order when the inevitable rows took place. Actually, there were no serious disorders. Gratz got a bit noisy but there was nothing in the shape of rioting or bloodshed.

Then Schusschnigg made another desperate move. Seeing the power of control slipping from him, he went to see Moel, Director of Public Security in Innsbruck, who gave him a piece of doubtful advice. This was to effect a three-day plebiscite as quickly as possible; no one under the age of twenty-four would be allowed to vote. This eliminated a large portion of the Nazi element and also gave them no time to organise counter-measures.

It was this plebiscite that decided the Germans. On Thursday, 10 March, a rabidly patriotic Austrian living on the frontier typed out a message to me, which he sent by a friend, saying that two columns were advancing from Bad Toltz and Rosenheim towards the Austrian border. But punctuality is not an Austrian virtue and the message did not get delivered until nine o'clock on Friday morning. Within an hour I had transmitted the news to London.

With profuse congratulations and appreciation I was told that this was the first news received in any of the Allied capitals of the advance. The means of communication available to me for hot news of this type was both primitive and risky, as it implicated the local telephone exchange. The call which I was obliged to make took an hour to come through and since the Gestapo had their agents in all the Austrian communication services it was not surprising that my cover was broken and my identity discovered.

Confirmation of the advance reached me by various means throughout the day. The half-thawed roads made travelling very hazardous. The Germans had concentrated an army on their side of the Kufstein frontier; a body of civilian technicians had already come in to take control.

The entry of a large force of mechanised troops at this sector and another at Mittenwald, to occupy Innsbruck and the country west of it as far as the Arlberg Pass, was expected every moment. It actually happened at 9 o'clock on Saturday morning, 12 March.

As I stepped out of the small store owned by an anti-Nazi woman where I had done my telephoning, I ran into Rudolfo and for once it was my turn to give him some hot information. He hurried off and soon the news was around Kitzbühel. The aristocracy and the Jews hurried to pack and leave for their respective homes to save what they could. I met Baron Louis de Rothschild and Graf 'Chappy' Silern hastening to the station. The latter called out to me that the Germans were coming and repeated verbatim what I had earlier told Rudolfo.

Meanwhile, a very visible change had taken place in all the towns of Tyrol. Some people were bold, even arrogant, while others had frightened looks on their faces. In this latter category were the Jews, the *Vaterlandische* fronters, the social democrats and, of course, the Communists. Many of them changed political views overnight and awoke on 12 March with new convictions and prepared to be good Nazis. The peasants retiring into their mountain homes took no part in the whole proceedings, while in the towns and villages Nazi flags flapped from the roofs of most of the houses and the main street of Kitzbühel was filled with red and white swastika banners.

The American widow of an English industrial peer gave a dinner for a couple of New York society girls. It would have been a dramatic moment for such a party. But her staff had forestalled her by drinking all her champagne in celebration of Austria's liberation. This so enraged the hostess that she fired them all on the spot and then, allowing her Irish-American temperament to get the better of her, went out to tear down every German flag she could seize. This, I thought, was not the moment for a show of bravado, so I, for my part, retired gracefully from the scene. But it was not so easy. My hostess was now thoroughly aroused and was shouting '*sal Bosches*' at the people in the street.

Next day at noon, Rudolfo and I listened to Goebbels on the radio. His speech was momentous and seemed to threaten Czechoslovakia next, which would mean war with England and the immediate internment of all British subjects of military age. Most of my contacts and acquaintances had either fled or been arrested as anti-Nazis. I decided to send Christina and Theresa to Switzerland and to follow them as soon as possible. I had lived a playboy's existence as much as possible so as not to attract undue attention, while at the same time being obvious. It was thus normal for me to go to Switzerland at this time; in fact, I had done so every year after the snow in Kitzbühel had disappeared from the ski slopes.

I had learned in my boxing days that the moment for taking advantage of my opponent was between two movements, in that interval of suspended animation. That was the time to exploit. Theresa and Christina therefore boarded the 3.34 p.m. train for Buchs on that very day and reached Switzerland without so much as having an exit stamp in their passport. I caught a train that night and by next morning fanatical Austrian Gestapo officials were ripping off the soles from passengers' shoes in their search for money and incriminating documents.

It was hard to keep an open mind for one was inclined to be prejudiced. An overall view of the situation was not possible to the ordinary individual. It was amazing, to some people, that Cardinal Innitzer had visited Hitler at the Imperial Hotel in Vienna and that a Jesuit had broadcast a radio speech from the Vatican urging the wisdom of attacking the Nazi regime from within, rather than mounting a futile frontal opposition.

Some days later in Davos I overtook Rudolfo as he zoomed down the Parsen ski run. He was an excellent skier but a little too fond of his wine and food for fast running. Nothing radical was going to be done about Czechoslovakia, he beamed, but the Sudeten Deutschen were going to press for independence and the so-called Gross-Deutschland Reich would insist upon the autonomy of the German population of western Bohemia within, say, two months, failing which the same tactics as they had recently employed in Austria would be applied for the seizure of their country.

I was only half-conscious of the beauty of that day as the sun played upon the frozen surfaces of the mountains. We retired from the slopes and relaxed in a café over coffee.

'Have you noticed,' I began, 'that there are things about this Hitler programme which very much resemble the techniques of the Communist regime?'

'Yes, of course, the control of the masses through indoctrination based on fear of some danger.'

'Exactly,' I pointed to my head, 'first implant a sense of fear or guilt.'

'Ah, ya, guilt.' Rudolfo's eyes twinkled as if I had scored a vital point. 'Mit guilt one becomes unsure of one's self. If you can get a person to feel guilty about what he thinks he is, you've got him.'

'The mind of man – that is sacred ground. No human being has the right to invade.'

'Yes,' said Rudolfo slowly, smiling his broad grin again, 'the Nazis, however, regard such people as the Jews (who might well agree with you) as a barrier to their programme of expansionism and will eliminate them. They are obsessed with the idea that the Jews are conspiring to undermine our cultural and moral standards; in fact, they say the Jews wish to demoralise the Gentile altogether as a means of achieving world domination.'

I found it hard to focus on the idea of genocide, world domination and war on the scale the world was heading for. The laws of man ostensibly protect the human body against hurts and exploitations, but the human mind, which is his only potential means of salvation, they allow to be dominated, exploited and deluded without restraint. The insidious use of psychological strategy was still in its infancy and yet more effective by far than a shooting war. Under the cloak of publicity or propaganda, the human mind can be raped and invaded, crammed with distortions of the truth and thoroughly poisoned. For after all it is but a potential, an instrument for good or evil and its fabric and defences can easily be broken down if care be not taken.

Organisations of every sort, including religions, have staked their claims on the human mind and, I mused, did some one really mean 'Give us a child until he is seven and you can do what you like with him later'?

It was the middle class, the bourgeoisie, to whom the Hitlerian creed appealed, for it had a superficial plausibility. But the opportunist and those who had the capacity for converting all situations into personal gain, were the enemies of freedom. They regarded the rising tide of human emotions as a force to be utilised. They had it within their power not only to convert the situation into a great blessing, but also, alternatively, into a devastating calamity. Subtle as it is there is a difference between exploiting a situation for your own gain and moving in at an opportune moment in the interest of good.

An Austrian lady, in Zellam See, who was in some measure financially indebted to me became bankrupt and offered me her castle at Mittersill for a nominal sum. But though I was very tempted, I was unwilling to commit myself at that time.

The castle stood on a rocky shoulder overlooking a great valley and had a complete panorama of the Höhe Tauern Alps, which included Austria's highest peaks. For size, architecture and site, it could not be beaten. It comprised a residence, a dower house, servants' quarters, stables and a chapel, complete with witches' dungeon, all ranged around a courtyard in the centre of which was an attractive well. Around the battlements was an archer's gallery. The castle contained a quantity of antique furniture of the period, including a four-poster bed of such beauty that it was almost impossible to resist. There were Renaissance paintings, too, and a library of manuscripts. But there was no plumbing in the castle whatsoever. An enormous tiled bathroom, yes, in which at least a half dozen people could bathe at one time – it even had an elaborate spout – but it was not connected with any water system. It would have cost five times the original price to convert the residence into a modern habitation.

Not long after this a number of young Austrian noblemen, with a dollar-backing, purchased and reconditioned the place and turned it into a kind of country club. It was one of these, a princeling who had joined in the usual round-table political discussions with his compatriots, that now turned out in the complete uniform of a storm trooper and, flying a Nazi flag from the car of a wealthy English woman guest, proceeded to denounce the other members of his set.

There was much of this shameful behaviour and much anxiety in those obsessed by the possible loss of their money and possessions.

To my close acquaintances in and around Kitzbühel my interest in international politics had been obvious. I was not likely to escape notice. The comings and goings of an individual could be lost amid the rush and bustle of city life, but in Kitzbühel, a holiday or residential resort, people had little else to do but to discuss their neighbour's affairs. So it was clearly a moment to remain out of the way and to let things simmer down.

Kathleen's will was under discussion in Dublin and the fate of Monivea, the ancestral home, was in the balance. The whole legal matter was, as it were, undergoing a period of gestation. The machinery of the law was working imperceptibly and it was again a time for patience. Nevertheless, I decided to travel to Great Britain.

My journey had been long and the crossing over the Irish Sea choppy. I was tired and inclined to be intolerant. From behind his desk in the Dublin solicitor's office a little man in a pince-nez was being taciturn. 'The Attorney General,' he said, 'had the matter in hand.'

It was a very complicated will in which Kathleen had left Monivea Castle to the Irish Free State government to be used as a home for 'old Ladies of noble birth and artistic tendencies'. The little man was afraid that the government of Ireland was not much interested in that section of its population.

'Hearing of our national disorders,' he said, adjusting his pince-nez, 'Miss ffrench believed that Monivea might share the same fate as her Russian possessions and evidently thought to forestall a second calamity by dumping her castle in the lap of the Free State.' His thin lips curled into an expression of mild disdain. 'Miss ffrench has left you, however, five hundred pounds and some jewellery."

The dream which I had so long cherished, the vision of holding and living at our ancestral home in Ireland, was vanishing. Monivea was on the way out, passing with the snows of yesteryear. A few

months later, Rozzie was carried out of her bedroom in the old Castle
Tower and laid in her coffin. With her death, the Castle walls seemed
to crumble as if her spirit had upheld them. The government of
Ireland had rejected Kathleen's bequest and the Castle had passed
automatically to her next-of-kin Rozzie and subsequently to the
sole beneficiary of her will, an old spinster who lived in some rural
district in England. Being poor, this old lady was glad to sell Monivea
Castle and its thousand acres of park to the Irish Free State for virtually
nothing. For the first time since it was built, Monivea passed into the
impersonal hands of bureaucracy.

The tide of class prejudice having turned, the park was broken
up into small holdings and the Castle, all but the so-called Milesian
Tower which resisted the house-wreckers' hammers, was demolished
and used for material to build roads.

Today there remains only the marble mausoleum to Robert Percy
ffrench standing defiantly in the open in a broken terrain which was
once a magnificent beechwood. And so did the former things pass
away.

For a long time I was filled with resentment. I returned to London
and briefly to Kitzbühel. Although I had left nothing there of an
incriminating nature I still had much of my personal effects at the
chalet.

The furore of the new regime had somewhat abated, but there
were ominous gaps in the population of the town. Two shopkeepers
and my lawyer had been imprisoned in the Kitzbühel gaol. Learning
that they were to be set free, one of them, a grocer, inveigled their
custodian into allowing them to have a party. Good things were soon
forthcoming from his store including much wine and before long a
banquet was in full swing. As the wine circulated freely the gaoler
joined in and soon songs of the wrong political brand were heard
in the street by passers-by. A hotel was just across the way and its
Nazi proprietors, armed with flags, soon organised a counter-demon-
stration outside the prison, shouting 'Dachau, Dachau' in unison,
with the result that the jubilations were suppressed and all taking
part sent to that now infamous concentration camp.

Back in Switzerland Rudolfo got a message through to me from his
home in southern Germany where he was apparently in some trouble.
I unhesitatingly drove there by car to see him, arriving late at night
and experiencing no difficulties beyond the military convoys which
had obstructed the roads.

Having decided to leave Kitzbühel for good, I had recommended Theresa, my cook, to Countess Toerring at her castle in Bavaria. She was now giving her mistress every satisfaction. I passed by to see them en route to Rudolfo's and found my late cook-housekeeper looking well, her sturdy little figure indefatigably toiling, sweeping, rinsing or chopping when she was not cooking. Since the Countess was an ideal person to work for I felt better about parting from such a devoted retainer, but on leaving I found her in the kitchen weeping into the salad. She was finding it impossible to adjust her domesticated instincts to the unsettled political state, the comings and goings and evidence of unrest everywhere.

I felt very conscious of the distress of this regime and what it was instilling among the natural peasants of the country. I sped northward to my destination. Moreover, the countryside I found to be in the grip of a rule of soullessness. Everything seemed to be put to some material or military use. The mountains had been organised for the enticement of tourists and the lakes into hydro-electric schemes. Roads, trains and power lines straddled the countryside. The 'would-be' beauty spots had multi-balconied hotels upon them. Steel pylons interrupted the vistas. The rivers were canalised, the cascades diverted, rapids weired or dammed; every rustic walk marked with some commonplace sign. Nothing was left to the imagination. All was 'order'. The higher valleys were used for *luft kurorts* for the diseased; the lower valleys were busy hives of industry. All fruits of the human mind. Everywhere there was evidence that man thought he owned the world as much as he possessed his own body – whereas he originated neither.

Rudolfo was in a state of nerves. Germany was looking covetously towards western Bohemia. A rich Jew who had several homes in Vienna and had recently built himself a mansion in Marienbad, for five million Czech Crowns, was so sure of a German invasion that he was ready to sell it at any price, including the art treasures that he had evacuated from Austria. The Jews, Czechs and anti-Nazis, said Rudolfo, were all fleeing from those parts. I had stopped and booked myself a room at a simple and rather charming village inn on the way to the Von Gerlach villa, rather than compromise them by sleeping at their house. This done I drove on to their abode where we talked until past midnight.

The Czechoslovakian-German political conflict was hanging over Europe like a threatening cloud – the Germans staging frontier incidents to goad the Czechs. Owing, however, to the total unrest and disorganisation in Austria, friction, corruption, graft and all the usual aftermath of occupation by 'invitation' were manifest. The German staff were feeling that the moment for attacking Czechoslovakia was not propitious. Thus, when Chamberlain proclaimed in the beginning of June that if Germany occupied Czechoslovakia by force England would join France against them, the matter was pigeon-holed.

Rudolfo had some vital information which exposed Hitler's intentions. He would continue discussions with Hodza, the Czech Prime Minister, over the Sudeten Deutsch question, but should he be superseded by a military dictator, or any such control, Heinelines's party would immediately revolt and Hitler would march into Bohemia just as he had done in Austria. The situation was so tense that Germany had called up its reservists and all military classes up to sixty-five years of age, which, incidentally, had included Rudolfo. This tallied with information from other quarters and I knew that, with the seizure of Austria, Czechoslovakia's strategic position was untenable.

It must have been one o'clock in the morning when we heard a sharp rap on Rudolfo's door. His wife, who had retired, looked out of her window to see two men in S.S. uniform standing outside. She hurried downstairs to warn me of my danger. I had taken the precaution of parking my car in the courtyard at the back of the villa, so hastily jumped into it without switching on my headlights and drove off into the night. As I turned the corner into the village I saw several more S.S. men and others surrounding the inn. I quickly turned the car and headed for Switzerland with all haste. It was four-and-a-half-hours drive to the border, mostly done before daybreak.

Outside Bad Toltz I took the by-pass skirting the greater part of the town. My Ford V8 had an English sports-model body and an unusual turn of speed. As I approached Fussen a car caught up with me, or so at least I thought. It followed me into Immenstadt where I drove into the heart of the city to lose it and got lost myself in the maze of narrow streets. At one point I found myself stuck in a lane with a garbage truck blocking the way, so turned into a warehouse gateway, knocking over a pile of crates as I did so.

At the main road I was stopped by a policeman who asked for my papers, but on seeing my Austrian number plates he merely pointed up to a sign which said it was a one-way street. We saluted each other politely and once on the open road again I headed for the frontier post at St Margaretha with all possible speed. It was not far from where the Rhine made a bend giving Switzerland a salient which bulged into German territory. Here countless Jews and other frightened fugitives from Nazi terror lost their lives trying to swim to safety.

It was now daylight and as I approached the black and white barrier I could see that I was the only car on the road. A frontier guard came out from the Posthouse, strapping on his automatic and fastening his collar. He seized the car documents and my passport and carried them into the office. A minute later I heard the telephone bell ring. There was another lengthy delay and I was considering running the barrier. Now one of his comrades came to the door to have a look at me. He disappeared and then a third emerged with my papers in his hand. He passed them to me through the car window, cranked up the gate and motioned me on. Never before had my heart pounded so violently; never had I felt so light-hearted. Then suddenly the light-heartedness left me as some shots rang out behind me and I heard shouts of '*Halt!* *Halt!*' I put my foot down and almost failed to stop at the Swiss control post. In fact I would have kept going but for the gesticulations of the Swiss guards. Once I had reached the safety of Switzerland I began to realise that my hazardous activities were over. I was more or less off the chessboard.

12

Art and Alexis

I sent off my dispatches by airmail and then sought out Ella Maillart whom I trusted and whose sane viewpoint always seemed to illuminate a darkened way. She sent me one of her books and wrote with it:

> You said more than once that a child lives in a world more real than ours. I went far, looking for that reality among nomads, who also are big children and I am searching out that reality in everyone I meet. A thing that is impossible to talk about but which one can feel when silent. If only we spent less time grasping and devoted more time to groping for this Light which is just beyond this big scheme of things – which is on the other side of the 'crack' as Blackwood calls it! Maybe one day I shall be able to make it understandable to others – what is really important. It is easier to grasp in the Hindu Kush or in Canada. That is why I am not so keen about Europe and all that. Time granted to us is so short in which to feel it, to learn and to understand enough. This desire to express my yearnings, to enlarge my limited consciousness . . . What can help me! Men lost in war schemes and all their entanglements are obviously so far from what counts . . . what is the good of trying to avoid wars and death when most people don't know what Life means, or is meant to mean? This unconscious human material is all wasted . . .

I sat on a bench by the waters of Lake Lucerne reading her letter and the message struck deeply home. Ella understood. It was still only an indication, however, and not the goal, but it comforted me to know I was not alone. There was a fascination about it like a voyage of discovery, conquering an unclimbed peak or penetrating to the ultimate secret, the ultimate mystery. It was salutary and led upwards – there was always going to be more.

But I felt physically and psychically uprooted and lost and my one thought was to help those of my acquaintances who had been put in concentration camps in Germany. But frustrating this desire was the fact that as an agent I was now compromised. I remained as close to the Austrian border as I could in the hope of something turning up. Rudolfo was still at large and periodically able to supply valuable information. I located myself in a small *pension* not far from the Liechtenstein border where I found an odd assortment of fellow guests assembled, for whatever reasons. One of these wore a bushy grey beard and spent the day in violet pyjamas, a kimono and straw hat. An old lady of between seventy-five and eighty years had the longest, sharpest and reddest nose I had ever seen. Her feet, too, were long and her legs thin so that her movement suggested a human landrail. There was an English judicial peer who endeared himself to me when I found him reading my sister's new biography of Ouida. The only really objectionable visitor was a man from the Gold Coast who had a room under mine. He was nervous and his manner extravagant. He dressed for dinner and expected the whole household to spring to his calls. If he did not receive immediate attention he would ring his bell again and again, generally while the maids were waiting in the dining room. He, too, seemed to affect pyjamas in the daytime, but in his case they were black and white. I enjoyed the English lord's point of view in politics although he seldom vouchsafed an opinion and mostly contented himself with asking questions and then making guarded remarks well backed by academic references. I began to wonder what I had put myself in the midst of.

I made several visits to Liechtenstein and then down the Rhine to Diepoldsau where the Swiss had a camp for refugees from Nazi oppression. Altogether the sector Sarganz to Lake Constance was of interest, though most of the unhappy individuals who crossed over at this point – many of them having swum the Rhine – were too frightened to give any information.

Switzerland could absorb no more Jews without money or passport for over 2000 already were being fed by Jewish organisations. Some were being pushed over by the Germans with dreadful threats if they dared to return. Others were brought over in the middle of returning hay loads by the Swiss farmers who possessed outlying fields in Reisel. Many Swiss families had relatives in what had become part of Gross Deutschland and had little sleep for months, smuggling Jews across into Switzerland.

I had seen many wrongs done to the Gentile by the Jews in Austria and so much that was un-Christian done to the Jews since Hitler's occupation, that I gave up all attempt at judging the matter. Was one to judge the Jews by their Mosaic law as it was intended to be or by the teachings of Jesus Christ? Both the Christian and the Jewish religions had been prime focuses of deity on earth and both the Jews and the Christians had departed from the sacred essence of their teachings and their religions had deteriorated or lost touch with the essence of spiritual expression. Man is always perpetuating that which was, and seems ignorant of the fact that that which was, although perfect for those conditions, is not necessarily perfect under existing ones. He appears to have a concept that God created the world in seven days and rested, leaving it at that forever more.

Looked at too closely, international politics became mixed up and the observer, blinded and biased, is unable to detach himself with ease from prejudice. He is influenced by a sense of national and traditional patriotism or loyalty to some ideology. But from a cosmic standpoint such things make no sense at all.

The principality of Liechtenstein, while not Swiss territory (though more or less under Swiss administration), was seething with intrigue and was a hotbed of espionage and counter-espionage. Diplomatic representatives of insignificant powers with suspiciously large staffs were merely information centres for larger states. One of these outwardly, was a Consul-General for a Middle-Eastern country, but turned out to be nothing but a German agency for spreading Nazi propaganda in German Switzerland.

I sat in the lounge of the Vaduzerhof or at the Waldams Hotel with their suspicious atmospheres of *va et viens*, of busy conniving, of watching and of being watched . . .

'The green-sweatered motor cyclist in the bar doesn't look Swiss. Haven't I seen him taking notes in Ragatz . . . Who was dictating to him on that occasion . . ?'

'Who are the two who have just arrived in a German sports car? They passed my Ford last night on the Sarganz-Buchs road while I was doing 90 m.p.h.'

'And that other car, with Persian numbers, which followed me and flashed a light on me as they overtook me . . .'

This sinister side had also its pathetic counterpart. There were Jewish families watching mountain paths across the valley – watching and praying for the safe arrival of relatives coming over some smuggler's route out of Fore-Arlberg down into Liechtenstein. It was now or never, for winter was approaching and the passes would soon be closed. Already the grapes were ripe and fresh snow had fallen upon the hills.

The Nuremberg gathering was nearing its end. Hitler's speech on foreign affairs was awaited. He finally spoke with great determination, but though he made many high-sounding threats and phrases and said that so far as the situation in Czechoslovakia was concerned he had reached the limit of his patience, there was actually nothing in his speech which materially removed the pressure on the nerves of Europe. Neville Chamberlain went to Berchtesgaden to see him. To those in Europe who dreaded another war, he symbolised a dove making an appeal for peace.

Close by my lodgings, Leonardo, a hypnotist, held a seance one night in what was called the Grosser Saal. About two hundred and fifty students and adults attended and their roars of delight, as a selected company from the audience were being hypnotised, attracted my attention. It was quite clear that more than half the company were gleefully and voluntarily playing into his hand, while the rest were either following like sheep or truly hypnotised. Leonardo told them to open their mouths and then told them that they could not close them and the whole company gaped until released from its absurd posture. He told them that a fly was buzzing above their heads; they all looked up and then he told them to catch it, and they obeyed, snatching vainly in the empty air. Then he told them that it was no fly but, in fact, a bee, a swarm of bees that was very angry and at this the audience fell into a state of panic which could be heard out in the street.

I could not help drawing a parallel between Hitler's control over his audience and Leonardo over his. Hitler was saying that the bees, which happened at this point to be the Czechs, were a menace. They were going to harm the German people. There were those in this audience whose interests were well suited by the lie, but the majority believed it or weakly obeyed and went along with the herd. When England and France persuaded Czechoslovakia to cede part of their country, occupied by Sudeten Germans to Germany, they accepted the plan. But would that satisfy the now rampant Hitler? Did he want the whole of Czechoslovakia as a stepping stone in the course of his march to the Black Sea? The thought was an ominous one for Hungary and Rumania.

At Ragaz, the secretary of the Golf Club introduced me to Mr Knittle, who lived with Robert Hichens in his very charming villa in Germany. Having considerable frozen assets in the Reich, both these authors were in a bit of a spot. They discussed the possibility of a Czech withdrawal from Bohemia and General Cyrovy's installation as head of the Czech government. The Czech army had taken up its position on the German border and was asking for guarantees that if it evacuated Bohemia there would be no further demands upon its territory. Meanwhile Poland and Hungary were clamouring for their minorities within Czech frontiers.

Mrs Hichens seemed perturbed about the political situation and, while tea was being served by an Egyptian servant wearing a fez, it was announced on the radio that Russia had declared that if Poland entered Czechish Silesia they would repudiate their non-aggression pact with her. So far the moves on the vast political stage had been made by politicians and adventurers, but once war was declared – whether the head of the government was an Emperor, dictator or ruling nabob – the control would automatically pass into the hands of the army. Therefore the aspirations of the army chiefs were worth studying.

It was clear that Czechoslovakia was the strategic key to Europe and it struck me as highly improbable that Hitler would resist the opportunity now offered by the situation. It was therefore not surprising when, shortly after 8 p.m. on 26 September, 1938, the Führer delivered a momentous speech in which he gave Czechoslovakia six days in which to accept his terms. After that, if they had not come into line with his wishes, he would march into their country. Obviously there was no enthusiasm among the Allies. Neither the French nor the English were emotionally involved in the quarrel. Hitler knew this, of course, but he understood little of the British code of ethics, nor did he seem to remember how they react to rampaging dictators, especially inside Europe.

Of course, one could see how both Hitler and Mussolini misunderstood the British point of view. Whether we like it or not, there is no such thing as a common acceptance of ethical standards on earth and, although those meetings to discuss international problems might be flexible and understanding about the other's point of view, the general public, their governments and armies, were not. There was no basic yardstick, no true groundwork for agreement. Even in spiritual matters there was no accord, and religious creeds were as much in disagreement as were ideologies and politics. Yet I was certain that there was but one primary cause, one truth, in which there was no possibility of schism. It now became more pressing than ever for me to come to an awareness of it.

I was again due to report in London and, having done so, I asked myself down for the weekend to my brother Alexis's attractive cottage in Kent.

An autumn wind battled with the remnants of the garden flowers. It was a foggy night and spider webs in the hedgerows sparkled in moonlight. There was already a carpet of dead leaves and it was wet underfoot as I approached the cottage door. Inside the fire burned a bright welcome.

In the sitting room which was pleasantly lit and filled with precious things, antiques, one felt enfolded in an early Victorian atmosphere with the frills and tassels which were being revived in a longing for securer days. Alexis was playing his piano when I arrived and his great friend Hardy Amies was sitting before the fire relaxing after a strenuous week at his boutique in London. Both were rapidly becoming well-known, Alexis as an interior decorator and Hardy as a dress designer.

As I unpacked in my bedroom I felt instinctively soothed by the harmony of colour and choice of ornaments surrounding me; there was as much an inner tranquility to be had from good interior decorating as from the contemplation of a master's painting. The first enfolds you, the second invades you.

I could hear the heavy touch of my brother as he continued his playing of the piano. I had brought with me some literature from the government of British Columbia and took it down with me to the sitting room. Alexis's foot was on the loud pedal as he played a composition of his own. I listened for a while; it had a familiar French flavour to it, perhaps influenced by Ravel, but his powerful treatment of the notes made me nervous. I began to read some columns of statistics about Canada's most westerly province and became increasingly sure that I intended to make British Columbia my home. The Western bug had been germinating, all unrecognised, in my system ever since my days in the Mounties and now by force of circumstance was asserting itself. England had passed the zenith of its imperial prime and, like Rome, her moral values had declined causing me to long both physically and spiritually for purer air to breathe.

As Alexis rose from the piano stool, breaking my Western reverie, I gathered up my papers and stuffed them into their envelope; his fastidiousness bothered me and yet I admired his polish and culture. I would have given a lot to have been able to get closer to him, but we revolved, as it were, in different orbits and perhaps even around different centres.

We made each other uneasy, slightly disapproving of the other. While I was still orbiting round Rollo, Alex was obliged to associate with the women of our family. I had been subjected to vigorous military discipline and the world of art was still pretty vague to me. To Alex, on the other hand, tradition, wars, international politics meant nothing, and during his war service he was in constant trouble over matters of discipline such as overstaying his leave. However, when serving in the ranks in the First World War, he proved himself to be brave and responsible. He was clever, intuitive, emotional, a true artist, but spiritually immature, and lest I be misunderstood in this I realise that one cannot judge spirituality by religious standards. One can be deeply religious, obedient to the strictest rules, believing all dogma and participating in all ritual – and still be completely spiritually immature.

I had come across many of his social sphere and they appeared to be intensely gifted and imaginative, but without inner preception, expressing themselves in fastidious fashionable design. Alexis had attended Andre L'Hote's Academy of Art in Paris and it was he who later introduced me to it, but there was nothing 'Lothonesque' about his work. He favoured Queen Anne style of house design, decorating the interiors with murals and flower paintings in a manner mildly reminiscent of Douanier Rousseau, but in a Swan Lake idiom with romantic swans, lake and distant pavilion set among low hills. As foreground he sometimes had balustrades combined with heavy curtains and the ceilings were striped to resemble an awning. It was most effective and much appreciated by the smarter set of London. He later became known as one of the pioneers of the Regency revival.

His house was in Knightsbridge and he had decorated it in this manner with here and there a mural or a mantlepiece, a wool rug designed and executed by himself, a baby grand piano and a Queen Anne style corner-cupboard filled with carefully selected china from his antique store in Belgravia, or an Old Master painting which blended happily with the rest. All this betokened creativeness and artistic imagination, yet he excelled in the buying and selling of antiques rather than as a composer, painter, or interior decorative artist.

Those who knew him best – Yvonne, Hardy and his devoted wife Anne, as well as a number of his artistic associates — were able to understand his complex nature. He was generous to a fault and extremely sensitive. He longed for love and understanding as do so many who wander through the purlieus of conventional society. The proper study of mankind is, however, man. Alexis often boasted that he knew himself, but what he really knew was his own outer characteristics while his real self, until the approach of his death, remained an enigma. He passed through a phase in which he craved recognition from the very society most likely to deny it to him and ignored the fact that by so doing he was no better than they. Then, suddenly, changing his tactics he would flout them as if he would free himself of their opinions. He was terrified of things that offended his aesthetic tastes, yet he rather enjoyed the uncouth and could tell a risqué story in a manner in which vulgarity became the garlic to his brand of charm. Sometimes his stories made me wince just as my lack of sophistication must equally have offended him.

No one knew less, cared less, about international politics than Alexis and if he went abroad it was to some less conventional spot in the south of France or Italy and his means of getting there would be luxurious. A journey to Canada was as horrifying to him as a trip to the North Pole and the very thought of it made him shudder. It was beyond understanding to him how anyone could want to live in such places. Most of the better London shops knew him and his maxim was 'the best that you have is just good enough for me'.

By now I had visited all the obvious art galleries of Europe and many private collections as well and was therefore personally acquainted with a great many rare and valuable art treasures of the world. They represented to me then, the highest tangible form of expression on earth, yet I wanted to emerge from the relative into the realm of the absolute. Man appeared to have to approach the absolute by a process of letting go in himself of previously accepted standards.

Leaving Burlington House shortly afterwards I ran into Claude Dansey, my chief, and as we walked down Piccadilly together I could not help noticing how depressed he looked. I quizzically watched his face and thought I noticed traces of ill-health. 'If only I could persuade the government to take those wads of cotton wool and prejudiced complacency out of their ears,' he wailed. I was sorry for him for he certainly had a most unenviable task and the public, refusing to face facts, was branding any who attempted to do so as 'scaremongers'. On the human level it was obvious that serious problems existed, but it was also clear to me that their solution did not lie in policies, ideologies or human organisations. The cause, rooted in human nature, was easy enough to see if one was courageous and honest enough to look beneath the surface or face oneself in the mirror the world was providing but, then, what was one to do about it? The public seemed to dread facing itself and was inclined to be dilatory in facing up to the cause of evil; rather like a house owner who, being conscious of his mistake in not putting in damp courses when he laid the foundations, decides to live with the damp and dry rot in his home.

When I was a child in school I once made the error of mistaking a figure in a simple addition. The mistake was slight for it was in the beginning but it increased a hundred fold before I realised it was wrong. It seemed to me that human beings, rather than admit an error made in the genesis of their story, had followed the same course, while attempting to cover up, persisting in the false way and in the absurd belief that it would eventually bring them to the correct result.

I removed all my belongings from Kitzbühel and stored them in a bonded warehouse in Switzerland and, having resigned from M.I., was now free to move about at will. There was one restricting factor, however. Rudolfo, who was now in Holland, had to be taken care of. He was still getting occasional scoops of valuable information and refused to be contacted by anybody else but me, so, pending my final departure for Canada, I held myself available for that purpose.

The interlude was spent mostly in London. Although I felt drawn to Canada I also toyed with the idea of going to Cyprus, Tunisia or Portugal. My eventual decision to return to Canada was made mostly because of my happy memories of that country in 1910. I was only seventeen at the time and awakening into manhood in a man's world – just as the vast central plains greened with life again after a frozen sleep – and the land had made a lasting impression upon me. The dry and sweetly scented air intoxicated me, blending with a vital rhythm which moved in my environment. Anyone who has not witnessed a prairie spring, especially in the days of the wild west, cannot possibly understand the force of its attraction. I had a longing to renew my acquaintance with that sense of union in nature, away from the restricting limits of civilisation. My soul was dilated by the open spaces. There was no resisting it, I strained to be gone.

But evenings were, meanwhile, passed agreeably at dinner parties and entertainments. Ella turned up in England and, as an alternative to her usual life of hardship on trek in Central Asia, was very social and gay. Thanks to her popularity, we dined with and met celebrities outside my normal sphere. From George Bernard Shaw and Somerset Maugham to Labour M.P.s and faith healers. The situation in Europe was avoided like a skeleton in the cupboard as if mention of it would precipitate the final crisis.

Parliament was mostly concerning itself with routine business and as for the masses, who were gradually gaining control in the administration of England, they were better equipped with radios and pensions and their leisure time more dedicated to the screen than ever before. But their school teachers were grossly underpaid and their education did little to lift them out of the growing belief that less work and more pay was a sound philosophy.

They had a rooted belief in an arbitrarily conceived Utopia on earth – a practically planned heaven – while in their hearts and minds no such heavenly state prevailed. The churches were mostly unattended and orators in Hyde Park preached the gospel according to Karl Marx.

Britain's budget had shown a deficit ever since the beginning of the century. There had been more imports than exports. Her fabulous riches had been able to take care of the deficit until the great depression of 1930, but thereafter the fatal leakage had become a matter of concern. The alliance with the United States had proved to be a blessing on the face of it, but her virile younger partner was also a competitor and every time they allied on some momentous enterprise, the United States emerged the stronger. There were other factors involved, of course, yet with every succeeding year Uncle Sam's voice became more and more vibrant in international affairs and seemed, moreover, inclined to set the patterns of diplomacy to which Great Britain, in spite of her experience, had to conform. It was fair enough that the one who paid the piper called the tune, but the United States had not yet acquired an ear for diplomatic music. Of course, at this point, Great Britain was hardly indicating by her behaviour that the centuries had taught her anything.

A postcard from Holland reached me, written in Italian and in Rudolfo's hand. '*L'orizzonto politico non mi piace per niente per Maggio,*' it said and went into detail as to why he thought May was going to be zero hour.

That night a group of young Englishmen, whom I met over after-dinner coffee, spoke openly of the Fascist coup they hoped to pull off in England. Their leader, Oswald Mosley, was speaking in some outlying district of London and they were going to support him. One of them, Tony, unable to attend the meeting, took me to a night club of which he was the manager. He introduced me to a Spanish dancer who had come to exhibit her skill with a view to a contract.

She came from Red Spain and was, in her own words, 'as red as a radish'. She whispered 'Salud' over the glass as she sipped the ruby vintage. More of her group joined her at the table. Casting aside her shawl, she took to the floor and gave two national dances in a Sevillian idiom. She then impersonated a gay and coquettish lace-seller from Andalusia. The very spirit of national Spain, she got her contract.

The next day at Chesterfield Gardens where my night club acquaintances of the night before had met, I visited an exhibition of Spanish art called from 'Greco to Goya'. I was interested in one of the many pictures of Philip IV by Velasquez, but very little else. The thought kept haunting me, as I turned away from Goya's pictures of the inquisition, as to whether Fascism and Communism did not have more in common than otherwise. Their aim was in both instances to control the masses on the basis of greed, either through religion if useable or by taking its place if necessary. Both attempted to bring about an ideal state on earth by a means which excluded its creator. What a hopeless muddle it all seemed. Yet the waters were beginning to clear in my own consciousness adequately enough to see the futility of trying to perfect the relative without knowledge of the absolute. My sense of perception caused pressures which forced me to let go of previous concepts and I found myself going through a period of transition in which there was no vision and I felt I would perish or go crazy in the void.

13

The Sun Rises in the West

A new political fuss was starting up in Poland. The Danzig question was coming to a head; France and Italy were quarrelling over Tunis and the Savoy just as Chamberlain, whom the French had now nicknamed *J'aime Berlin*, was due for talks in Rome. The world's convulsions were working towards crisis. Remembering the last war with horror, however, the opponents moved stealthily round each other like two ferocious yet sagacious dogs. The heads of governments flew back and forth making direct contact with each other – a procedure which inevitably robbed diplomatic representatives of their initiative and placed immense strain on the leaders. Yet the urgency of the situation demanded prompt and radical treatment. I watched the developments closely. I was in a better position to do so than most, for I was still closely in touch with headquarters and was able to get a detached view of what was going on. The point of view of the heads of governmental departments was influenced by national policy and, therefore, prejudiced.

I knew that the Germans had uncovered my activities in Europe and that I was a marked man and one who would compromise those with whom I associated. My name was placed on the Gestapo's list of war criminals. Consequently, my departure from the scene to Canada was approved by the director of Military Intelligence. The spring seemed to be the appropriate time for the venture. After examining my maps of British Columbia for hours, I placed the point of a compass on one of the islands between the southernmost tip of Vancouver Island and the mainland, described a circle with a radius of 200 miles, and decided to settle within it.

Having a little time, I passed it visiting people and places associated with my youth. Bradley Court, where between the ages of thirteen and sixteen I had been sent to learn something about agriculture, was one such place. Memories of youth are presented in brilliance of colour and design, but time plays havoc with the form. Returning, one is often sickened with disillusionment. It was a sad experience

179

and being December and cold, with Mayhill newly covered with snow and standing out against a grey sky, I found the country stripped of much of the beauty I remembered.

The house, now dilapidated, stood gaunt and naked in a neglected garden. Some of its windows were broken and the bellpull was out of order. The stable and coachhouse were in bad repair and showed a lack of care and understanding. When I had been a student there the horse was still flourishing as an essential part of country life, yet already with the increase of technology and the use of the motor car a new spirit was superseding that of live horsepower. Even at that time I found a decline in interest and feeling for the horse and my new interest in equitation was for something rapidly becoming obsolete.

I was invited to a scratch meal served and evidently cooked by two buxom stable girls. The rooms were cold and unwelcoming – the plaster peeling from the ceilings and walls. The house was only half-furnished with broken furniture. I therefore left Bradley Court with a shudder and headed down a snowy road thoroughly chilled and miserable.

Driving on I passed through Monmouth and Brecon, arriving at Stackpool Court in brilliant but frosty sunshine. The evergreen oaks which surrounded the house, the lakes and lagoons lent a particular exotic grandeur to the impression.

The fires in the beautifully appointed room were heaped with Lidney coal and burning brightly and there was a warm welcome awaiting me from my host and hostess. Out of doors there was a record frost. Thousands of wild fowl sheltered in the lakes: widgeon and flocks of heavier duck ranged and circled in the cloudless sky. But there was a futureless note in it all which was expressed by my host in the words, 'What is the good of struggling and scraping to keep a big place going for the sake of one's heirs who will be taxed out of existence after this next war?'

In London, smog and the flu were adding to the political and financial depression which invaded everyone's mind. The hub of the empire was filled with foreboding.

Late one evening in March I stepped into a cross-torrent of vehicles and human beings – and felt like a man who had begun again an entirely new life. In my pocket was a ticket for Victoria, B.C. As I hurried westwards towards where a setting sun silhouetted Nelson's column, I felt that the journey had already begun, for the agonies of packing and leave-taking were over.

The *Queen Mary* made a record run and reached New York in the early morning of 10 March. The skyscrapers towering over Manhattan reflected sunlight from their windows in a dazzling display. I had friends whom I hoped to see before leaving civilisation behind. New York was, I thought, a European extension in America and once I had left it behind me I would increasingly become caught up in the rigours of the West. I telephoned Hope, a Paris acquaintance, a young American whom I had known while she was at the Sorbonne. While waiting for her I watched some workmen planting a solitary elm tree and I could not help wondering whether it would survive in that canyon of carbon monoxide fumes.

Hope met me by the Statue of Atlas at the Rockefeller Center and took me to a bookstore where she was working and so together to an Italian lunch where we were joined by a young Frenchman, Pierre Matisse. We resuscitated all our Parisian and Tyrolese experiences. They came to life out of the past and stood as garish witness to a sequence which had, however, moved into oblivion.

The weather turned cold. Snow sailed horizontally down the streets before a wind which piled it into drifts. I was crossing to the St Regis for a cocktail and stepped into slush almost up to my knees. My attention was arrested by a girl in blue jeans and sandals riding a scooter on the far side of the road. I could not see her face but that body could only have been Jane's. I rang up my host and learned that the girl on the scooter had probably been her. Was this sheer exhibitionism? Had she gone crazy? I learned that she had gone 'primitive', and had become a nature girl. She was now more beautiful than ever, still using neither cosmetics nor millinery to adorn herself. She had been refused entrance to most of the hotels of New York and had frequently been summonsed for unseemly behaviour. I felt I wanted to meet her, talk with her, and find out what it was all about, but my friends warned me that she had an embarrassing way of throwing off her clothes without warning. Nevertheless, I telephoned her, but she refused to meet me except in the privacy of a hotel bedroom. She sensed that I was hedging and quickly took the offensive. 'You are no better than the rest of the conventional idiots in New York.' I was a false hypocrite who couldn't understand. She pelted me with abuse. I hung up. Jane seemed to be carrying on her own private crusade for sex – not for material gain nor for sensual satisfaction, but because she believed in it as a mode of expression for the feeling of initiation that it could give her. She was very matter-of-fact and completely unsentimental about it. It was, to her, a creative act. As for me I could only see it as an admission of promiscuity and shrank from the embarrassment of being seen in public with such a notorious Venus. But the whole incident made me feel rather small.

Rushing home I got into my dinner jacket and ploughed through the snow to an address on 53rd Street where I arrived late, with many apologies. I sat next to a willowy socialite. We rose from the dinner table in time to miss the Philharmonic Orchestra's performance of Handel's Concerto Grosso at Carnegie Hall. Mozart was about to be played. The hall was filled with an interesting crowd common to the world of music lovers, but I could not help but be struck by their cynical expressions.

Later, outside the concert hall, a council of war took place in an icy wind and my host decided that I must hear some good swing music. I meekly protested – the idea of swing after Mozart seemed sacrilegious, but I was in the minority. The Coconut Tree was reached with another taxi and I felt my spirits ebbing. A circular counter surrounded the loudest jazz band I had ever heard, situated in the centre of a room where the walls had been painted to represent a jungle. We sat within inches of the band and drinks were called for. 'What would I have?' ... I needed a strong one. I wanted to lose consciousness, cover my face with a handkerchief and blot out the whole scene. The percussionist, all animation, was chewing gum in rhythm with his drum.

I watched the faces of the crowd, their eyes registering a cross between resignation and stupefaction, their bodies convulsed by an ecstasy of syncopation. This was the antidote to an office life in some lofty and soulless building. I began to understand Jane's disdain for convention and civilisation.

A woman was playing the piano and singing into a microphone. She was shrill enough without it, but now she was positively ear-splitting. The willowy socialite prattled trivialities. The pressure on my head was unbearable. The decorations around the room became deformed and started swinging as if a tropical storm was sweeping through them. The woman's voice grew shriller and the willowy socialite more persistent with her cliché-ridden conversation. I got up and said, 'But for the pretty girl playing the harp I would like to shoot the lot. Let's go!' I called for the bill.

The journey from New York to Victoria, with its many incidents and garbled scenic interests, was passed in the company of a stalwart

Superintendent of the Royal Canadian Mounted Police and a Deputy Commissioner from Scotland Yard who, like myself, were travelling to the West. The Superintendent was a fine type, tall and tough with a square jaw. The Scotland Yard man, who could have been taken for a Methodist preacher, was taciturn and conscientious and wore a bowler hat. They were travelling along the route which would be followed by the King and Queen of England on their anticipated visit to Canada. I gave the Deputy Commissioner a book on Canada which he accepted with polite caution – force of habit no doubt. The Superintendent then offered me a pull at his flask. Liquor was forbidden on board the train except in the dining car. The Scotland Yard man neither drank nor smoked and his expression was one of blank amazement.

At Regina, some of the Mounted Police brass were on the platform to greet the travellers. One of these, a Superintendent Salt, had married Jenny Quinn whose father had kept her so strictly from me when we were down at the Battle Creek detachment in the winter of 1910-11.

After a brief stop in Vancouver I took the ferry for Vancouver Island and on reaching Victoria the whole trip became a kaleidoscopic blur out of which my brain, tired with new impressions, could distinguish no details. A bus took me up island to Duncan where all unsuspectingly I met Fitz, an acquaintance, who dragged me into an adjacent hotel bedroom to meet some of his friends. There were bottles of rye whisky, a radio, together with handshaking and many voices varying in vibrancy and direction from very English to very Canadian.

I could not make it out at all. Why should they all meet in a bedroom? Why not downstairs in a bar or some public room? But it was against the law to drink in public rooms in B.C. My recollection of it is very indistinct as they all wanted to tell me about the country I had just arrived in and, in particular, the part they owned. It was ideal. It was a paradise. My spirits rose a little. Then I met one who seemed less enthusiastic than the others and from him I got a different story. I had arrived at a place denuded of trees by a gang of wantons, stripped of its wild life by a mob of armed hooligans, fished out by a handful of greedy opportunists and wracked by government incompetence. From somewhere in that smoke and vapour-filled room, Fitz's voice penetrated in its unmistakable Orderly Room pitch, 'It's a scandal, and I tell you, it's all due to graft.'

Then all at once, as if in sudden contrast, the silence of the wilds

rushed in on me as if a million harp strings had burst within the
compass of my skull, leaving a blank hush. I was out in the West
at last! I persuaded myself that I was now away from discord and
among the harmonies of nature.

When I left that hotel and by what means remains a blank, but
the next thing I remember was the spring song of a solitary robin.
Somewhere under tall firs by the water of Maple Bay, my head still
throbbing from the hectic tempo of the past few weeks, I realised
that I had at last escaped from the sphere of convention to one of
peace and that I had come to rest on a soft camp bed in a cabin overlooking a landlocked bay; scents reached me through an open window.

The robin carolled on in his thrushlike manner and I slowly sank
back into a sleep from which I was only awakened by a call to breakfast.
The voice was that of Ian MacKenzie, one of last night's guests who
had driven me to his home – a fox farm overlooking Maple Bay. It
was still fairly early in the morning, but the sun was shining and the
water was like a sea of glass, totally serene.

The bay, encircled by wooded mountains, looked like a lake for
the shadow of the mountain hid the narrows which connected it with
the Pacific Ocean. Towards these narrows, and now lit by the sun,
stretched a point over which a haze was hanging.

'What an ideal spot to live,' I said casually to the MacKenzie family
at large.

'There is a house on that point which is for sale,' they said. 'Why
don't you go and have a look at it?'

Of course, I could not wait to do so.

Soon I was in the land of hot smells of juniper and cedar bark.
The salt water of the rising tide lapped happily at the rocks nearby.
Dense forest climbed into the hills as I followed the trail through
woods carpeted with ferns, salal and flowers, interwoven with honeysuckle.

I had stepped, all at once, out of a world fashioned of human intellect into one wherein the laws of nature still predominated. Never
had I seen such trees; on either hand the firs reached up to at least
one hundred and fifty feet. The impression was that of walking up
an aisle of some vast cathedral. Perhaps there was the scent of incense
and a reverent hush as breezes stirred the crowns of trees. Now and
then bird song resounded among those immense trunks. The rocky
coast line curved and, as I approached it, I came to still stranger
trees, their smooth bark tinted with orange and mauve. By some

caprice of nature they were casting their leaves as the others were bursting into spring foliage. They were the arbutus or mendroza tree, stretching out red tormented limbs towards the sea like the arms of Indian maidens reaching for departed braves. Under those trees I found midden heaps where the coastal Indians had camped in the days when they used to maraud along the shores of the Pacific in dugout canoes.

The deep green waters, coming and going with the tide, drenched or withdrew from the barnacled rocks, exposing and returning again to its scurrying creatures in the coves and crevices. The beachcombing crow, the watchful gull and the salmon in the pools were all part of its beauty, yet none so striking as the amethyst and gold of the starfish that stared up from the bottom of deep green water. Rounding a bend I came upon a house. It stood in an open clearing with the mountain behind it, a rose garden and lawn in front which ran down to a small cove.

There were a few fruit trees and a vegetable garden, a cabin and a shed for chickens and goats. But the joy of it was the large basement which contained quantities of tools and garden implements. Every care had obviously been given to the necessities of life in the house but little to its aesthetic potential which was very great.

An old man came out to greet me. The place was for sale, he said, but, he quickly added, there were many disadvantages. He showed me over the house, while his wife, a delicate little woman, prepared some tea. They had been caretakers there for several years, the owners having returned to England to educate their son. There were, of course, a number of snags to be considered, but the price was certainly not one of them.

I was anxious to possess a place of my own, some acreage, a far-ranging outlook, a place where one could enter in, close the gate behind and shut out the world with its dangers and discords. I wanted a sanctuary, an escape from the cacophony of human minds and the end of civilisation as I knew it. That evening I made an offer to the owner by cable and within a few days I became owner of the property. It was called Arbutus Point. There was a lot of land and about a mile of south-facing water frontage. The disadvantages enumerated by the caretaker were all of a minor nature and, at any rate, quite outweighed by its assets. Never before had such a plum fallen into my lap. In the hollow of the bay was the village in which there was a rustic hotel. I now moved in there and would walk over to my property each day to plan some alterations. It was tremendous fun, for I could see how beautiful it could be made. Meanwhile the caretakers were pleased to remain on and look after the place for me.

More and more I could see that the Second World War was not far off. Paradoxically I wanted to be free to take part in it. Arbutus Point provided me with a wonderful background – somewhere to look upon as home to which I could return for peace – for it possessed a restful self-contained atmosphere.

I worked hard throughout the late spring cutting down trees and bushes that obstructed the view of the bay. The hotel radio provided me with an outline of what was going on in the world. Germany had occupied Bohemia; the Hungarians were pouring into the Carpatho-Ukraine; Hitler's pledge of last autumn had proved as worthless as England's had to protect Czechoslovakia.

Every day I walked along that enchanted forest road to the entrance of Arbutus Point; there I would pause and allow the tranquillity of the scene to possess me. A small dam just inside the gate supplied the house with water and also worked the electric plant. It flowed over a fern-choked spillway and on down a gulley under large maples and yews. I never saw this scene without its affecting me deeply. I sometimes caught myself being humanly sentimental and even possessive, for I had never owned land before and here was a beauty spot which was mine, even to the centre of the earth, for I also held mineral rights on it. Such good fortune, I said to myself, was not a matter of chance! Then I reflected that it was only a step beyond this to the possessiveness which was now precipitating the great war upon the world. For no man can own the earth, for it is there to be appreciated and enjoyed.

It was the time of spring flowers and the first fruit trees around the house were in blossom. Birds sang in the forest and the sound of returning geese came out of the sky. Millions of salmon were wriggling up to their spawning grounds, there to spawn and die, their carcasses providing a feast for the herring gulls. But elsewhere, just as Rudolfo had foretold, great concentrations were taking place which were to prove tragic.

German troops were massing upon the Polish frontier. The bone of contention was Danzig and still England would not conscript. In Canada there was an almost unanimous vote for conscripting capital in the event of war, but those in favour of rushing to England's aid if she got involved were, as yet, limited. Drugged by the fascination of impending calamity, many became blind to the true significance of the trend of events. Each thought of how it affected him or her. By this I, too, became affected. This inverted vision narrowed my awareness and I lost an expanded understanding of the whole. My first impulse was to serve. Lord Tweedsmuir, then Governor-General of Canada, was an old associate of M.I. days. He wrote introducing me to the appropriate official. I immediately offered my services, but was told that there was no opening for experience such as mine. There were plenty of young Canadians for Canadian jobs, I was told.

Canada's winter climate, so far as it is determined by its longitude, is essentially cold, but its west coast temperature is influenced by the warm Japanese current. This causes great condensation and heavy rainfall. The humidity has a slowing-up effect on the inhabitants who become relaxed and phlegmatic. I bought a car. It had a radio and was a quicker means of getting back from Arbutus Point to the village hotel after a hard day's work. Sometimes I drove through the forest, listening to the news or to soft music.

The caretaker's wife looked so frail and ill at times that I did not like to ask her to cook my meals. I felt sure, moreover, that before long war would break out and that I would be glad to have them living there. Roosevelt's ten points for the preservation of peace were being used by Chamberlain as an ultimatum to Hitler. If he did not accept them by 29 April, said Chamberlain, he would have conscription in England. However all this would eventually affect my

life, at all events I now had the means and the freedom to explore.
The ferry services between Vancouver Island and the mainland would,
I knew, make it easy to visit the interior of the province.

The alders and maples were just bursting into leaf as I drove up the ·
Fraser Canyon toward the Cariboo country. At a wayside inn by one
of the bridges over the Fraser River, the innkeeper sat with me listening
to the radio. Like so many in British Columbia he had emigrated from
England.

The road wound up the canyon through dense vegetation. I met
a wrecking truck towing a badly battered Ford car and its occupants.
They had gone over the edge and down some three hundred feet into
the Fraser River whose swirling muddy waters flow between steep
rocky cliffs through the mountainous country of British Columbia.
At Lytton I saw a number of men panning for gold and from that
point northward I was quickly in a dry belt that runs parallel to the
coast all down the continent. Looking back over the cloud-enveloped
country out of which I had risen, I was suddenly glad of the clear,
dry air and the brilliance of sunshine. There were pine and poplar
in the hollows of the sage-covered hills and heading the valley were
peaks still covered with snow.

My car sped on, no longer through rain puddles but in rising clouds
of dust. I left the great Fraser and followed a tributary along but
forked away again until I found myself among low hills and open
valleys. The road passed through poplar groves, an Indian reservation
and finally to where some ranch buildings occupied a strip of land
between two lakes. I entered the ranch store and found the book-
keeper sitting in his office. Although he had been out West most of
his life, Mr Leith was still very English. I looked around the store.
There was everything there that would gladden a cowboy's heart,
including ten-gallon hats of every style and shade, stock saddles,
Mexican spurs and bright coloured shirts. I had been given a letter
of introduction to a rancher, Frank Ward, whom I found having
coffee on his verandah in the company of his manager. With them
was a girl and an older woman. A breeze from the lake fluttered the
aspen leaves and sunlight played on their faces. Frank poured out
another cup.

'You'll stay the night, I hope. Brian Chance here will show you over
the place.'

The girl, Mary Bosenquet, in very English tones, asked whether

she could come too. We drove off by car. The ranch, which is now
over 430,000 acres in size, then graced 10,000 head of cattle. Mary
was mostly interested in horses for she was intent on riding across
Canada from west to east and needed a good mount. Nor was she
disappointed, for Frank gave her one of her own choosing. Mary
eventually got to the east, though the horse which she chose on this
occasion did not reach the end of the journey. Her book, *Saddlebags
for Suitcases*, describes the adventure.

I awoke next morning to the liquid notes of the Japanese starling
in the trees and then, shortly after daybreak, a ploughshare at the
back of the bunkhouse kitchen was struck by a hammer. It resounded
like a gong and drove from my mind the thought of packrats in the
ceiling during the night. I dressed and was amused to find the Win-
chester Coat of Arms on a coat-hanger in the cupboard. This, some
photographs and a little drawing of the Devonshire moors, were links
with England. The ample ranch fare of porridge, eggs and bacon with
grilled cakes and maple syrup provided a good start to an active morning.

It was chill and the poplars stood motionless by the lake. Cowboys,
mostly Indians now, streamed in from the bunkhouse, their bright
shirts and jingling spurs lending harmony to the scene. We saddled
up and rode out with Brian and reached a place among the hills where
a few hundred cattle were bunched in a corner by a lake; we joined
in with the cutting out of thirty-three of the best, as well as one who
had his nose pierced full of porcupine quills. My pony was a marvel
at working cattle and together we peered through the dust and the
sunshine at steers that stared right back at us. Then, all of a sudden,
there was great animation, Brian had selected a beast to be cut out.
The herd deployed and then bunched together again like the opening
and closing of a great fan and then, as if by magic, the selected steer
galloped up to join the others now grazing apart on the hill. I was
utterly happy and felt well in my body and mind.

Brian had selected his cattle for special feeding and now turned
them over to the cowboys and we rode off on our own until we reached
a bluff to the north from whence we got a panoramic view of the
region. As far as could be seen, distance upon distance of hills ended
in a snowy ridge which separates Douglas Lake from the Okanagan.
Some of these hills were covered with trees, others were rolling pasture
of grassland and sage. In the folds of the distant mountains were
thickets of poplar and pine and here and there valleys filled with
orange and gold of willows ready to burst their buds.

It was now noon and we rode down to one of the subsidiary ranches where a woman refreshed us with lunch. She lived a gun and frying-pan existence but she gave us of her best. She told us moisture was needed and this was evident, for the dry breeze that swept the hills was scaring up a brownish cloud of dust. Yet, despite this, the young grass was growing and the stock was putting on weight. We heard the melancholy call of a loon from the lake and a coolness came out of the east which caused some ranch guinea-fowl to give a rain warning.

Clouds gathered and we headed for home. Brian Chance explained how they had to nurse the pasturage and keep the grass in close bunches; how and when to eat it down and when to save it. But his words were carried away on the chill wind that now increased. We reached the ranch house in rain.

Mr Leith was leaving after eighteen years on the ranch. His age was seventy-two and he had been pensioned off. He looked very English in his tweeds as he shook his boss's hand – a typical military man of the old school with all that accumulated cunning of an old campaigner, 'hair and hide, with a jug full of arrogance thrown in', as my companion put it. He probably felt this uprooting very much, not that he dared to show it. He had to catch the stagecoach at Quel-chena. When it swung in it contained a 'mopsie' in red pants who was being cuddled by a beery cowpoke, and a rabbity-faced youth who sat next to the driver. Leith had him out of there in an instant. 'By gad! there's no room for a fellah!' The youth joined the cuddlers inside whilst Leith piled golf clubs, guncase and a lot of very English-looking luggage on top and then climbed on in front. When we waved goodbye, the old fellow looked straight ahead to a horizon of retirement and uncertainty.

Mary came out. 'Visitors!' she cried, pointing to a Cadillac which had just parked under the trees. I heard the sound of clinking glasses from inside and thought I should join the company. A Colonel and Mrs Green of Victoria had dropped in to say hello to our host. They talked loudly and aggressively in terms that laid down the law about polo and climatic statistics, or argued amongst themselves about trivialities . . . Did I play polo?

'Men should play polo,' said Mrs Colonel. She herself was president of a ladies' polo club.

'Look here, ffrench.' said her retiring husband, 'I've been here twenty years. I know the country like the palm of my hand, its people and its habits and I can't see why you shouldn't play polo.'

'What's wrong with the man?' queried the woman with an obvious sneer. 'Doesn't play polo! Doesn't even drink!' Then, turning to me, 'How do you spell your name!' She took another draught from her glass. 'I used to know a Lady ffrench, any relation of yours? They had friends called Boreing in an Irish Regiment.'

Making a wry face, she flicked her cigarette ash on the floor with a puce lacquered nail, while, in her other claw, she grasped her whisky glass.

My next trip into the interior was up the Cariboo Trail. I started by following the same road as before, picking up information as I went of Mary's escorted progress on the first leg of her trans-Canada ride. Her exploit had great appeal to Canadian youth and many an ardent cowpoke had offered to accompany her.

As I drove north, the road deteriorated. I picked up a young fellow to whose sentiments I was thereafter obliged to listen. He wanted to die, he said, with a gun or a fishing rod in his hand. 'No sick bed for me!' My car radio was playing a Haydn symphony. He pointed to it with his pipestem. 'We gotta listen to that stuff now? Boy, oh boy, am I ever glad when they give hockey matches on the programme!' He was going to see his girl. 'Her sister is full of learning,' he confided, 'but Bet looks pretty good beef to me!'

I suppose he was a fair example of the young of western Canada. On the other hand, I had met an isolated individual on my last trip who had with his own hands transformed his modest bungalow into something in the style of George III. He had panelled his walls, parqueted his floors, tiled his open fireplace with Dutch tiles and filled his home with an aesthetic harmony of antique objects of art, with cut glass and with rare china in his corner-cupboards; paintings, samplers or miniatures on his walls and period furniture. I recollect that evening – its rum and ginger ale, and its moonlit garden heavily scented by the rambler roses and honeysuckle, because it was an attempt at European culture in a misty sea of raw practicability.

14

The World Catches Fire

It was early summer. The country grew wilder and yet more beautiful. I drove through a thickly wooded and rolling land which was, nevertheless, well provided with open grassy tracts called, locally, 'parkland'. The road climbed to about 4000 feet and as it dropped toward 100 Mile House a panorama of distant hills covered with snow opened up towards the north. On reaching the floor of the valley where the road crossed a stream I found a lodge, a barn and some corrals. Tired and hungry, I wondered what sort of a welcome I would receive.

Close to where I stopped I could see a muskrat swimming in the stream and not far from him a cinnamon duck rested on the bank. For a while there was no other sign of life. I watched a kingbird making sallies from a fence post. Then an opening screen door arrested my attention and I saw Lord Martin Cecil coming out to meet me. What seemed to be an unimportant encounter was to prove the crucial step into a period of my life which brought to light new and greater purpose in living.

Martin stood before me; in his regard was depth of sincerity, perhaps a little shy, for he was neither cold nor effusive, neither was he talkative nor taciturn, gushing nor indifferent, but there was a quality which touched me immediately, something mysterious. At first I was a little on my guard, but instinctively I knew that he had stimulated a responsive chord in me.

Had I evaluated him socially as a Cecil, of noble parentage, I would have lost him wholly. As a rancher, too, he was well thought of throughout the West, yet ranching pure and simple gave me no focus on this man. An Englishman, a gentleman, a rancher? These were useless measures which did not scan nor fit his true proportions, although he answered to those descriptions. But none of these did him justice.

He gave me a sincere handshake and the friendliest of smiles which evaporated any doubts I might have had about my welcome, and introduced me to his wife. Thus, in a few moments, was a new beginning made.

Some Austrians, who were old friends of my family, now turned up, having travelled north from Vancouver by car to investigate the purchase of some property in the Cariboo-Chillicotin country. Their estates in Austria were on territory occupied by the Nazis so they had abandoned them to seek a new life in Canada. We met in the lodge which had been built by Martin with some local help. It consisted of an entrance and lounge with kitchen and dining room behind it and a number of bedrooms upstairs for guests. On either side of the lounge were other apartments used privately by the Cecils.

When later Martin reappeared it was to invite me to join them for dinner. This, our second meeting, confirmed my first impression of a quality in him which was greater than his inherited state, a positive authority emanating from some intense inner source. I was at a loss to encompass something for the first time in my life. It was not what he said or did, for outwardly he was quiet and unassuming. I judged Martin and his wife Edith to be in their late twenties.

After breakfast the next morning, as I sat with the Austrians, we were joined by our host who suggested a drive to show us the surrounding country. It proved to be as beautiful as could be hoped for; flatter than that of Douglas Lake and yet varied with surprising physical features – creeks, lakes, hills, ravines, open grassland, dense forest, all mingled in harmony. From the top of a rise we saw Lac la Hache in the distance, lying in a beautiful vale of mixed scenery.

Some ponies, having been brought in from grass for our benefit, were offered to us as mounts and I was asked to act as guide. I was interested to learn that the pony I was riding had only just been broken. The Austrians, who were less accustomed to such mounts, fared as best they could. On the whole the ride went off pretty well, my horse making only one attempt to buck which I frustrated by tying his halter shank to the horn of the saddle. Clouds gathered and thunder rolled and we decided to return and, as is usually the case when heading towards home, the horses became more amenable.

Next morning the Austrians continued on their journey to the north while I decided to stay on and, asking for sandwiches, took a trip to Lord Egerton's ranch at 105 Mile where a deserted house stood two miles back from the road. I passed groves of poplars, their silvery stems contrasting with the deep blue of the lakes. On the lakes were wild duck of many varieties. Plover flew around me menacingly as I walked along the fringe of the lake. They seemed to say . . . 'Don't! . . . don't! . . . Please don't!' fearing that I might tread on their eggs among the short rushy grass. They did all they could to lure me off after them, which was easy as I was going in that direction anyway. But no doubt it gave them some satisfaction to see me follow them.

When I reached the deserted house, which had stood empty since its owner had been killed in the First World War, I found it inhabited by the little creatures of the woods. An old ground-hog stood erect before it like a sentry, diving into his hole only when I passed through the wired garden gate. And even then he came up again to have another look at me. The door of the house was open, the locks broken. The rooms were large and well-built with cedar panelling and carved mantlepieces, but grit from fallen masonry or plaster mixed with the droppings of little creatures crunched beneath my feet. The foundations and cellars, too, had partly collapsed and were riddled with tiny holes and burrows. Thus this pretentious Edwardian mansion with its stained-glass windows, no longer sustained by man, had yielded silently to nature save for the scraping chirrup of the cliff swallows under the eaves and the occasional scuffle of tiny feet across its parquet floors.

I sat on the verandah rail and gazed across the lake. A snipe was drumming, a fleeting speck amid the clouds. Somewhere below him, among the reeds, his mate sat on her nest completing her small creative cycle.

The next day I was invited by Martin, Romayne his sister and her friend Dianne, to accompany them on a ride through magnificent country to Buffalo Lake.

It was wild land, inhabited by bear, moose and deer. Being overtaken by a sudden violent thunderstorm we rode under a large Douglas fir to keep dry, but the lightning played around too closely and it seemed increasingly dangerous. Soon the sun shone again, casting a rainbow broad and low across the murky sky and illuminating the bright green foliage and silver stems of the poplars. We were all very wet but had enjoyed it immensely, especially the thrill of emerging from a forest to find ourselves in a beautifully open space fringed by aspen, a lake or a creek. Such surprises await one at every turn in that district, still permeated deeply with the pioneering spirit and an exquisite living vitality.

I took my leave of Martin reluctantly and, a few days later back at the coast, sat in the home of my friends, the MacKenzies, of Fox Farm at Maple Bay. On the radio King George VI and Queen Elizabeth were making their parting speeches before leaving Canadian shores.

The King, half in French and half in English, spoke with improving ease, while the Queen, using the first person singular, spoke straight from her heart in a manner that could not fail to cause the stiff upper lip of her subjects to tremble. Ian hid himself in a cloud of tobacco smoke. Mary was in tears.

I employed Johnny, a half-breed, as co-labourer at Arbutus Point. He worked hard, but while I tried to keep pace with him, ominous political and religious thoughts ran back and forth through my head. Things in Eastern Europe were coming up to the boil again. Coming down the drive to where Johnny and I were building a terrace in front of the house, I noticed a couple who looked un-Canadian. The man said that he was Swiss, and that they were looking for a place to buy which was off the main road and which had a deep sea anchorage. The depth off the tip of Arbutus Point was 150 fathoms. He came from German Switzerland, he said, but when I asked from which district he came, Shaffhusen, Appenzel or Schweitz, for instance, he hedged. I was surprised when he spoke with the accent of a Brandenburger. Needless to say, I could not accommodate him.

I received mail daily in the usual tin box that stood on its post in line with others opposite the landing stage. Close by was Maple Bay store where one could buy groceries. Each day I would look into the mail box on my way back to the little hotel where I spent my nights. It being mailtime, I cadged a lift from this 'Swiss' couple. I found a letter from Ella and my daily newspaper, and sitting on the landing float began to read them. A Canadian destroyer glided in and dropped anchor. Across the velvety waters, her ship's bell rang out the 'Dog Watch'.

Ella wrote from Afghanistan, but the news from the paper was that a strong anti-Polish breeze had arisen in the Nazi press concerning Danzig. Italy was concentrating troops in the south Tyrol. My feelings were quite dead about it all, although I knew that Europe was inevitably on the brink of all-out war. It all filled me with a sense of hopelessness. A Chinaman was coming along with a vegetable cart; it plonked along in tune to the pony's hooves over the wooden pier.

Sir Neville Henderson, British Ambassador to the Reich, had just flown back to Berlin with the British reply to Hitler's note filled with its 'I must have's.' He had previously said, 'I must have the Ruhr and there will be peace.' Then, 'I must have Czechoslovakia, and there will be peace.' And now it was the Polish corridor. It was finally obvious to everybody that Hitler's word had no value.

While all this was going on two distinct movements, which cut diametrically across grain to each other, intrigued me. On the one hand there was the anti-Comintern Pact, instituted by Hitler, and, on the other, a secret pact between Russia and Germany.

On 31 August, England ordered general mobilisation and all children were evacuated from London. Two days later, German troops were pouring into Poland. Hitler's speech, delivered to the Reichstag, was as momentous as it was shrill. He screamed defiance at the Allies and abuse at the Poles, but for his erstwhile enemies, the Russians, he had nothing but soft words. Paradoxical as this may seem, bringing to a rational world amazement and horror, it was judged with great approval in Nazidom.

It was Regatta Week and the hotel was filled with bronzed yachtsmen and intoxicating drink. Accordingly, I slept little and in my wakefulness I could not help thinking of war. When I arose it was a reality, for the next morning found England, France, Poland and Germany in the arena. An English couple, overcome by an equally restless night, were having their breakfast in bed in the next room to mine. The hotel was astir. Great white clouds arose above the pine-covered hills, the yachts offered their full canvas to the breeze and the Regatta was on.

Stunned by the realisation of being at war, the world awaited developments which now seemed all too slow in appearing. Things were outwardly at a standstill. I wrote to various friends in authority, offering my services. It was a young man's war, they said, and advised me to stay put and offer my experience to Canada. This I immediately did, but since I was technically only a landed immigrant my services were not accepted and I was again told that any jobs that were going would be given to young Canadians.

The British army had landed in France and had been placed under the orders of the Supreme Commander, General Gamlin, a sixty-three-year-old product of St Cyr Military Academy and a military genius who knew by heart every order ever given by Napoleon.

Overlooking the cove was a rustic seat among the roots of a great fir tree and here I would sit and read whenever I could find time. Before me lay the open expanse of the bay. As autumn advanced the sea breezes grew chill and I discontinued the practice. Silently the petals dropped off the last roses and I could not help but think of the many young men who would fall on the battlefields before spring.

The dreadful thought of a Second World War, the horror of human ruthlessness on the rampage, the persecution of others in pursuit of their own ideals, the concentration camps, genocide and other atrocities were causing, not only outside Germany, but also among Germans, a desperate search for a saviour in our time, a leader of men who could be followed into a state of peace and sanity, into a state of safety against man's potential for evil. But if such a superhuman being did appear on earth would he not be persecuted even as Jesus was, and even if he was not would not his followers discover that they had escaped nothing since it was they themselves who had precipitated the ill condition in the first place?

If ever they did manage to achieve their 'ideal state' it would be found that it was not the condition, nor some other person who had changed, but they themselves. This was a fact which had dawned on me once or twice while in Central Europe but which had been swept aside by the deeply entrenched concepts in which I had been indoctrinated from birth.

Rudolfo's warning for the spring was now corroborated from another source. Pope Pius XII, having learned through an anti-Nazi source in the German army that Hitler intended to invade Great Britain, had warned Sir Francis D'Arcy Osborne, on 6 May 1940, of England's peril. D'Arcy, an old acquaintance of mine from 1917, now Minister to the Holy See, had wired in code to the Foreign Office as follows:

> The Vatican expects a German offensive in the west to begin this week, but they have had similar expectations before, so I do not attach particular faith to their predictions. They say it may include not only the Maginot Line and Holland and Belgium but even Switzerland.

'Switzerland?' I thought to myself, 'that will be a tough nut to crack.'

About this time Martin came to visit me and as we sat one morning among the daffodils on the bank watching the ebb and flow of the sea, together we discussed such matters which we called the 'things of reality'. He had brought with him some papers written by one called Uranda.

Uranda, he told me, represented the spirit of truth. My immediate reaction was 'And so do thousands of other self-appointed prophets, especially in the western United States. They all claim to expound "the truth" '.

'But,' added Martin, 'this man is different. He manifests it in his living.'

Martin then changed the subject, 'Are you going to get involved in
this war ?'

'Yes, they don't need me here. Besides I like the idea of helping
in the war effort. I suppose it is just an idea of mine, probably wishful
thinking. But Britain is really up against it this time.'

I sincerely believed in the right of the British cause, mostly because
it was British and when I had served England as a soldier or later in
British Intelligence I had done so in all good faith. But now, having
resigned, things were not quite the same and I could see Britain's
cause objectively and how it had frequently followed policies of self-
aggrandisement rather than self-defence and all too often moral
issues had been secondary; and here my Irish heritage asserted itself.

Insofar as justice is concerned, if indeed it existed at all in the
world of man, I, as a soldier or as a secret agent, merely acted upon
an idea that the Allied cause was just and I was therefore prepared
to risk my life and the lives of others in that belief. I enjoyed excitement
and, above all, the idea that in this romanticised game I was frustrating
the international policies of a maniac.

Martin listened to me gravely. He threw a pebble into the amethyst
depth of the bay. It landed with a 'plonk' in a pool just below us.
Finally he said:

'Right and wrong, according to Uranda, are degrees of judgement
on a human scale. In the state of order or perfection there is neither
good nor evil.'

'Who then does he say is responsible for the state of order ?'

Martin was silent. He threw another pebble into the water. It caused
a bigger splash this time from which concentric rings spread outwards.
'There is always a cause to all effects, you know.'

'As for causes, what is good and what is bad ?'

'In the First World War each side was asking God to bless their
arms for them against the other. The only thing that is real is that
which is part of the state of order and the state of order is the nature
of that which functions in and controls the universe, including man.
Beyond that I can see no truth in anything.'

'I understand,' I said.

Martin fixed his eyes on me steadily as if to say, 'That's right, but
do you really know that ?'

'I feel it, I feel that it is right,' and as I said it I felt we were sharing
something so basic that it would be a bond between us forever.

Then I thought to myself regarding Uranda: why should there not be on earth such a clear expression of truth? It would not be the first time nor, I felt, the last.

Martin had apparently been awaiting such a revelation for a long while. He hungered and thirsted for the truth unlike anyone I had ever seen before and although he had not yet seen the whole of it, he felt he had here touched the central evidence of it in the writings of a living human being.

Suddenly I caught a glimpse of a new dimension which put nationalisms and human family quite out of focus. And from then in my heart I became a citizen of the world more than a citizen of a single country or federation of states. And even as I did so I got a vague idea that this was but a step towards becoming a harmonious part of a universal order.

About this time my caretaker's wife was taken ill and died and her family left Arbutus Point of their own accord. I was thus able to occupy the house and I completely reconditioned and redecorated it, hiring a retired Finnish mariner as cook and caretaker. So I took up residence on my property.

Fred Bjerkbom had sailed around the Horn seven times before the mast in square riggers. He had an endless supply of yarns about the sea, where the setting was usually a seaport tavern with plenty of grog and a good clean fight to end it all off. He was usually carried back to his ship just as it was about to cast off. As for the rest he was strictly co-operative. His right eye had been knocked out by a marlin pin, but he had practical hands and a philosophical outlook, with only one flaw. About every eight months he would get amiably drunk and stay that way for some days. Of course there was no fixed date either for the beginning or the ending of these bouts and so, as the time came round, I would have to stay by in case I had to do his work.

Fred's English was far from perfect, but it was extremely picturesque. He worked tirelessly with effortless efficiency and yet always kept an eye on the kitchen stove. When mealtime came, there would always be something ready, even though it was only parsnips, a roast potato and some tea, maple syrup and homemade bread.

The rainy season came and we woke to find fog over the bay. As the day ripened, dark masses appeared and the hills came in sight, first their wooded crests and then their rocky feet around the fog-blanketed water. Gulls flew out of the mist and were just as quickly lost. Ducks and grebes, emboldened by the lack of visibility, came into the cove in search of food. The peace of these surroundings was soothing and yet a pall of depression hung over the future as civilisation entered another phase of self-destruction in the name of God knows what.

I had decided to return to England in the spring in the hopes of getting a war job there. I bought Fred four pullets for company and he could not have been more pleased had I handed him a thousand-dollar bill. He was soon on personal terms with all of them. One rainy day he returned from the fowlhouse with dampened spirits. 'Dem chickens are so doggorn mad at me today, they're growling at me all the morning.' When I asked the reason, he said with a sigh, 'Guess I'se got a different pair of pants on today.'

And so the weeks passed until one day in March I found the point covered with snowdrops.

By the middle of April, Gayda was blowing up some trouble in the Italian press. Norway had been invaded and Narvik was in British hands. Finland had been over-run by the Russians. The best piece of news, as far as I was concerned, was that Uranda was coming to Vancouver and would speak there, Martin and I attending. It was our first meeting with him.

It was cold as Fred accompanied me to the garage some distance from the house.

'The north wind is cold, notsomatter waar she blow from,' he said cryptically as he placed my suitcase in the car. As I drove to Nanaimo to pick up the ferry for Vancouver, I found myself vainly probing the depths of this remark.

Uranda's talk took place in Vancouver on 15 April 1940, and my first impression of him was as a truly remarkable and compelling man. Exercising a genius for analogy, he approached the subject of the human condition from many angles, seeking to engender in our understanding a sense of his vision of human being. He told us that man's mind had become like a window pane through which the sunlight of the spirit was scarcely able to penetrate, so thick was the coating of self-centredness that clouded it.

'Man,' he said, 'is accordingly in darkness, with his vision so obscured that it has left him with a desolate sense of abandonment and insecurity.' Continuing with his theme he indicated that it was not a hopeless condition, but that if man were to cease using his mind as a means of polarising himself in the outer form of things, lusting after his material environment, the state could clear, his consciousness could again become translucent and allow the sunlight of love, the most potent of all creative forces, to radiate into the world.

Man, he taught, has the power of free choice allowing him to transfer his response from his outer involvements toward a true polarisation in the sun-source within him, the light of his being. To me this was plain speaking. I saw in it the true meaning of the first great commandment that one should love the Lord with all thy heart, and with all thy soul, and with all thy strength, and with all thy mind. From the solar system and the universe through the infinitesimal entities of the worlds beyond the atom, the same principle of radiation and response prevails. It could be observed between planets and sun, between the moon and the earth, between electrons and their proton and between male and female.

He spoke of fear and hate and their influence upon the human organism, creating chemical changes in the blood stream.

'Hate,' said Uranda, 'is a slow form of suicide.'

The human mind is a good instrument but a bad master – like a car which starts off before you have touched the controls.

The threat of planetary spasm is by no means new and is in common coin with the soapbox reformers as a means of proselytising; the idea being that when there is a threat of danger from outside, the herd bunches together for security. Hitler used the threat of Jewish and Communist domination to rally the Germans to the Nazi standard. Russia uses capitalism and others have used imperialism to stir up their people's animosity, the idea being that there is something about to destroy you unless you hearken to my philosophy.

Clearly that approach had been overdone. And yet here was I compelled to listen to this simple prophet's offering. I told myself not to be a sceptic but to allow the matter to prove itself. If the pattern of order was within me, as he indicated, then the truth of the matter would be made clear once I allowed it to be experienced.

I sat next to Martin during these talks, and wondered a little at the contrast in backgrounds these two men represented; yet they were united by this magnetic power. Later on I brought this point up. 'Backgrounds, social levels, or race, have nothing to do at all with the one law,' he said. 'If at this time the spirit of truth finds a clearer passage in Uranda than it does through me, I accept him as my leader.'

This was stupendous and if followed out might carry one to the point of no return wherein one might be obliged to move on into a state wherein the values, conventions and ethics with which one had been saturated throughout one's life became no longer valid. The image of a Daddy God up in the sky was gone and replaced by a principle, a primary cause, an aspect of which was in all creation – that was far more like it. It was within me too, not far away but very close. So close indeed that I, we all, could become one with it. Now we could work together, now I could live God all day long and all night too for that matter, and step in line with Him in every detail and be part of the universal order.

Martin and I parted as I boarded the boat for Vancouver Island. The passengers were all lining up outside the dining saloon and I treated myself to a hearty meal.

I thought a great deal on these things as I watched the deep blue waves sweep past us, in brilliant sunshine, while we shortened the distance to Victoria. After my meal I went on deck gazing, as I walked, at the snow peaks of the Olympics across the straits. It seemed incredible to me that we had been created with the capacity to reject our creator in this fashion, and yet it is written that we were created in His own image and likeness with a capacity for free choice which we can exercise to our own destruction.

My meeting with Uranda was the turning point in my life.

When I reached Arbutus Point I found that there was a plague of ants in the house. They had got into the store cupboards. Fred, who did not see too well with his one eye, was eating stewed prunes when, to use his own words, 'Dom went crack, crack in my teeth.'

So he declared war on them with tobacco ash from his pipe. This, and epsom salts were his remedies for pretty well anything. Ants or no ants, it was good to be home. The garden was full of tulips and narcissi, and some of the fruit trees were still in blossom. The scent of the flowers came in through the window.

Fred had rowed across the bay to fetch the mail and some stores. I had checked his list: 'Matses, angens, pis, radiu, Fraiser Wale botter', which I had translated as matches, onions, peas, radio and Fraser Valley butter. The tide was low and he might try to dig some clams on his way back. I piled an armful of arbutus wood on the open hearth and sat before the crackling fire. It was peaceful and I was able to do some quiet thinking. The arbutus wood burned brightly till its charred scales looked like a heap of raven's feathers.

When Fred returned, he brought me some letters. One came from a shipping control office, telling me that a passage was available for me to England. This opened before me the vision of an England threatened with invasion and calling to me from across the sea. I went out and sat on the verandah. The tranquility of the scene tugged at me inside as I thought of the turmoil I would be going back to. What was it that made me want to go, but a deep-rooted desire to serve without really understanding how or why I should do it? Had I relaxed into this pattern of natural beauty into which I had so distinctly been led, I might perhaps have become the means of releasing into my environment, if not the world at large, some of the healing power humanity so badly needed. Had I learned nothing from Uranda? I did not yet know how it should be done, how significant the peaceful acts of one man can be.

To sit on a bank among the bluebells, watching the rising salmon ring the surface of the bay was all very fine, but it could easily become a means of indulging one's self and of burying one's head in the sand whilst the greatest war of all time ravaged the world. I believed I could and should become an instrument for the expression of universal order in this chaotic age, but I still had a very great deal to learn about the truth and how to apply it in living before I became fit for such a task. Or so I reasoned.

There was, too, a fear of missing out on a segment of history; of not taking an active part in the dangers of war, and the credit of victory. I had been robbed of that, I felt, in the first war. I knew that this would be a far more terrible conflict than the previous one; I had, after all, seen the preparations, but I had a clear feeling of assurance about its conclusion.

In Central Europe the national spirit of the middle classes had been infected by National Socialism, but I also saw that one of its causes was the impracticability of democracy, or the majority rule, because the majority is still inclined to feather its own nest. The world was full of ideologies which looked good on paper, but fail miserably when applied. The flaw in these things was undoubtedly human nature, that part of man which he regards as himself but which is only a counterfeit of his true self. I had seen Communism as well as various brands of Fascism in theory and in practice and was convinced that as long as man's first love is for himself, or his party, they would all end in disintegration. Of all the most self-centred people I know, a child, an artist, and a patriot are the worst, for they are all seeking security for themselves or their folk at the expense of someone else.

15

Lure of Patriotism

On the morning of 10 May 1940, while the British Parliament was in a hullabaloo and trying to get rid of Neville Chamberlain, the Germans invaded Holland, Belgium and Luxembourg. These countries had been afraid to co-ordinate their defence plans with the Allies for fear of committing a breach of neutrality.

A few days later, I was doing voluntary submarine watch on the ss *Sythia* bound for England. Every now and then I would level my binoculars at some smoke smudge on the horizon or watch a porpoise fin cut the steel-grey water. Sheerwaters skimmed the trough of the great waves as the ship churned on into the failing light. We were on a northern course. My relief, a young apprentice, came and we stood for a while staring into the passing twilight.

'Oh, it's no use worrying,' he said, with a veteran's calm. 'I'd live in a forest of periscopes if I thought about them. Until that one comes along which has your name written on it, you're safe. The one which is meant for you will get you however much you may worry.'

I turned from the sound of such fatalism to the comfortable warmth of the lounge and the radio. A terrific battle was in progress in northern France. The Germans were advancing on Paris. Mussolini, finding the Allies at a disadvantage, was deciding to come in against them. He finally declared war from his now famous balcony on 11 June. This, in a way, was a relief, for nothing is more ominous than an animal, no matter how craven, which is merely waiting for an opportunity to spring.

There followed a series of heroic events which were epic in stature. My friend, a brother officer, Claud Nicholson and the brigade he commanded, were captured by the Germans at Calais as they were covering the evacuation of Dunkirk. Then came the Battle of Britain. I reached London at the peak of that crisis, but found myself slipping into clubland life as a hand does into an old glove. There were changes in my social sphere and some tragic gaps had appeared. The strain of the past ten months had told on everybody; it was a cleansing fire

204

separating the dross from pure metal. There were those who had committed suicide, others were in gaol for participating in Fascist activities. England had gathered up her strength and would tax the fibre of every branch of its population to the limit. There was, as one might say, a strange and sinister feeling in London, a doggedness, a calm triumphing over an atmosphere of defeatism and nervous jitters which had mostly been introduced by the refugees to whom England had opened her hospitable doors.

On the other hand, France was suffering from political fragmentation. She rationalised where she lacked single-mindedness and was occupied by the Germans. On Friday, 13 June, Paris had fallen into their hands. Poor France! My heart went out to her for accepting a course which would hurt her pride far more than devastation. Lady Maxwell-Scott wrote to me from Abbotsford. Herself a Frenchwoman, she said, 'On French soil, near the market town of Crécy Aisne, stands a house which bears the following inscription:

The White House – built in 1728
Looted by the Germans in 1814
Burned by the Russians in 1815
Rebuilt in 1835
Looted and burned by the Bavarians in 1870
Rebuilt in 1877
Looted and later razed to the ground by the Germans in 1914-18
Rebuilt in 1920'

She went on to plead for trust in the French who, she said, had lost faith in themselves. As true and as tragic as this was it should be remembered that there had been no fewer than seven invasions of German territory by the French during the eighteenth century.

I heard that Rudolfo was now in London and soon arranged a meeting with him. We strolled in the park to exchange our news and he told me he had seen King Leopold five days before at Laaken; he was in full possession of the facts relating to the collapse of Belgium. It would not serve now to reveal these, except to say that King Leopold had been deluded by false peace proposals. After some misunderstandings he felt that he lacked the support of the British; then, taking a drastic step without proper advice, he threw in the hand of his country. That the Belgian monarch had acted unwisely seemed a widely accepted fact, but his action is understandable when the truth is known.

Rudolfo went on to reveal Germany's strategy and foretold much which was later found to be true, including certain schemes we now know the Germans were not able to put into effect. So England had been forewarned. On 17 June, the French ceased fighting. Old Marshal Petain took the lead and the Allied chances of victory at that point went down to zero.

Bombs began to fall. Raid followed raid as the Luftwaffe plastered the east and south-east coast of England. After being offered several jobs, I chose one as inspecting officer for censorship and was given the whole of Scotland as my area. I needed a car and was allowed to wear uniform; having neither on the English side of the Atlantic, I had to make that initial outlay myself.

These sporadic air raids on the British Isles by the Luftwaffe were a preparatory measure for the invasion of England. The United States were openly assisting us with all possible supplies. The U.S.S.R. on the 'qui vive', but still helping Germany; Japan was busily invading China and Spain was sitting on the fence. The French government, which moved to Vichy, was conniving with Hitler. Within the territories controlled and occupied by Hitler's minions, nothing but ghoulish pictures appeared. Otherwise those countries lay like the dead. Out of the stillness came rumours, faint but ominous, of preparations and diplomatic moves for Britain's destruction.

Then from Maple Bay, sad news reached me of Fred. He had suffered a stroke, lay paralysed in hospital, and had little chance of recovery. I wired that he was to be given anything he wanted and eventually heard that he had asked for a bottle of champagne and that he had died in a very contented frame of mind.

My work in Scotland consisted of inspecting firms and individuals who had applied for export permits for goods going to countries under censorship. Scotsmen did not enjoy having their ledgers scrutinised by a government official and I used to have to do a lot of coaxing and smoothing down of indignant directors before and after the ordeal. The hours, too, were long. I had no help and had to do my own typing until the small hours of the morning. For six months I was unable to have a day off and worked Sundays and holidays to bring my reports up to date. The bombing attacks intensified, especially over London and the large cities of England, but Glasgow and its shipbuilding yards got its share. At first I lived in a damp stone-built village pub in East Kilbride among the hills east of Glasgow and found out abruptly that it was on the direct air route taken by the Luftwaffe when bombing the Clyde.

The banshee-like wail of the sirens woke me out of my sleep on the night of my arrival. I stared into the blackness of the night, unable to find anything; I admit it stampeded me at first. Having eventually found my clothes and dressed, barked my shins and bumped my head, I got down through the bar and out into the street. Except for the drone of planes overhead, I neither heard nor saw anything in the darkness. It was two o'clock in the morning and there seemed nowhere to go, no shelter nor place of safety. And what is more, the village folk seemed unconcerned about what was going on, no one was about.

Then, over Glasgow, the darkness became streaked by shafts of murky light and the sky lit by a rash of flashes as anti-aircraft batteries went into action. The noise was terrific. When it ceased the scene again darkened, leaving only here and there spotted glows which spread and flickered or became obscured with smoky billows. I realised with horror that hell had been let loose and that hundreds had perhaps been killed. I returned to my lonely bedroom above the bar and felt cold and a little sick and could have done with a good Irish whisky.

The reflex action of the sound of the sirens, whether in daytime or at night, always brought a slight sense of panic to me thereafter. Getting about after dark, especially in bad weather, was trying. I had a lot of driving to do and found it hard to find my way about the blacked-out streets and highroads of a country unfamiliar to me. Austerities, ration cards, permits, identity cards and wartime red-tape increased, causing frustration and inhibiting the normal course of life. But I received Uranda's letters regularly which seemed always to provide the just solution to the circumstance of the moment.

I was in many air raids after that. Bombers, V1 and V2s rained their death upon Britain in a manner that would have dismayed a people of lesser courage. In the South Kensington district of London, while I was spending the evening with some members of the American Ambulance Corps, the capital suffered one of the worst raids of the war. I sat in the sitting room of an apartment while the house jumped and rocked; showers of plaster came down from the ceiling on to our heads and the rumble and blast outside was deafening. After that first raid in East Kilbride I had disdained the dugout shelters of the basement, for it was a question, I reasoned, of being killed outright or of being buried under the debris of a collasped building in the event of a direct hit. And yet I never really felt I might be hit.

I remained seated in my chair, unswayed by the human emotion rampant about me, coldly and determinedly preserving my sense of

identity. I felt I must at all costs not become subject to the hell that
was being let loose around me. Some of the girls were lying on the
floor covering their heads with their hands. I felt a great sense of
assurance flow strongly in me, radiating outwards about me, a peculiar
sense of being encompassed, enfolded in an all-pervading peace.

One of the girls sat up and crawled towards my chair, placing
her hand in mine. She was brunette, half my age and normally as
buoyant as a brook. They called her 'Crookie' and she was frightened.
Little wonder.

The raid subsided and then, by the light of the great conflagration
which lit up the whole district as if it had been day, I walked home.
Though somewhat battered, my club provided me with shelter and
I realised then how much it had become a home to me.

I had known some of its members for almost twenty years and
regarded many of the staff with respect and affection. My letters
all came to me there and I greedily devoured them. It seemed difficult
to those living in countries remote from this strife to understand
what it felt like to live one's life in the possibility of getting a bomb
upon one's head at any moment and how everything that the people
of England thought and did was related to the actual life-and-death
struggle going on around them. How very grateful I was for my letters;
how comforting the feelings which passed between friends in moments
that might easily be one's last. Yet at the same time the inner world
in which I was now beginning to dwell was strangely remote from strife.

I was no longer so concerned with petty problems. I knew that
what mattered was facing situations squarely without getting involved
with tangent matters that sought to claim first attention. In the past
it had always been too easy for me to become implicated and to worry
over problems, but now I began to realise that every problem contains
its own solution. I sometimes wonder to what degree problems become
a way of life – one can reach a point where life seems empty without
some kind of difficulty. 'Sweet are the uses of adversity,' wrote Shakespeare. Blessed, indeed, is the usefulness of pressure so long as we are
in control of it.

Ella wrote at great length from India where she was sitting at the
feet of Ramana Maharshi, the sage of Tiruvannamalai. I read her
letters carefully several times, for I was always deeply interested in
her opinions. I asked myself then, 'Do people really wish to find the
truth?' There were, of course, the cut-and-dried creeds available
within the confines of which it was comfortable to live. Everything

was laid out; you got into these religions free, so far as the requirements for personal transformation here and now were concerned. If you lived simply according to their rules and dogmas you had a reserved place in some hereafter, your future assured. Personally, that sort of future held no attraction for me. I knew that 'The Kingdom of God is at hand,' not up on a cloud some time in the future after death, perhaps, nor beyond the horizon somewhere, but here and now or nowhere. I had wandered too long in darkness seeking after the truth, but never facing myself right where I was.

Romantic adventurers go out into the wide world to seek a fortune, having to hunt for it sometimes at the cost of their lives, but the state of order which is peace and fulfilment cannot be bought or bargained for. It inevitably asserts itself, for it is natural and therefore available in every instance. Each has to find it for himself and it is very much a real thing when it is found. This idea is attractive, but not until it becomes a living reality in the practical affairs of living can it rightly be offered, by example, to others. Generally the last thing people want is to be parted from their comfortable concepts and beliefs . . . they do not want to change.

With time my work increased and conditions grew worse. My headquarters were transferred to Edinburgh where I was given the courtesy of a temporary membership to a social club. It was now mid-winter and the enormous rooms were heated only by small coal grates around which the members huddled sometimes two or three deep. They were mostly lairds whose ancestral homes, like Monivea Castle, were filled with the spirit of their forefathers, steeped in tradition and deeply entrenched in ancient rites and conventions, but with very little warmth.

As an Irishman I found them reserved and stiff and had visions of their dismissing their wives from the dinner table after the pudding course where, in the chilly drawing room, they would await their lords for a game of piquet and nine o'clock retirement.

A gunner, who had been a prisoner-of-war with me while he was still a subaltern, came into the club one day in the uniform of a major-general. With him were several of his staff. When I greeted him he looked through me as if I had been transparent.

One night in the middle of an air raid, as I took shelter from falling shrapnel in a doorway, I noticed by the reflected beam of searchlights that I stood next to a girl in the uniform of the American Ambulance Corps. I looked more closely at her face – there was no mistaking it, it was the girl I had comforted the night of the raid in London. We seemed destined always to meet under these conditions. 'Alright, alright, it's only me,' said Crookie. After a brief exchange of news she asked me down for the weekend to her home in the Lamamure Hills.

Her father, who had been a colonel of an Irish regiment of the line, had retired on their estate with its home farm and its good shooting and fishing. Crookie's background was therefore materially secure, comfortable and harmonious if a bit conventional, which gave her the poise common to her class.

On the night of my arrival it started to snow and continued to do so for the next three days and nights. The roads became blocked and I found myself marooned on their property. In one sense it was a godsend for I was tired and welcomed the rest. However, before long, business called me to London, Liverpool and Manchester. The first carried a dreary feeling of impending calamity, the second a certain doggedness and the last devastated but nonchalant. The wounds of these large cities had to be seen to be believed. At Liverpool, I saw hundreds of little children being tearfully led amid the ruins on their way to the docks, there to embark for the U.S.A. or Canada on an evacuation scheme.

Later on in March I met Crookie for dinner at St Giles Grill in Edinburgh. We were having coffee when the sirens went and there followed a very heavy attack on Glasgow which lasted until morning. It was a perfect night from every other standpoint. Edinburgh Castle rose ghostlike above the city, under a full moon. The air was warm and springlike and there was no breeze. Crookie, looking prettier than ever, shook her curly head in teasing defiance. It was past midnight as we walked down Castle Terrace. The sky was filled with search-lights and the hum of German bombers as wave upon wave of them passed overhead. Bursting shells spangled the night and tracer bullets streamed like tiny meteors in all directions. Crookie was thrilled and only wanted to see more. The droning of planes kept up all night with only occasional anti-aircraft fire and sporadic machine-gun bursts. She called her headquarters and was sent speeding in her ambulance to Glasgow.

One evening, not long after this, I was looking at a collection of watercolours of an older member of the club who lived in one of the apartments at the top of the building, when the alert sounded. This was immediately followed by a terrific explosion. A picture of Agra, which we were viewing, almost jumped off its hook. Straightening it, my host said in tones of hurt dignity, 'What cads! They must be after Rosythe!'

Downstairs in the big smoking room a group of uniformed members were intently listening to a news broadcast of a *coup d'etat* in Yugoslavia. French batteries had opened fire on British ships off the coast of Algiers and there had been a naval victory over the Italians in the Mediterranean.

I was due at the theatre where the Sadlers Wells' opera company was giving Johann Strauss's *Die Fledermaus*. Next to me sat Crookie. She was strange and silent. After the theatre I dropped her at her quarters, but around midnight she rang me at the club.

The rain had stopped, but the wet pavements reflected the meagre light of the blacked-out lamp at the street corner where we met. Arm in arm, we walked and talked, in the company of her Samoyed dog until, with the coming of the dawn, her depression wore off and was replaced by drowsiness. The new grass was coming up in the meadows and the castle silhouette with its sombre hardness reached towards a ceiling of mist. I drew her closer and she did not resist, but the mouth I kissed was laughing. I walked home frustrated and curious. Was I lonely? The formula found in the third chapter of Titus, 'to be discreet, chaste, keepers at home, good and obedient to their husbands, that the word of God be not blasphemed', seemed not to fit the girls of war-torn Europe. Yet it was their world and they had to make their own choices for living in it.

Newsboys were already depositing their bundles when I reached the club. Charwomen were at work in the various rooms. I seized upon a *Daily Mail* and for once had the blazing open fire in the smoking room to myself. Yugoslavia was refusing to obey Hitler. Churchill, now famous for his impressive pronouncements said, 'She has found her soul.' And so she had, but at the price of losing her body, so it seemed.

What guts those mountain peasants had! They would first establish a kingdom in their hearts and then trustingly wait to see it take material form. But in the meantime Germany, Hungary, Rumania and Bulgaria had all set upon her like a pack of wolves intent on devouring their prey. A German drive towards Monastir was also in the news. They were attempting to rescue 300,000 Italians besieged by the Greeks. In short order, the Germans had driven down the Struma Valley and had swept aside Yugoslav resistance and were now turning their attention towards Salonica, trapping 30,000 Greeks in the three dismembered provinces of Thrace. Coming on top of a German landing in Libya, which swept onwards towards the east, capturing Benghazi, Derna and pressing on towards Tobruk, this increased the pressure on the Allies' morale. Such seeds of discouragement could so easily be sown by the gremlins of defeat and it was more than ever important that they should not take root in the heart. Battles are lost or won in the heart.

About the middle of April, I was called to London to confer with my boss and, forseeing an end to my Scottish interlude, I drove down by car. Coventry lay in my direct route, but it had just received another severe 'blitzing' and I was advised to skirt it. I drifted down side roads, but found them so congested with exhausted and homeless refugees that I could make but slow progress They were escaping from a city still in flames, stunned and wounded and unable to get sleeping accommodation. Many of them were preparing to spend the night by the wayside. Tired as I was after my drive from Edinburgh, I decided to press on to Woodstock, for I learned that Oxford too was crammed full of refugees from London.

It was a cold, starlit night. Orion was low on the horizon and on all sides the sky was drawn with beams of searchlights. Occasionally a vivid flash could be seen far to the south-west, but the purr of my Jaguar drowned the thud of the projectiles. I rested in the Marlborough Arms, where I breakfasted as well as food restrictions permitted, then pushed on to London. There were signs of spring, untouched by the holocaust that was sweeping England. Snowdrops and blossom dusted the banks and hedgerows. I saw some martins, too, gathered on the telephone wires. I filled my tank at a wayside station for there was more chance of getting petrol in the country than in the towns and there I learned that London had just been bombed more ferociously than ever.

I found my club still standing although a bomb had landed just behind it. I telephoned my sister Yvonne who told me of the previous night's raid and the devastation it left. 'Words cannot describe the row. I don't think that anyone in London closed an eye the whole night . . . Poor London,' said Yvonne. 'So much that was ugly has gone and will go, but some precious exhibits have gone with the junk – Chelsea Old Church, for instance.'

I closed my eyes in an attempt to forget it all. My native city, I would not mourn her lest I shut out the dawn.

As an outcome of my conference I was instructed to spend some time with the Imperial Censorship in Trinidad and, feeling the need

to visit Arbutus Point now that Fred had departed, I returned first to
Canada. This time I crossed the Atlantic in a whaler. Our first day
at sea found us zig-zagging off the coast of Donegal. I read, painted,
did some laundry and settled down to the routine life on board. On
the first of June there had been a beautiful sunset and a few of us on
deck had seen a sperm whale spouting off the port quarter. Way out
to sea we joined a convoy of forty-three ships and from that time on
we were under escort of R.N. and R.C.N. units.

A few days later while in mid-Atlantic we learned that the German
pocket battleship *Bismarck* was approaching us from the north-west.
The Atlantic looked merciless and grey and flecked with white, with
a strong north wind roaring and piping in the rigging. That night,
while travelling at low speed, a ship loomed out of the darkness on
our starboard bow. It gave the third officer of the watch a bit of a
start. She was so enormous and yet so silent, passing ghostlike in the
faint moonlight abaft the beam and coming up to port not three
hundred feet distant. Her searchlights winked immediately and we
were flooded in a blaze of violet and green light.

Meanwhile a huge convoy of over fifty ships was gliding off towards
the northern horizon. We were now travelling side by side with HMS
Hood. An exchange of messages was winked out in code. I took up
station on deck near the radio operator's shack and heard him mutter
the letters as he read them off the light. She bombarded us with
questions which were answered from our bridge by the Captain's
flashlight. What was our name, our destination, the number of our
convoy, etc., which finally ended with the usual courtesies, to which
our Captain answered, 'OK, once seen, never forgotten.'

The spectacle of the ship which had brought us helter-skelter up
the companion to the bridge was indeed unforgettable and we descended
now to the warmth of the messroom somewhat elated and with a feeling
of security.

Soon afterward we heard that the *Bismarck* had been intercepted
by a British naval force, so we altered course to the south-west.
I sat in a sheltered corner on deck watching a gunner clean his hotch-
kiss. I pulled out a letter which I had received on the day of our departure. It was from Uranda. He wrote:

> Those who trust in guns know that the right kind of ammunition
> is required for each type of gun, that the gun must be loaded, that
> it must be pointed and discharged according to the gun's method
> of operation if it is to cause destruction. These are, therefore,
> well-defined requirements necessary for the operation of a gun. In

other words, the laws of the gun must be obeyed if the gun is to function. Now note- those who are ready to agree to the points outlined about the operation of the gun are inclined to think that if there is a real spiritual power, then that power ought to come into manifest operation without giving consideration to the laws by which it operates! Is that consistent? No, indeed. Men are trained to use guns, but when I suggest that men should be trained to use the power of God, people who claim to trust in God look upon my statement as being foolish.

I folded the letter and put it my breast pocket. The radio operator ran out of his shack and up the steps to the bridge. The gunner and I exchanged glances. I followed him up. The Captain read the message. 'HMS *Hood* has been sunk by a single shell from the *Bismarck*,' he said. 'Now we can expect fireworks.'

From that time on all hands took a keen interest in the running battle that followed, until finally the *Bismarck* was pounded to scrap iron and sank. After that we breathed more easily.

The Captain was my frequent companion. A Hebridean, he had a jovial personality, with dark laughing eyes illuminating his ruddy features. Never had I met anyone with such an endless run of stories. Yarns of the harpoon, of ambergris, or of Freetown. The convoy travelled at a slow five and a half knots, yet, by the time we reached Halifax, he had not once repeated himself. On the 29th, the convoy was attacked by a U-boat, and our escort dropped about twelve depth charges, the action lasting most of the afternoon. We left a corvette over the spot, watching like a cat over a mousehole, in case the submarine should surface. Meanwhile, the convoy plunged and rolled its way onwards. On the fourteenth night, we sighted lights on the Canadian coast ahead of us.

It was late and the air on the bridge was cold. I turned in for a short sleep, but soon all was animation. Derricks and donkey engines thundered into life and the anchor was let down with a mighty splash, a rattle and a plunge. I opened my porthole and heard the comforting sound of horses' hooves on cobblestones. We were alongside the quay at Halifax at last. The sun was streaming in on the tables in the little white messroom where eggs and bacon were being served. I ate with greed before the army of port officials had time to invade us. I was indeed sorry to take leave of the Captain and his shipmates, though grateful to feel the security of Canadian soil beneath my feet. On reaching Montreal I purchased a station wagon and drove across the dominion to Vancouver Island.

16

Censorship Amid the
Palm Trees

Canada was warming up to the war. She had not, of course, been ravaged and casualties had so far been slight, but she was gearing herself to an effort which was to be unsurpassed. I saw a column of troops go by in Halifax. They looked green, with office-bleached faces, but very proud of their uniforms. I felt I would have liked to tell them to what extent Canada's backing was boosting Britain's morale in her life-and-death struggle. Crowds of civilians, coming out of the shops and restaurants, stood on the curb and clapped their hands as the troops marched by. It was all still romantic, the grim reality of it not having yet struck home. But taxes, wages and prices were all mounting. I indulged in sweet frivolities in the semi-French city of Montreal and now, after the dreary ride across the prairies and the exhilaration of the Rockies, I sought out my various friends.

Heading the list was Lord Martin Cecil. We had breakfast at the Empress Hotel in Victoria when he stepped off the night boat from Vancouver and then we drove up island to stay a few days at Arbutus Point. In the afternoon Martin and I walked to the point where, in a spot secluded from keen February winds, we sat in the sun watching the waterfowl dive and the fish jump. We had many things to talk about, things we had done and how our various experiences had affected us. Martin was by nature more reserved than me. His point of view, his approach to every subject was its relevance to the state of order, so much so that I found myself revising my thoughts before sharing them with him. This process revealed to me how trivial most conversations are. There were others, of course, I wished to see, but my ability to make small talk was waning and my interests and conversation were being more and more prompted by and limited to those ultimate concerns. I wondered at first if I had become obsessed by

215

'that subject', but found that nothing was really worth considering that did not spring from the power which governed and controlled reality – of which I was now beginning to become so conscious.

But the unreal was yet deeply entrenched in my heart and, having for so long become conditioned to the trials and pressures, not to mention excitements of war, I soon began to find life out of the mainstream of international conflict and intrigue painfully dull and I longed to get back to it all again. These were, of course, signs of my immaturity, and my desire to be an active and vigorous part of the current trends of man blinded me to the importance of seeing circumstances correctly and taking all the facts into consideration from the perspective of reality. 'Experience is the proving ground of concept'. But I still was not fully awake to the reality of experience and tended to fall back. Some might have interpreted my desire to return again to war work as a form of nervous restlessness, a permanent seeking after adventure. Adversity generates pressure and pressure produces nervous energy or thrills. People are, of course, doing this all the time, seeking their fulfilment within the range of their material environment, or their happiness just over the horizon somewhere. But it is an exhausting quest and fruitless too for it slumps one back into a disillusioned heap. It isn't the right approach to fulfilment.

Shortly after Pearl Harbour in the winter of 1941, I left Canada again and travelled to Panama on a cargo boat which was laden with acitone and dynamite en route for Trinidad. Apart from the fact that we were literally sitting on dynamite and that the ship was captained by a neurotic little Welshman, I enjoyed that trip through tropical waters immensely. After leaving San Francisco, I spent much time forward watching the prow dividing the waters. It had a soothing effect. While abreast of the mountain ranges of Mexico, the radio came in clearly and we were able to keep in touch with the news. The Japanese had attempted a second Pearl Harbour in Colombo, Ceylon, but had met with such resistance that they had lost about fifty planes.

I never tired of watching the flying fish, the 'Boobies', the tropic birds and frigate birds, just as I had been fascinated by the effortless gliding of the black albatross in the more northerly waters, and in the vast fields of Portuguese man-of-war. As a contrast to the birds of freedom, there was the Chief Engineer's pet canary which he sometimes let loose in his cabin. The Chief was a great reader and the bird used to roost on his book as he read, obliging him to slip each page from under its claws when he turned it over.

At Panama most passengers for the east travelled by air and we flew over the top of South America to Trinidad, one of the crossroads of the world. Scuddy clouds caused our plane to bump as she flew over the Canal Zone. We flew blacked-out for security purposes for a time. Then the sun flashed on the rotating blades and metal wings as we left the fortified zone behind us and my ears yielded and yielded again with a pop as we climbed. Crates of day-old chicks in the baggage compartment chirped like a million chattering sparrows in an evening grove. They had come all the way from Canada. We flew across the face of Santa Marta mountain, the plane's tiny shadow following an undulating course over the dense jungle beneath. We flew across the plains of Venezuela, parched and unearthly, the trees looking like bleached bones and then, as daylight rapidly faded, we swooped down to Trinidad. The name, 'Imperial Censorship', worked like magic and I was the first to take my place in a car bound for Port of Spain.

The hotel was full up and arriving guests were asked if they would mind sharing a bedroom with someone else. By seven in the morning the hell that had reigned all night had subsided. Drunks, babies and catfights were succeeded by barking dogs and crowing roosters, the last starting at daybreak and, as the sun rose, mounting into a clarion fugue. It being my first day I was allowed to have it off so as to find some accommodation and settle in.

Before the hotel, a park or savannah stretched out towards hills at the foot of which was Government House and the botanical gardens. After a weary day of room hunting, I stretched out and rested under an enormous samman tree. I had found a bedroom in town at a house called the Hall. Its only window opened on to an inside staircase up which bronzed and barefooted legs of black servants could be seen as they went to the upper floor. Next to me, a retired bishop had a permanent lodging while above my room lived an American girl who worked at the U.S. mission. It was not ideal, but rooms were hard to find. The new American base was causing congestion.

I had not long been stretched out under that tree when I was accosted by a coloured man whose name was Albert. In flowery Oxford English, which lapsed occasionally, he offered to show me around the gardens. It was hot, and I felt disinclined to move. To see all the trees would be exhausting so, after some hesitation, I asked him to show me only the native trees and shrubs of the island. But in spite of this, our tour lasted over two hours, ending with my pockets bulging with betal nuts, coffee beans, Napoleon's buttons, cow beans, almonds, bay and

pimento leaves, camphor and nutmeg. Taking his stand before a tree, Albert began with, 'Allow me, Sah, to lecture you on this tree heah.' He did not say 'cattle eat this,' but 'cattle partake of this,' and so on.

He showed me royal palms and a kind of tree he called weeping willow. Explained Albert, 'It derives its name from the sound of weeping made by the wind passing through its foliage.' This must not be confused with the melancholy tree on willow-pattern china. We saw iron trees, banyans and flamboyants and a poisonous tree from Malaya. But the most unforgettable was the immortelle . . .

Having exhausted his repertoire, Albert then accompanied me to the gate. I realised we had seen every tree in the garden and I suppose that he had been unable to break the continuity of his regular round and that I might as well have expected a student of Spenser to recite the *Faerie Queen*, leaving out all verses starting with a vowel.

It was close on midsummer day, 1942, and a taxi came to the Hall to drive me to the Imperial Censorship office, there to start work. I was shown into a room which was large with open shutters on either side, through which I could feel a slight movement of air. Censors sat at long rows of trestle tables covered with files and their paraphernalia. I was in the trade section and was handed a file of French and German correspondence to read, so as to get the feel of it. The subject was Swiss watches, the atmosphere suffocating and not one breath of human relief throughout the morning to stimulate one's

interest. Moreover, watches only remind me of time and how very slowly it was passing.

This educational phase of my training lasted some time and was only relieved by an occasional practice air-raid alarm. But one Sunday a censorette invited me to join a party of her friends at a bathing beach on the north side of the island. There the native houses clung to the steep incline of the hills. Blue sea and rollers came into view and then a sandy beach, with a small stream grooving its way down from the highlands. Over the hard sand rolling surf rose to meet the bather, tumbling at him or tugging at his legs as it ebbed. Pelicans in single file skimmed the broken waves. The warmth of the waters was not exhilarating, but very soothing. Sea grapes, growing over a cliff of red cavernous rock, made shade in which my friend deftly prepared a picnic, with food to suit all our tastes.

When it was finished we packed up and returned to Port of Spain, reaching the summit of the hills as the sun sank and night engulfed us almost immediately. As we approached the town a strange variety of odours reached us from the fragrance of sweet lime to the musky fumes of burning cowdung. Natives, homeward bound, all carried bundles on their heads. From a cabin I heard the sound of the tom-tom and the cymbal. The Southern Cross was high in the sky of a tropical night before we reached our quarters.

The following day was office routine again. The bishop who lived in the Hall turned on his light at 4 a.m. He washed and then cleared his throat – a raucous noise – dismissing sleep from all within earshot, which was most of us. His light started a chain reaction in the rooster population of the district.

As day after day passed in sweltering heat, relief from my office life came when I was sent to examine the correspondence of passengers alighting at Piarco airport. Likewise, those Spanish ships which were brought into Port of Spain to have their cargoes examined by Contraband Control, would have their passengers interrogated. In this way I met many interesting people including some former acquaintances, politicians and diplomats. The hours were long, entailing early morning rising in order to catch the government jitney to the airport or dock.

My landlady was deaf and used an old-fashioned ear trumpet. But the instrument so amplified background noises that she virtually could not hear anything distinctly. She, accordingly, did not go to the market to do her catering if she could possibly avoid it. This, of course, had an effect upon our diet and eventually upon our health. I went to see a doctor.

His waiting room was always crowded with sick and sorry-looking people of all shades. One bumptious socialite with a cigarette and a 'Government House manner' came in, and was shown into the consulting room immediately. But, for the rest of us, we waited. Yes, those black faces were most expressive as they sat around commiserating with each other's long-named illnesses. For one and a half hours I sat in that circle of sickness before being called in to the little man in a white coat. 'Acute enteritis,' he said, writing me a prescription.

The waiting patients looked at me sadly as I passed through their midst on my way out. They put me in mind of a pet dog with a stomach ache, for they wore on their faces expressions of resignation, fear, indulgence and self-pity. Many of them, quite unable to afford the dollar charge, enjoying the occasion little more than they would a funeral, wholeheartedly entered into the morbid spirit of a consultation even though only a few of them got as far as seeing the doctor.

The East Indians are plentiful in Trinidad. They can usually afford to pay, but like to bargain with the doctor for a cheaper rate. How much of their trouble would he heal for fifty cents? If they prayed for him or only had half the treatment, would it be less, and so on. A little Indian girl squirmed in her seat. Near her a mangy old dog had followed its master into the waiting room and lay panting in the heat.

She drew herself from the animal as far as she could, tucking away her pink skirt disdainfully lest he should touch it. She made wry faces so that all would see that she was a good Hindu.

One day things were busy at the airport and I missed the jitney back to Port of Spain. My only other means of getting home was the van which carried all the airmail to the censor's office, so I thumbed a ride in it. The airport was heavily guarded by a regiment of American black troops. As soon as we were clear of the gate I heard a scuffling from within the van. Looking back I saw several black soldiers emerging from underneath the mailbags. The idea of a Royal Mail van with registered mail in it being used as a means of smuggling troops out of barracks tickled me, but I saw it could also lead to serious trouble. At the Hindu settlement of Tunapuna our stowaways got out and were joined by a waiting bevy of brown girls, while the driver pocketed his illicit fares. This was the moment to deliver my blast! I knew that this simple Trinidadian lad was no match for his American brethren. I had not listened to the Amos and Andy programme for nothing. I barked and barked loudly.

The sequel to the episode came on the following Sunday. It was my slack day, as a rule, and a good opportunity to explore the malarial swamps which surrounded the airport. So, with binoculars and camera I set forth in search of scarlet ibis, little doubting that I was probably straying into a prohibited area. I had not gone far before a coloured sergeant arrested me, and I was marched off between two black soldiers with fixed bayonets. As they prodded me along through the marsh, I tried to explain that I was one of the airport staff.

'Ah doan know nuttin abaht that,' he said, 'you'se all got to come along with us.' And so, protesting, I was marched off to the guard tent. Then, as a last resort, I took a gamble. 'Did you all enjoy you'se all at Tunapuna the other night?' said I, imitating the dialect in a jocular vein, as if I had a bit of information up my sleeve. The sergeant's jaw dropped and he stopped short. 'I was sitting right in front with the driver of the mail van.'

'Well, dat changes everything,' he said with impunity. 'Guess you'se free nah.'

'Oh, no!' I bluffed. 'I'm coming to see your captain. I surely am!' His features grew green.

'No,' he said, the corner of his expressive mouth registering desperation. 'That ain't necessary no mo.'

But I persisted that he should do his duty. We found the captain in the guard tent. I greeted him cordially, for I had taken lunch with him in the mess each day. I then asked him where I could safely do my birdwatching in future; and the colour returned to the sergeant's cheeks.

Back at the Hall, things were looking up for me and I moved into an attic bedroom with a magnificent view across the harbour. Shipping was something one did not talk about lest one unwittingly became the cause of getting it sunk. But one morning the sun gleamed upon the white hull of the *Gabo Di Hornos*, a Spanish liner bound for Buenos Aires which had been brought in by Contraband Control for inspection. On such occasions, a group of censors went on board to interrogate the passengers and examine their papers.

To the average individual, censorship consists merely of opening letters to see whether they contain any information of a military nature. This is what censors do, of course, but it is an infinitesimal part of their wartime activities. Censorship makes a minute study of the endless means of sending or collecting information and exploits them in the interests of its country to the full. Their methods are tireless and meticulous and sometimes a great deal of time is spent for what would appear to be a very small yield. But, grain by grain, it is garnered and filed. A great deal of it is only corroborative, but censorship is like a vast machine with its antennae sensitively feeling out every known form of communication, checking and double-checking what passes through it, until it is able to produce a minutely accurate and informative picture of the military, political and economic situation, mostly compiled from a mass of carefully sifted grains of information.

The passenger list, having been carefully scrutinised by experts, with a veritable library of records at their disposal, and certain individuals having been selected for interrogation, a group of censors, assisted by stenographers, would each have a list of these passengers to examine. Meanwhile, Contraband Control would be going through the hold, baggage rooms and cabins. We worked as a team, passing information back and forth as each made some discovery which would be of interest to the other. Under cross-questioning by a censor in the ship's luxurious saloons, a passenger might let something slip, which would be worth mentioning to the Security Control officer on board who, putting two and two together, might find it important enough to pass on the word to the Contraband gang. Acting on this or on some other matter, they might then make a corroborative discovery which might in turn reveal something else and so on. This might all end, for instance, in a passenger being removed from the ship for further interrogation or internment or, what might be more likely, the information about the passenger would be cabled on to his destination where, under appropriate observation, he would perhaps disclose other members of a spy ring or some such activity antagonistic to our interests. All very involved, but all very necessary.

Most of the personnel of the Imperial Censorship had not been long on the job. Many of them were better-class girls, unaccustomed to routine and long hours. To put it mildly, they were more accustomed to leisure. They were always going off for coffee and were easily distracted by men. The stenographer on this particular day was one of those who would drop everything and rush to the window if a plane flew by, in case it was Johnny or Richard piloting it. When, therefore, I finally got down the gangplank at the end of my day's work, I felt tired and in need of peace.

On one such evening, I walked to the botanical gardens. The air was spiced with herbacious scent and I felt that the spirit of life and growth was abroad. Albert came out from among his trees. He, too, sensed the coolness that had come up from the sea.

'I am a lover of beauty,' he said softly. 'You, too, like it, I believe.' He led me off to where a lily pond was surrounded by thickets of flowering shrubs and dark bowers of overhanging vine. Here, sitting on a bench, was a flower of India, her pretty face framed in a sari, her brown legs dangling above the water. Never had I seen such beauty. Albert left me to work out my own doubts and desires.

Above us on the hill was a wooden tower, like a decapitated piece of some extravagant palace. From it the panorama of Port of Spain opened out towards the sea. Beyond it, the southern extremity of the island was clear on the horizon while, on the other hand, the distant hills of Venezuela stood silhouetted. It was a scene which was soft, caressing and warm, the glow of the setting sun penetrating and melting all resistance.

I looked at the girl who stood beside me. Perhaps she was sixteen. The lemon-coloured sari had slipped back from her dark hair. Gold ornaments adorned her small neck and ankles. She gazed at me steadfastly and presently her eyes burned like fire. Her sari fell from her shoulders as we returned to the lily pond which now reflected a rising moon in its waters. The leaves trembled as a breeze fanned them. Her heavenly face, her body so thinly veiled, made me want to merge

with it apart from the inferior world. I hesitated for an instant only
to yield to the gradually increasing volume of the urge; sweet and
involuntary influence seized us, breaking through the thin hedge of
resistance into a warm and smooth paradise.

The mornings usually started well, divinely calm and balmy. But
there came a change towards noon with the shifting winds to the
south-east. Then it faded out altogether and the lull was filled with
greyness and humidity. It grew oppressively hot towards early afternoon, a moisture-laden breeze freshening thereafter. The distant hills
were blotted out and then came rain. But it was soon over and there
was a grateful hush over the trees broken only by the twitter of birds.
With a clearing sky, only the swollen gutters bore witness to the
passing mood. Among the wild mango trees behind the airport buildings, I saw blue tanagers and the love note of a dove came from the
jungle. Then scissortails flew across the open sky, reminding me that
I was still a censor.

On this day three passenger planes arrived at the same moment,
causing congestion in the baggage room while at the same time menacing
black clouds burst and tipped a deluge upon us. I dealt with the
literary matter of a professor of the University of Michigan, then
passed M. Pierlot the Belgian Premier and Roger Taymens, his President de Conceilles who, of course, had diplomatic immunity. They
were on their way to the Belgian Congo which entailed crossing the
Atlantic from east to west and then crossing the southern Atlantic
from west to east. However, they seemed little travelworn and ready
to be sociable. From them I received news of my Belgian friends,
Queen Elizabeth and Antoinette De Ligne, and learned that Baillie de
la Tour and his son had both been killed in a plane crash.

Clare Booth, at that time a journalist for *Time-Life* magazine passed
through on her way back from North Africa. Luckily it did not fall to
my lot to have to impound her briefcase. Nevertheless she did have
it taken from her which saved some red faces in high command in
Tobruk. Another arrival about this time was Count Carlo Sforza who
had been carrying on an anti-Fascist campaign in South America and
who later became Premier in post-war Italy.

It always saddened me that the turn of events had set the Italian
people, amongst whom I had been raised, against the British Common-
wealth and I felt warmly towards this courageous politician who later
led them back into democracy. I felt that I would like to help him in

his crusade and sought a means of revealing what I thought were the true sentiments of the vast majority of the Italian people. I felt that whilst they had been content with the creative phase in the beginning of the Fascist regime, they were not at all happy with what it had latterly become. We spoke together at his hotel in Port of Spain and I later gave a press conference to journalists of the *Montreal Gazette*.

During this period of rains, the mosquitoes were very troublesome and I was terribly bitten at Piarco. But I liked my work there and enjoyed the contacts I made. The food, too, was good at the American Officer's Mess compared with what we put up with at Port of Spain. It was now the beginning of September. Somewhere new snow was falling on the mountain tops and leaves were beginning to turn.

Back in Port of Spain I walked around the lower part of the savannah with a fellow censor who, in normal times, was a film director in California. A cynic, he saw no merit in anything Trinidadian although he had to admit it was a beautiful evening. A giant cumulus cloud shielded the setting sun, its crown so lofty that a stratospheric wind was smudging it into an opalescent halo. Its filmy quality was shot with yellows, like the Indian girl's sari – whom I remembered with a pang. An old coloured woman stopped to ask if it was a sign from God. My companion laughed at her. We sat on a bench watching the phenomenon while a cool breeze fanned us from the hills.

'I am an agnostic, sometimes atheist and a materialist,' he said and came out with an overwhelming parade of facts to which I had no answer. With his head of grey hair resting in the palms of his hands, his eyes half-closed behind the bifocal lenses of his glasses and with a voice as precise as the tick-tock of a pendulum, he set out to disillusion me. He produced chapter and verse, statistics and quotations which were calculated to explode my dearest creeds. 'Christ,' he said, 'was a little Jew, a poet and a rich man, his teachings completely ill-recorded and misunderstood; his death a fallacy; he fainted upon the cross and was only hidden by his rich uncle for safety in the tomb. His resurrection was therefore no miracle, but a deception.' The immaculate conception he dismissed as a myth.

On the following Sunday we went to Arima where there are remnants of the Carib inhabitants of the island. Here we visited Mrs Merges, the Carib queen. She lived with her daughter in a small plasterboard home on the outskirts of the town. She seemed uncertain of her age but I was told she was eighty-six. Her features and her gestures were refined, her skin the colour of a well-baked biscuit. There was something neither Spanish nor Indian about her. Her nose was small, her cheekbones large. It was an animated face full of life and expression, and her coal-black eyes were distant, revealing a mind wedded to the mysticisms of her tribe and its adopted religion.

They had not been converted, she said, but had become Catholics of their own accord and Saint Arosa was their patron saint. The Saint, she added, had been found in a spring of water and had been with the tribe ever since. She showed us a silver staff and cross which Hy Arima, their one-time chief, had possessed as a symbol of leadership. Otherwise, the old lady's house contained no fineries. There were odd photographs or china ornaments of personal interest only. As we talked, her daughter, sitting on the sofa, stitched a dress of mango-patterned material. Pictures of cats and other animals had been worked on rugs and hung upon the wall. The tribe and its queen had evidently become westernised, a very difficult process to resist.

It had been an interesting day but, as we drove back to Port of Spain, I began to feel ill and before reaching that city of bicycles and donkey carts was in an ague. I remained in bed for some days with a sharp attack of malaria. The houseboy attended to my needs, bringing me fruit juice and changing my bedding which quickly became sodden with perspiration. Many of the symptons of phlebitis now returned, and on 22 October 1942 I was flown to Bermuda in a Catalina on the first leg of my journey back to Canada.

When at length I arrived home, I found the house and garden in tip-top condition. Never could one have wished for greater care. The house was painted, the doors varnished, the floors polished, the kitchen and its utensils shone, cupboards were filled with preserved fruits and shelves stocked with jellies. My clothes had been cleaned, mended and pressed; linen ironed and socks carefully put away.

The trees were well pruned and the lawns tidily mown. Food was stored in the basement which was as clean as a parlour. The garden was in a dreary winter mood, but it was well cared for and neatly tended. It was good to see my new Scottish caretakers looking well and happy; good to see new pullets all in good lay; good to see the dead timber felled and the woodshed filled with kindling.

The drive which I had built was swept clean so that not a dead leaf was in sight. There were grouse in the thicket and deer in quantity on the hill. Yes, it was good indeed to be back, yet there was something missing.

I thought of Crookie and of England and I wanted to be where there was activity, ignoring that it was a form of hypnotic attraction towards discord. Among the tears and tragedies, the rubble and blast of a life-and-death struggle one would have to be supremely attuned with creative power not to become overwhelmed and subject to the spirit of destruction.

Hitler's annual speech before the Reichstag was interrupted by bombs dropped by the R.A.F. and, as I listened to the radio, I heard the detonations. Churchill had met with Roosevelt at Casablanca to discuss the future course of the United Nations.

We were rapidly approaching a crisis in world affairs and there had to be a clear-cut attitude towards the true meaning of peace. I believed in a universe of order and that order and not chaos was the norm for the individual as for the world. Peace to me consisted of coming into a oneness with the natural state of order at its central and creative point and revealing this inner point of peace in one's living. It seemed to me that if others were to adopt a similar attitude, peace and goodwill towards men in a general sense would become a reality. I did not stand with those who prophesied the end of the world, but I recognised that cataclysms did occur and the question of why they did was a matter deserving attention.

Midsummer 1943 came and once again I set off for England. I spent some days in Vancouver and Banff, and then in Montreal awaiting the departure of my convoy; it was while sitting on Mount Royal watching the distant shipping that I entertained grave doubts about leaving my home again.

My instructions had been to be in Montreal not later than the first of June. It was what I had awaited, so anxious was I to help in the war effort and its postwar reconstruction. While still at Arbutus Point the thought of leaving the safety and gentle beauty of my adopted home to travel for weeks in crowded trains and on the hazardous Atlantic, had not been at all attractive. Before me lay uncertainty, a vague programme of service, perhaps a meeting with Crookie. Yet I did not hesitate when space in a cargo ship was offered to me; not that my rapid decision was not fraught with a pack of fiendish doubts closely following it, but on the whole it remained staunch.

Sometimes, I had argued, it was crazy to exchange those simple interests, that ease, for a leap into the grey and merciless Atlantic which had already swallowed up more than 400 British ships or, reaching the other side, to be haunted by a hellish nightmare of murderous dreams where death and madness staggered hand in hand. Yet, shining above the warped horizon, was the hope that I might be of service. And what was more the thought, that adversity taken the right way was maturing, encouraged me. These ideals had become somewhat dimmed as I packed and toiled to get ready, but they nevertheless cast their light through all. I had not taken any steps to make my stay at home permanent, so had nothing to cancel or regret, but all the same it was a wrench to leave my sanctuary. On my final walk through the woods to the Point, the leaves had seemed so fresh, the grasses so green and slender, bowing their seeded heads; the wild flowers at their best and so appealing. The first were tipped with green shoots and the woods were scented with the spirit of summer. A deer stood watching me as I moved in and out of the shadows. I spoke to her from a few paces' distance.

While passing through Vancouver I went to the Marine building and found that my ship had been delayed. I spent a few days at an hotel of pioneering days but the discomfort and noise drove me to more comfortable quarters at the Vancouver Club where I was extended the courtesy of a temporary membership. I was invited by various members to their homes on Granville Street. One famous Russian pianist, married to a wealthy Canadian, was hospitable and while at their apartment I was introduced to Kipnis, the Metropolitan singer. We discussed many subjects, including war and revolution, during which my host grew so excited that I became a little startled. He got wild-eyed and his hair stood up straight like a Gollywog so that as his face got closer and closer to mine he sprayed me with saliva. He finally cornered me between a marble-topped chest of drawers and a lamp and punched me so hard in the chest that I had to laugh to hide my embarrassment.

I was asked to many cocktail parties, a form of reunion I abhor and at which one meets people whose names escape one promptly, but I saw some good shows and went to a concert given by Kipnis.

I was already middle-aged and knew that this was a young man's war, yet there was this urge to take part in it. A woman at one of these parties asked me, 'Why do you want to return to a sinking ship?' to which I replied, 'Because I don't know of a ship which is sinking faster.'

I had written to London to the Ministry of Information asking for a job and received a reply from my old boss of Trinidad days: 'I am not very hopeful that anything will come of it as we have stopped recruiting men for some time in the department . . .'

Austin, a moving spirit in Vancouver, was at the Ministry of Marine Transportation, but he could not help me get to England, neither could the C.P.R. shipping authorities, nor the Manning Port where I offered to join the Merchant Marine in order to reach my native land, but there they told me I would need an M.M. discharge in order to join ship.

I ate many of my meals at the cafeteria of the Hotel Vancouver where I chanced to meet again H. B. King who was then Inspector of Schools for the government of British Columbia. We had previously travelled together in a transcontinental train from Ottawa. And it was partly this meeting that started me thinking of education as a means of reforming the young idea in Great Britain.

On arrival in Montreal I met with further delays and would have become frustrated were it not for the events and the way they turned out.

I looked for lodging and found, in the apartment of a French-Canadian spinster, a room with a divan bed. But the room was scantily furnished and dark. Then I remembered the advice of one of my neighbours at Maple Bay, 'Go and see my cousins the Stokers.' Mary Stoker was widowed but she had three sons living with her. Being of Irish descent they accepted me as if I had been one of their family. Their apartment was within a short distance of Montreal's Sherbrooke Street and the art gallery. They introduced me to the President, then one of the Group of Seven, Arthur Lismer, and finally, Ellwood Hosmer, who showed me his collection of Canalettos, magnificently hung in a room specially designed to show these treasures to their best advantage. There were also other pictures of the French post-impressionist type. And so I passed a very pleasant morning. But Montreal is full of interest to an artist. It being Saturday the Stokers took me up into the Laurentians where Mary kept a charming farm aided by a French-Canadian couple. The brown earth, the undulating softness of different shades of ochre, the greens of fresh meadowland and the hollows strung together by a mountain stream and their little lakes with ruffled surfaces, walled in by stern faces of rock or gravelled banks, the azalia, trillium or columbine scattered under a blue sky, a sky streaked with winter's last breath – it was an ecstasy so moving. It was cool and my underwear was being washed and I was wearing one of Paddy's silk vests. But it was warm indoors, a special warmth of Irish hospitality. The walls were panelled with natural pine and a log fire crackled and spat on the hearth and there was an atmosphere of peace.

17

Out of the Frying Pan

When I reached London my attention was drawn to R. A. Butler's new Education Bill, which had promised to reorganise national schools. But the Bill aimed at an intensification and not a change of the old methods. I felt that if the world were not to suffer the same tragedies again then some radical changes would be necessary in the education of human nature.

Accordingly I went to Oxford, not with the idea of converting the pundits of learning to my way of thinking, but more to study the principles followed and to see what changes were feasible without wrecking the whole system. I was received by Sir Richard Livingstone and Sir David Ross, and later in London by Sir Frederick Clarke, whose articles in the *Spectator* had greatly impressed me.

I felt that youth had been encouraged to cram its mind with knowledge in somewhat the same style as indiscriminate collectors fill a museum without respect to the wisdom of relativity. I could see that classified knowledge had its uses in providing lines upon which truth could express itself. Nevertheless, education should start by clearing the path in the mind and heart as outlets for the wisdom which is inherent in each one of us, so that wisdom might be the keynote and guide to further advance into the field of knowledge. Knowledge for knowledge's sake is dangerous or, at best, a waste of time. Those who seek wisdom without giving full credit to its author are little better than those who have learned to write cheques but have never opened a bank account.

At present it is fashionable to explore the realm of the spirit by the use of the intellect, through the medium of theology and philosophy, but intellectuals are not always humble folk. Indeed, they tend to ignore the fact that the things of the spirit must be spiritually discerned and that intellect in and of itself can blind them to the things of the Spirit.

At this stage these ideas were mere speculation on my part, but, as I allowed them to materialise in me, I saw how well founded they were. I could see how nature expressed beauty in all its forms.

I walked one afternoon over Shotover Hill to visit Dr L. P. Jacks, the editor of *Hibbert Journal* and found this deeply spiritual man out in his garden; the maid called him by sounding a little bell. *Hibbert Journal* was well known for its high literary standard and contained the writings of many well-known theologians and philosophers. I thought this a suitable outlet for what I had to offer. There was undoubtedly a dawning of spiritual thought in England, no doubt stimulated by adversity and the hardships increasingly borne by its people. There was, too, a move away from the dogma and ritual of orthodoxy in Christian thought, and the Jewish and Mithraic influences so evident in Christian religions.

I was hungry after my walk, for in my over-emphasis I had overshot the house on Shotover Hill. Tea was brought in and dispensed by Mrs Jacks in true English style with teacake and thin bread and butter with lots of jam, and mustard and cress sandwiches. The house was comfortable and well furnished, and contained original Burnes-Jones paintings.

Dr Jacks asked me to write for his journal on the spiritual approach to educational reconstruction, which I was glad to do.

I had letters of introduction to the author of the Village University scheme, who was also President of the Board of Education in Cambridge. He, in turn, passed me on to the principals of the colleges in that University. Whilst they endorsed my views, I found them too wedded to the old order to give me any particular support.

The summer was waning. I had luck with the weather. The large trees were growing weary, and their ripened fruits ready to scatter; the lawns and parks were dry. Swifts cleaved the air, screaming at the advancing autumn. The beasts gathered together in the shade, bloated and fly-tormented. The avenued vistas and architectural harmony of Cambridge were eighteenth century. There was something languid and soothing about the river flowing past those elegant colleges, the banks and paths overhung with willows and populated by young people in punts or canoes. The onward flow of its waters here and there was gathered in the apron of a weir, or crossed by a low bridge from which boys hopefully fished with dough and float. Strolling throught he meadows, between appointments, I was overtaken by a Samoyed dog who, in his undemonstrative fashion, showed me recognition. I turned in time to escape being jumped on by Crookie. I

caught her and whirled her around like a top, in sheer delight. Her
ambulance unit was operating in that area. We had lots of news to
catch up on.

'Why didn't you write, you ass ?' she said.

I shrugged my answer. 'Why didn't you ?'

We passed through a country churchyard beneath yews and oaks
and out into a field of corn down to a copse-enclosed pond with a
mill and an old barn. In the beauty of the evening I quite forgot my
appointment with a don. We came to a gate. She draped herself on
it, her cheek resting on the top rail, her grey eyes on mine. Something
was coming to point that would link me with the conventional life
of an English country family. A period of reverie fell upon us, and a
moorhen played upon the pond, flicking the whiteness of her tail as
she picked at the vegetation on the surface. The day was spent, the
moon was rising.

Crookie stood under the outstretched arms of an old oak where
the bank jutted out into the silvery water. I took her in my arms – I
wanted her, who had so often given herself to me in looks.

'I do love you so,' I said. But we were both laughing. For one brief
moment we might have taken ourselves seriously.

I caught her again and held her to me. I looked into her face, and a
sly prettiness looked back at me.

'You are a little monkey,' I said, putting her down.

And we both knew we would never take each other in earnest.

We walked arm in arm to her rooms as a haze settled in the hollows.
We said goodnight at her door and I returned to my pub. A group
of interested listeners was gathered round the radio. Italy was suffering
under the German yoke and also under the lash of our bombers.
General Alexander had made his headquarters at Bolsena within sight
of my Hill of the Irish upon which stood the monument to King
Donough; and General Kesselring was conducting a German retreat
from Villa Torlonia when the R.A.F. had bombed it reducing the
casino to rubble. Russia was riding defiantly forward, rolling the
German army backward. I could not help wondering to myself whether
this was the beginning of a Communist triumvirate, and where it would
lead.

I did not feel it could last forever, for fundamentally the Russians
are a pious people with a filial affection for a Supreme Being. It was
said that Russia had found her soul but it was more correct to say that
a minority had wrested control over her vast resources of manpower

The Cottage, Fairholme Ranch, Banff, Alberta, 1947.
and below
Fairholme Lodge, 1948.

Far left, **Lord Martin Cecil;** *centre*, **Lloyd A. Meeker (Uranda)**
and Kathy Meeker; *far right*, **Lillian, now Lady Martin Cecil.**
and below
The Cottage, Fairholme Ranch, in winter.

Christina
at 18, 1950.

Below:

Rosie and
bear, Banff,
1964.

The author's son John at Fairholme, 1954.

The author's son Rollo, 1971.

Self portrait.

Sunrise Ranch, Loveland, Colorado.

The author at age of 80 in Vancouver, B.C.

and material. I felt strongly that nothing would stop the Communist advance except the unity of the so-called free world in truth.

The trouble was most of them thought they had the truth already but were unable to agree about it, which meant there was no real unity of purpose, and, since there are no divisions in truth, it was obvious that none of them had found it.

In the beginning of September I returned to Oxford where I contributed to *The Times Educational Supplement*. It was my parting shot in that field, for I could see that, after the passing of Butler's Bill for educational reconstruction, nothing more at that time could be done. All that did not conform to the findings of the human intellect was called naive. Perhaps David was naive when he tackled Goliath. No worthwhile reconstruction could, in my opinion, come out of the debris of a discredited system – the true value of a system being proved by its contribution to peace and freedom.

The new and better world we all hoped for could only be born out of a new and better basis. In other words, it was once more a matter of letting the order appear in us as individuals first before it could be expected to manifest in our education system. Once it had appeared among the ranks of educationists, they could offer it to their public, to their pupils. But our educational hierarchy, controlled by itself, had appointed its own executives and was closely allied and controlled by the churches and Greek philosophies, which do not themselves teach the whole truth. Had they taught the whole truth there would be unity and not a scattered enmity.

The general poll of opinion in Oxford as far as I could gather was that the White Paper was inadequate, but that one should welcome the millimetre advance and apply oneself to the full accomplishment of it rather than take the more distant and radical view, on the principle that if one is faithful over a few things one eventually becomes ruler over many.

My landlady in St John's Street came from the north of England. She was kindhearted, if a little intolerant and inclined to pessimism. Her husband was a retired chef. 'Ma oosband,' as she called him, had been knocked about in the First World War. 'Ee kem 'ome sick an' creaking like an old gate,' and then there followed all the gruesome details of his wounds, and his only remaining lung. 'An' talking of loongs,' she added, 'Doctor says I've got small "bronicals"; they've never growed oop, like.'

Breakfast was a chatty meal and one never knew who might be

present. There was a famous head injuries hospital in Oxford and many of the lodgers were those visiting their wounded relatives. I made the acquaintance of Hilaire Belloc, a Catholic and a Frenchman by birth, who viewed the British character much as I did. He was far from orthodox and detested all things stuffy – a genius and much to be admired. One morning he came down to breakfast in a heavy ulster coat and created a commotion by losing his pince-nez. He had us searching high and low for them until I caught sight of a black ribbon around his neck and, hauling on it, I brought them up from the inner recesses of his underwear, for which feat he rewarded me with a twinkle of his eye. I wished then I had known him in his more vigorous days when he lived in one of Oxford's small backwaters called Bath Place and wrote his great historical studies.

I met a great many dons during the months that I remained in Oxford. Some welcomed me as a nonconformist brother, others listened to what I had to say gravely, and then said I was an Oxford Grouper, or a follower of Rudolph Steiner. They heard me out patiently, looked wisely attentive and then advised me to write a book. Some spoke of the efflorescence of puberty and the powers of the psyche which seemed to me only to complicate the sweet simplicity of the truth. They spoke of karmic records and of consulting those who had 'gone before us'; the cultivation of their minds had obviously darkened their hearts. Those I met had come more to develop their minds and to collect knowledge than to learn how, in utter humility, to gain wisdom; how, in fact, to become as little children. Their minds and hearts were far too sophisticated to sound a common chord with a universal resonance.

In my research for further details of Kathleen ffrench's life I met a Swedish lady who had accompanied her on the first part of her trek across inner and outer Mongolia to Urian Khai in the province of Tannu-Tova. I also sought out the Very Reverend Archimandrite Nicholas, who spent part of his time in Oxford; his original name was Gibbs, but he had become a Greek Orthodox priest subsequent to serving the Imperial family of Russia as tutor to the Tsarevitch. After three attempts I found a handsome old man with a white beard and a black flowing robe. I knew that he had been the only friend of the Imperial family to witness their massacre at Ekatorinburg and carefully avoided that subject. What interested me most was his close friendship with Kathleen, and the fact that he had been frequently at her side in Harbin.

We spoke of those who were her constant companions there and also of Paul Dukes, whom he had known whilst in Petrograd; of his attachment with Miles Lampson's mission, and their later meeting in Peking; of his period in the Chinese Maritime Customs, where he had met my old companion Docia Logwinoff. But we were digging into the past and his memory was not very clear. We sat talking for some time in his odd bedsitting room, perhaps two hours or more, while night fell. We had tea, bread and margarine. The walls were covered with books, ikons and symbols of his faith, while furniture, crockery and apples from his farm filled the room.

I parted from him, so frail and stooped, promising to meet again, and so out into the darkness of a blacked-out street.

The news vendors were calling out the news of the recapture of Smolensk by the Russians; by spring they would have chased the disheartened Germans out of their country. Montgomery, too, was doing his stuff, for the Eighth Army was within striking distance of Foggia and the Germans, under Kesslering, were in danger of being surrounded. Seeing their inevitable defeat, a dense gloom had descended on the German people.

All this time I daily attended the Pitt Rivers Museum. Oxford in wartime was a different place to that which I had known in peacetime. Many of the colleges were occupied by troops: some American, others British, whilst others were turned into hospitals or quarters for the women's services such as the WRNS, WRAFS, or ATS. The streets in daytime were crowded: milling masses of all types and colours, very many of them refugees from Europe, or evacuees from the bombed cities of Britain. The local shopkeepers, usually so polite and attentive, were now tired and overworked, and sometimes sour with their patrons. But from the human torrent that flooded the shopping centre there were places of refuge, such as the quiet gardens of New College, Magdalen, or St John's. The river, too, in warm weather, offered an escape from the dangers of the crowded thoroughfares. But whatever the circumstances, Oxford was a model of distinction and of historical architecture, and one's interest never flagged.

Walking through the market one day I ran into Mrs Hodges who, when I was sixteen, had taught me to ride to hounds and care for my horse. She had not changed much, considering the thirty-four years which had passed since I had last seen her. She took me home to tea where I met a refugee from Nazi oppression who was a graphologist. I had first been introduced to the marvels of the science of character-reading through handwriting by Baron Trutzler von Falkenstein and it was bracketed in my mind with the influences of the psyche, and the vibratory nature of Being. I was not aware at that time that George de la Warr was active in a field which he called radieshesia, and had established a laboratory on the outskirts of Oxford for its research, on which subject he had published a book. I later visited him and his wife at their laboratory.

This theory, which later in 1960 received a great deal of publicity through the famous 'Black Box' trial in London, involved the reading of vibratory interrelationships between all the units of matter. George de la Warr claimed to be able to 'photograph' a distortion pattern or organic disorder in a body through the agency of a drop of blood, in spite of the distance separating the drop of blood and the body from which it was taken. On the particular day on which I visited his laboratories the kidney of a dog in Oxford, some few miles away, was being 'photographed' through the medium of one of the dog's hairs. I was invited to witness this and was accordingly present in the room where the photographing was taking place. But I was told that the camera, which had been attuned to the vibrations of Dr Cote and his photographic assistant, was being affected by the proximity of my own vibrational nature and was not functioning correctly in consequence. I was obliged to step into the corridor and witness the proceedings through a small pane of glass in the door.

Life was filled with revelation and incident. New discoveries and inventions followed amazing political and military developments. Sometimes they followed in chain-like sequence; at other times they came all at once, until one found more on one's dish than could lightly be digested. Moreover, the state of war seemed a permanent experience in my consciousness. Man was perpetually in deadlock with man, to kill or be killed.

Sometimes I was sapped by a sense of intense loneliness and a longing for the fellowship of someone with whom I could share these convictions. The world of man was in such desperate need, yet too intensely hypnotised by materialism to realise its plight. I longed to do something to change this downward trend, yet what could I do more than live moment by moment according to my own ideals? For surely, since universal order was the norm, all that was not of order would pass away with the passage of time. I wanted nevertheless to talk with someone about it – for sharing one's convictions is at least comforting, if not confirmatory. I kept in constant touch with Uranda through the mail.

An old skiing friend of Kitzbühel days had asked me in for a drink. An autumn gale was tearing at the trees and rain deluged down upon the darkened townscape of unilluminated Oxford, its pavements and crowds unseen and haunted by the wail of sirens.

As I reached the rooms in St John's Street and pulled the bell knob, I was conscious of the sound of music and of voices from an upper storey. In the dimly lit hall where umbrellas puddled the floor, I left my raincoat and lightly mounted the narrow stairs. As I reached the door, now separating me from the gaiety within, I paused a little to regain my breath – I was fifty years old and more conscious of age than I am today.

What a moment it is, one's entrance into a room containing the unknown – the breaking of new ground; the impact like an electric contact, thrilling the fibres of the spine. Then after the initial blur, the emergence of vague recognition, the room and furniture once familiar is now in a new context.

Grouped around the fire were some young people, among whom one, in particular, Rosalie, stood out in relief, causing a dim-out of the others in my eyes. One could not analyse her features any more than one can anatomise the love feelings that pass through the mind and heart at such a meeting. She appeared slim, shy, even timid, yet with a sensitive and intelligent face.

When we found ourselves irresistibly falling in love, I had a peculiar feeling that several kinds of forces were at work, some of which I could not understand for they were, as it were, concealed, yet there were others which, though I understood them vaguely, I kept secret. The desire for the full experience of union which I was experiencing was stronger than my need for honesty at this point. At all events we felt a desperate need for each other.

Looking back, I can see we both had a great deal to learn about unity. I, for one, had not yet learned to know myself and could not, therefore, be true to myself. Accordingly I could not be true to anyone else. I did not realise the nature of the situation beyond this, but only indulged myself in my new idol whole-heartedly, who also reciprocated in kind. She had struck a chord in me, whatever it was, which was to survive all the difficulties that lay in our path.

Our trysting places after that initial meeting were mostly in and around Oxford. We sometimes met at restaurants or at the Mitre for a drink, or on the New College lawns where undergraduates came to relax and eat their sandwiches between lectures. Sometimes we would stroll in Magdalen Gardens or along the Thames and, one day, there being good reason for going to London, we planned a meeting there.

I picked her up at Grosvenor House at eight o'clock and took her to a show in Leicester Square. We had not long returned to her hotel when there was a bad raid. Several of my friends who had gone to the Cafe de Paris narrowly escaped death when a bomb pierced the central skylight and burst in the midst of the dancing floor which was crowded with people. The casualties were heavy. But this we only learned the next day.

I had spent the morning at the Athenaeum Club with an old Scottish baronet who was so senile that I had difficulty in following his conversation. When later I met Rosalie at the Menagerie restaurant she acted upon me like a newly opened bottle of champagne. She literally made me tingle with exhilaration. I had lost my ration card and the old waitress roared like a lioness but, to our great relief, fetched some stewed herrings.

Naturally we were both eager to find out more about each other, a subtle game and highly entertaining, especially as there is always more to come. I found myself comparing Rosie with Crookie. How unlike they were. Crookie, whose progress through life was as uncompromising as a tank, with her strictly conventional upbringing, while Rosie, as I now called her, was guided by something uncannily intuitive within herself. Crookie was reliable, stimulating but independent. She would give one moments of loneliness, for she was not conscious of another's feelings, while Rosie was sensitive and gentle and as soft as a kitten's wrists and ever inclined to run away, feeling she was in the way. I had never heard her criticise or utter an unkind word about another though she would say in a mock-panicky voice, 'Dear so and so, I do hate him so,' when she feared aggressiveness in someone.

Crookie had a barb in her tongue, a quick temper and a sharp wit, with which weapons she won many a battle and many a heart. Would Crookie be genuinely monogamous I wondered, or would that be an ideal she set for herself. As for Rosie, on this score she would be utterly faithful in happiness, but should she be unable to find it she would give herself over to abject misery. Crookie would be rich in friends all her life, as people are who know what they want and go after it regardless; but she would never be dismayed if she failed to reach her goal. She was a plucky little fighter. Rosie was not any of these things, for she had neither the constitution to fight nor the desire to do so, yet she had a hidden toughness which the stranger might discover with a shock. On the other hand she would appeal very strongly to a man for protection. She needed to be shielded against the world and against herself, and this appealed to me.

After lunch we sauntered past the caged animals. I have never really cared for zoos. I am not a scientist and as a lover of animals cannot help but feel that they would be happier and look better in their own wild and natural circumstances. But perhaps I had a fellow feeling for them as I, too, had been caged, and was more at home like they in the freedom of the wilds. Rosalie shared this feeling for, sophisticated as she was on the exterior, she had a disregard for accepted usages and preferred the backwoods to the glamour of town life. She obviously had some kind of bond with wild animals for the ferocious and timid alike came to the bars of their cages and allowed her to caress them. I quoted Genesis, 'And let them have dominion over the fish of the sea and over the fowls of the air, and over the cattle and over every creeping thing that creepeth upon the face of the earth.' We both lightly agreed that man had taken the word dominion to mean exploit, instead of to extend the state of higher order to the lowly ones. As man was in the midst of the greatest killing war he had ever precipitated, that was further evidence of his topsy-turviness.

In the ladies' lounge at my club there was talk that summer of the Americans cutting across the Cherbourg peninsula and of the Fifth Army in Italy having reached Perugia. Assisi and Bolsena, they said, were once more in Allied hands.

On the following day Rosie was to visit her parents in East Anglia and that night we dined at l'Escargo in Greek Street with Arthur Waley and Byrl de Zoote, where I had so often been before; yet during this period of love and peril it seemed even more delectable. I parted with Rosie saying that I would take her to King's Cross the following day to catch her train.

When I returned to Oxford I became more than ever connected with the Slade School of Art which had been evacuated to the Ashmolean and I attended it daily. My landlady had hinted that if I were able to disappear for two or three days it would be a good opportunity for her to change my room to the lighter and airier chamber immediately above, a room until then occupied by an old Jewish lady refugee. So I went to Bath where I knew Crookie's old governess had some lodgings. One of her lodgers was a young WRNS who took me to Bristol where her squad was painting a corvette. We took a small ferry and crossed the Avon and from there up a hill where there was a fine view of the city with its tragic disfigurements of wounded and devastated buildings. Over all was the smoke, the noise, and the strife, with the barrage balloons tugging and swinging on their long cables. Bristol was rather more squalid than before but infinitely more sure of itself, an assurance which comes from a carefully built-up wealth and prosperity. One felt that whatever came there would always be a Bristol.

The girl at my side fitted in with the character of this great seaport for she, like England and its cities, could afford to be a bit untidy and nonchalant. No vulgarity, cheap technique or cosmetics, no effort, no smartness of line, she just was an English lady, the best that could be found in the land and I was very proud to be with her.

The following day I went for a walk. Bath, like all hollows and floors, is a cold, damp place in winter and relaxing in summer, so I walked up and over Claverton Hill. It was foggy and the visibility was not good. On the hill stood Claverton Manor which I used to know in the days of its owner, Gaythorn Hill. I remembered the avenue and stately gates, the lodge house and the great beeches spreading smooth arms over the lawns. Claverton, its front covered with magnolias, faced across a valley and a river on to a wooded hill beyond. I remembered the comfort of that house, its mahogany and its polish, its cut glass and its Georgian silver. The pictures and the port, the fire that burned in my bedroom from a grate full of nuggets of the best coal, throwing shadows over the rich ceiling and upon my evening shirt which was draped before it on a chair. I remembered the four-poster bed with my pink evening coat laid upon it flanked by silk socks and clean underwear. I remembered the Beaufort Hunt ball at Doddington and how Gaythorn had looked well in his blue coat and buff facings and knee breeches; the joyful assembly, the chandeliers, the marble colonnades, the cars, the meet on the next day, the sound of the horn, the covert, the cry of the hounds as they hurled themselves in a dappled torrent out of the thicket to stream across a sunlit vale. I came to the same lodge gates and there found a notice which halted me. This was a prohibited area of the R.A.F.

The shooting phase of the war was reaching its conclusion and, by the beginning of October 1944, the Allied troops had crossed into Germany. So went the military situation, but the conflict was by no means over. Such strife as this was not to be settled by armies, nor by crossing of national frontiers, for it was a conflict without confines

which caused a nation to be divided against itself. The world had
moved into a phase of inter-ideological strife. In a way it was a move
in the right direction, for it signified dissatisfaction with the old order.
Later it would be found that there was a further point to be reached
where it would be realised that peace is not to be had by force nor yet
by negotiation, but only when it is revealed from within the hearts of
men. My part, I now saw, was simply to let that state of order, or
perfection, reveal itself through me, for it is already established in
each of us. I had come to be convinced that perfect equilibrium is the
ultimate state of the universe. Human destiny has been controlled by
concepts and beliefs which man has carried forward and refuses to
relinquish, consequently obscuring this present reality. Such actions
as he takes and the ideas he projects are prompted by such fixed and
stale concepts that they hinder the moment by moment workings and
foul the trends of his life. The things of the past are beyond redemption,
but the potential beauty of the present moment is always with us.

By the beginning of 1945 I was feeling the effects of war again upon
my health. At first I did not take to my bed, resolving to ride it out.
Medical attendance was hard to come by, as all the available doctors
were needed to attend to the extremely heavy casualties which were
pouring in from the various fronts. Towards the end of January I
began to feel very ill, and my nights were tormented by fits of coughing
and fever. Rosalie practically never left my side; she fetched food and
in other ways acted as a hospital nurse. Nevertheless I grew very thin
and weak. My landlady was obviously anxious to get rid of me; a
lodging house was no place for a sick man. And yet where else could
I go? The hospitals were all taken over by the military, and every
nursing establishment had a lengthy waiting list of decrepit civilians.

An old friend in the New Forest found me a place with an Irish
nurse who ran a convalescent home. She had not expected anyone as
ill as I, and seemed dismayed at receiving a stretcher case. But Rosalie
saw me through that period – abandoned her studies and came down
and did not leave me until I was completely recovered.

The little Irish nurse, overcome by the departure of her American
boy friend for his native land, now took to her solitary bed and sent
a message by the old charwoman that she wanted to close down her
establishment and go on a holiday. The old girl with the mop and a
cigarette dangling from her lips plodded up the stairs heroically. She
had kept the place going throughout the war. Having croaked out her
message to us she volunteered the advice, 'Why don't you marry 'er

and take 'er back to Canada with you ?' She did not intend it as interference. It just seemed the obvious thing for her to say.

Rosie and I looked at each other. We agreed that she was right, and
so that is exactly what we did.

The spearheads of the British and American forces under Montgomery and General Eisenhower had reached central Germany, and
Hanover was within striking distance. The Russians continued their
methodical advance towards Berlin and Vienna. Franklin D. Roosevelt
had died and Harry Truman had taken his place. Peace seemed to be
just around the corner.

On 1 May 1945, at four o'clock, Rosalie and I kept tryst with our
two witnesses, one of whom was her tutor, and we were duly married,
after which we went to London.

The war was over and the sparrows chirruped among the May trees
in Green Park. We sat under one of the pink arbours playing with a
stray puppy. It was peaceful and calm and an atmosphere of repose,
if not of well-being, had returned to the capital. 'What,' thought I,
'can the shriek of a bomb or the wail of a siren matter ?' Things only
of yesterday, yet already fading from memory.

London was gaily passing by and Piccadilly was in jubilant mood.
Flags were flying and the outward appearance of that long-awaited
Victory Day was everywhere present after six long years of trial and
ordeal. In all our hearts was a sense of gratitude, mingled with a
feeling of insecurity for the future. On top of it all was the intense
fatigue of exhausted nerves which, but for the indomitable fibre of
the British, would not have survived the strain. Yet here was evidence
of mother nature again in full leaf, defying all the concepts and prejudices of man.

The eighth of May had been declared V.E. day and we strolled down
to St James's Park. The crowds there were thick and the ducks and
pelicans had retreated on to their island in the middle of the lake. A
coster cart and a few park chairs protruding above the litter-scummed
surface of the water were signs of rowdiness natural to the occasion.

We mostly avoided the crowds, but on hearing cheers from Piccadilly
we hurried across the park in time to see Winston Churchill with his
cigar, closely followed by cars filled with returned prisoners-of-war.

Shortly after we sailed for Canada.

18

How the Rest was Won

The Scottish caretaker at Arbutus Point met us at the gate to welcome us home. Everything was beautifully looked after and Andrew had even found time to go out fishing every evening. The tall firs seemed to have grown in height and the roses were blooming in the garden. I walked down steps to the cove and found the rowing boat on the slipway in the shade of an arbutus tree. I had written to Andy to scrape her bottom and repaint it. I turned the boat up to see if it had been done, but I found the bottom covered with scum. Tapping at the timbers my finger broke right through the bottom. When I returned to the house, the Scot was in the kitchen pensively picking his teeth and reading the family Bible.

'Andy,' I said, 'Are you a good swimmer?'

'No, I canna swim, why?'

'You've been out fishing in 150 fathoms of water in a boat whose bottom is as soft as piecrust.'

Andy applied himself more vigorously to his reading. He looked up, but in an instant the grin came off his face. Rosie had entered the kitchen in a pair of very brief shorts. Andy stared at her legs in evident disapproval. He closed his Bible as if to protect it from outrage; he rose and muttered 'Sodom and Gomorrah', to which Rosie gaily replied, 'No, Swan and Edgar'.

But Andy had been shocked. At the bottom of it all was resentment at the intrusion of a young and attractive personality into his puritanical world. In my absence he had grown to look on Arbutus Point as his own domain.

But it was evident from the start that the climate of Vancouver Island was not going to agree with Rosie. It was full of retired old people and the dampness of sea level was making her cough.

Remembering an earlier visit to Alberta with its 2000 to 3000 foot plateaux, its rolling hills, and its towering Rocky Mountains, I suggested a trip there to see what we could find; for there lies some of the most

243

beautiful scenery in Canada, especially the undulating foothill region where life goes on in a pleasant, unhurried way much as it did when the early settlers arrived. We went to Banff in among the mountains on a visit and eventually moved there. The air was stimulating, the altitude just under 4500 feet.

Banff, which is Canada's largest national park, seemed to suit Rosie; moreover, it had a drier and gayer atmosphere. We enquired from the park authorities about available building lots with the idea of settling there permanently, but received little encouragement. An inhabitant told us of a tract of freehold land five miles east of the town, and on that same day we hired saddle horses and rode out to see it.

It was an ideal situation, 4735 feet above sea level sloping towards the south-east. As none of the surrounding mountains overshadowed it, there was plenty of sunshine and a magnificent view in all directions. Water was apparently plentiful and the land was easily accessible by two main roads. Without hesitation we staked our claim.

Freehold land within the boundaries of a national park suggests all sorts of amenities and privileges without too much restriction or obligation. It was, in fact, one of those seemingly ideal situations which so rarely happen. I thought to myself that the luck I had had in finding Arbutus Point was holding. My friends had often referred to my Irish optimism.

I had longed since the days of my childhood at Villa Torlonia to reintegrate myself with physical beauty and tranquility in the belief that some of the peace in my environment would rub off on to me and sublimate, to some degree, the turmoil of my heart. It was an easy mistake to make. There are those who live in some neat and rustic chalet with a far-ranging outlook and others who are amid the grime of a back alley in an industrial city, and I would not attribute more happiness to one than to the other, for it is neither the view, nor the purity of air that brings joy.

Alas, in my desire to live in a world of health and beauty I rushed with great vigour into building a home which harmonised with the magnificence of the mountain scenery, so that the whole style, materials and layout gratified my ideal. And this was not all; I also designed the furniture and fittings to match the house.

A coal-mining company sold me the land at a time when coal was becoming a drag on the market, especially with the railways converting to diesel oil and the growing promise of natural gas as a fuel for household use.

The Parks Department in Ottawa consisted of men who had served their time in the wild magnificence of Canada's national parks. They were very conscious of the ways of nature both from a natural as well as a scientific standpoint.

'How can we control a park,' they asked, 'with an independent landowner in its midst?'

I saw their point, yet I was convinced that it could be done. It took me over five years to convince them that I was an ally, and to show them that I had not come to despoil the natural beauty of the park but, on the contrary, to enhance it.

The site we chose for the lodge, as such log houses are called, was upon a rise in the open upland from which could be seen an endless panorama of peaks as well as a view down the Bow Valley almost to the plains; a view which later inspired many of my paintings. The country around was rolling benchland, partly open but mostly covered with pine, spruce and aspen. The trees yielded here and there to lakes or rivers; it was a country which, by its irregularities, kept one guessing, and impressed one with its variety and beauty.

Rosie and I spent much time houseplanning and the plans grew or shrank until we thought that we had reached the mean level between modesty of funds and living space. When finally its size was fixed, we agreed that it should be built of pine logs, if possible those growing on our land. This proved impracticable, as our trees were all far too small. Our plans called for sixty-foot logs with as little difference of circumference as possible between the heads and the butts and such trees could not be found nearer than the western slopes of the Rockies.

It soon became clear that it would take us, provided we could get help, two years at least to collect materials and prepare the ground for our lodge. In the meantime, we argued, our hotel bills in Banff would run away with much of our money; they would, in fact, cost as much as building a modest cottage, near the site of the lodge, in which we could live until the larger house was finished and which we could then lease to a desirable tenant. What actually happened in the end was that we lived in the cottage and leased the lodge. However, by the time we had put in such essentials as electricity, dam and water system, pump, sawmill, workmen's cabins, drainage, stables and paddock, we decided that we could easily have bought an hotel for the cost.

We purchased a jeep and a trailer and set to work clearing the space for building. Cutting the roots of pines, we pushed the trees over with

the jeep and hauled and stacked the trunks close to the sawmill. We
left the aspens standing for they are beautiful trees and of little value
beyond the fact that they feed the wapiti with bark in winter. The
beaver had felled great quantities of aspen along edges of the streams.
They stripped them of their bark and left us quantities of dry firewood
for the hauling. In an open fireplace this wood burns brightly, without
either spitting or fouling the chimney with soot.

Axes flashed in the sunlight, chips flew and the crosscut saw could
be heard echoing through the woods. Then as winter returned and
the lakes froze again we went after the spruce trees, logging them off
the banks where, at high-water level, their roots risked inundation.

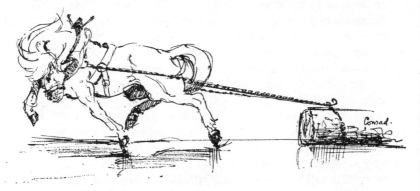

We skidded them on to the ice and hauled them to the Fairholme
Ranch as we now called our land. The lake is deep and we nearly went
through the spring ice with our last load.

As soon as the frost was out of the ground Harold Fuller, the axeman,
and I got busy on the basement, but it was tough digging. I combed
the district for help. Ex-servicemen were drifting through, but they
were mostly on holiday. A party of students came and camped on our
land for a week or more, but a bear raided their stores and they left.
Then a young Englishman turned up and lent a hand. He was unaccustomed to hard work and his physical condition was soft. When
asked what his trade was, he told the astonished Harold that he was
a magician. Harold's eyes brightened at this information.

'Can you really produce things?' he asked.

'That's the idea,' replied the magician.

'Then produce some dynamite,' continued Harold who knew that
the stuff was almost unobtainable.

'O.K.,' smiled the conjurer, as he hopped on his bike, and within a very short time he had got a case of it from a construction gang working in the district. This hurried things on a lot. With a portable forge we kept our picks sharpened, and by midsummer the basement was finished, the cement poured and the first round of logs in place. Log construction is thrilling to watch, heavy to work at, and probably the most expensive form of building. But at that period it was about the only uncontrolled building material available.

By September the cottage was finished and we had used half the spruce logs for putting up the stables! We did this because it seemed original to start each of these buildings with four rounds of logs and go up from there with lumber. The effect came off very well. Cedar siding outside and knotty pine interior provided the setting for bunkbeds and an immense open fireplace built of rock quarried on our land.

Cement was hard to come by; nails were rare but they turned up miraculously when needed, though sometimes our problems seemed for the moment almost insurmountable. At such times I would sit on a log bench in the sun, gazing at the wonderful scenery, watching an osprey in the sky or, in spring, listen for the fascinating roar of an avalanche.

By Labour Day 1947, Harold had scouted the vast forests at Kootenay Crossings for some really tall pine trees from which to cut the necessary logs for our lodge. The appropriate time to get the sticks out of the bush was between the end of the tourist season and the arrival of winter snows. The road switchbacks and wriggles its way through the mountain and here and there are dangerous curves and hairpin bends. Coaxing a load of sixty-foot logs around them is no easy task. We lost only one load down the mountainside with fortunately no loss of life.

It was early autumn and hardly had we laid the last of these logs on the building site than winter was upon us. Retiring to the cottage basement, I fitted it out as a workshop. I had lost all my furniture during the war and now needed sufficient for both houses. I designed cupboards, dressers, beds and corner-cupboards in a simple baroque style, decorating some with paint and using Western motifs inspired by Indians or by the animals in our surroundings: wapiti, moose, bear and many small birds and woodland creatures. Other pieces, such as ladder-backed chairs, chests of drawers and tables, I left in their natural colours, sealing the pores of the grain with chemicals which would prevent the wood from darkening.

Out of some old logging equipment we forged firedogs, massive door hinges and even lamp standards. On sunny days we decorated woodwork by using the burning point of sunlight through a magnifying glass; we made ash trays out of pottery and worked at tapestry by a log fire at night. Whenever I found a suitable hunk of granite, I hammered it into an Indian or animal head to be used as a doorstop. I painted pictures of mountain scenes and of animals until I had sufficient canvasses to cover the walls. I bought some carving tools and carved some relief designs on some of the furniture. Meanwhile Rosie stitched and hemmed the curtains and hangings for both houses out of English material procured in Calgary.

We started laying the logs on the lodge in November, stripping each log with a drawknife before laying it on. We reckoned on two rounds of logs, requiring as they did innumerable cuts and notches, every three days. The character of every log house depends on how the logs are united at the corners. There are many ways of doing this. The simplest is known as Hudson Bay corners and the most difficult and most effective is known as cupped saddling. In this case a concavity is gouged in the upper log where it crosses the lower upon which it rests, the rim of the cupping taking the bearing.

The first half of the winter kept fairly open. The temperature remained on the upper side of 20 degrees below zero and we lost no time in reaching the eaves, which we did with the twelfth round. The roof was set with a half pitch, steep enough to shed snow. We carried out the interior of the dormer upper floor with knotty cedar and knotty pine, sealing the wood as we had formerly done the furniture and thus preserving the subtle browns and pinks of cedar and those contours of yellows which culminate in the dark knots of pine and form a variegated pattern which is never tiring to the observer.

A few spruce logs left over from our cottage served as beams to support the large cedar ceiling of the living room. In this room, too, was a fireplace wide enough to burn four-foot logs. The opening was cut away, as it were, so as to enable the fire to be seen from any angle in the room. This was fitted with a false back concealing outlets so as to serve as a miniature central heating system.

Developing an urge for a change of scene, three of our horses escaped. Two of them were valuable mares and, knowing that there was a wild stallion in the vicinity, I had to get them back. This held things up for a few days as this is a big country and horses are hard to find among the trees, even if they are belled. I rode for three days, but found no trace of them. Sometimes I would tie my horse to a tree and climb a mountain to an altitude of 8000 feet so as to look down upon the country beneath – but saw no horses. A few days later a friend suggested hiring a small plane, owned by a bush pilot in Banff. The landing strip lay between us and the town and soon we were flying over likely terrain. At length we saw them, three specks, grazing peacefully in a slough. In a short while I was walking after them with oats and halters and so got them home again.

Before the roof was put on to the lodge we had already rented it to a charming older lady from Chicago who had been attracted by the fact that she would be the first to occupy the house. We had to work overtime to get it finished by the fixed date, 1 June. The job was done with every detail in place, and all as clean and polished as a new pin, on the appointed day.

Our tenant and her maid arrived by train while the chauffeur and butler drove up by car with the cook. Next morning he came over to us in the cottage saying that they had believed that they would be the first tenants. Mystified, I followed him to the lodge, where in the living room he lifted a cushion of a window seat and pointed to a family of newly born mice.

'They beat us to it!' he laughed.

The lodge brought us in a good income. Don Cameron, who later became a senator, was forging ahead with the formation of what has now developed into perhaps the greatest art centre in North America. He named it the Banff School of Fine Arts. Already there were six hundred summer students and he needed instructors. He invited me to join the faculty and I spent the summer of 1948 teaching a class of aspiring water colourists. The faculty consisted, otherwise, of well-known Canadian artists. Some were members of the famous Group of Seven. Only I, who was not dependent upon painting for a living, was an unknown. Canada was still in a state of artistic doldrums. To earn a living a professional artist would have to supply his public with paintings that they could appreciate. I was not prepared to do that and it was a godsend, therefore, that things worked out as they did, for the renting of the lodge made me financially independent and enabled me to paint when and how I felt moved to do so. My paintings represented the best I could do at that point. In the days when the really great art works were produced, the painter was usually under the patronage of the church or of some rich nobleman, and so not under any financial compulsion.

But it was not all work. The long-awaited Stampede Week came around and we went to Calgary to see it. The city of Calgary was beginning to feel that it was on the threshold of becoming a great city. It had been looked upon as nothing but a 'cow town' in the past, with a romantic Mounted Police history behind it. Now, suddenly, it was aware of its tremendous oil and natural gas potential. The sky was the limit!

Accommodation was still scarce and during Stampede Week all the wild and woolly West wanted to be present. However, we were lucky to find a room and to secure grandstand seats. There was no Ascot quality about the crowds. The exhibition grounds teemed with ranchers, drovers, cattlemen and cowboys and the inevitable tout who is identified with all race courses.

Perched on our lofty seats we were at the height of expectancy and we were not disappointed. Had we been born with twenty eyes, we would have had plenty to occupy them all, for there was not a second's hitch and events seemed to overlap each other with such rapidity that we were bewildered.

Of the various items, the Wild West were by far the most interesting to us. They were alternated by horse races, but always our attention was drawn to the whitewashed chutes, behind which, at any moment, a frantic bronc or steer might suddenly be released into the open, there in violent bursts of fear and rage to get rid of its rider. To make the scene more dramatic, occasional thunder-showers swept the field. On such occasions the tightly massed crowds mysteriously evaporated and by the same magic would once more flood the enclosure as soon as the shower was over and the rainbow shone in the east.

Of course there were other contests. There was steer decorating, calf roping and other thrills. But perhaps the most bloodcurdling of all was the chuck-wagon races; four teams of four horses each performed seemingly impossible manoeuvres at full speed. Within the cramped space of the arena they formed a figure-eight course around some barrels before galloping for first place around the race course.

Somewhere in the background, apart from the stampede itself, was a 'Midway' show. There was a section set aside for agricultural exhibits, too, and many innovations of interest to farmers and cattlemen. We returned to our hotel elated by our experience, if exhausted emotionally and physically by the outing.

Following this event of great local importance, and rather in contrast to it, comes the Banff Indian Days, during which practically the whole

Stoney Indian tribe treks up to Banff in horse-drawn vehicles from their reservations in Morley and pitch their teepees on some level ground amid the magnificence of the Rocky Mountains. There is more of a tourist attraction than a tribal rite in this, being a very rustic affair, haphazard, spontaneous and altogether charming.

A rodeo takes place each day in their camp to which, of course, the public is admitted. There are also contests of an amusing nature such as a race to eat a pie, and in the evening in the grounds of the huge Banff Springs Hotel tribal dances take place during which time a white benefactor is perhaps made a blood brother of the tribe with tom-toms and much ceremony.

Whereas the Calgary Stampede tends to become over-commercialised this Indian meeting is still unsophisticated. Their dances and wild songs are inspired by such creatures as the prairie chicken or the buffalo. One can imagine the buffalo quietly resting – the scene is peaceful – then two bulls rise ponderously and start fighting. The song of the wind – it sweeps through the trees and the mountains, over the plains, and brings life and fruition, rain and sunshine.

'O wind,' they sing, 'the invisible strength.'

In another song the deer follow the herd. Snakelike and in single file the Indians trot, bells ringing at their ankles, a squaw or two joining in the line; the tempo is merry and the music full of leaves and colour. Louder the drums and the chorus rises as the line winds in and out of the teepees. Many wear bonnets of eagle feathers, others crowns of porcupine hair.

We would go to Indian Days on our best horses wearing the gayest horse furniture and Western outfits. For my part, I did not much care for that which took place in the arena, but enjoyed blending with the scene. To me, these Indians carried the spirit of the wilds – something that harmonised and belonged to nature, and I was often moved by their close relationship with the land they lived in. But all too often they tried to emulate the white man – and so lost their identity.

I received word that Lord Martin had been called down to California by Uranda on some important business, and that he wished me to accompany him. We drove down in his Studebaker taking turns at the wheel.

We reached our destination amid the California hills south-east of Los Angeles in the early spring and Uranda came out of the small ranch house to greet us. We were, of course, a bit travelworn after a journey of two thousand miles. There were others there as well as those we had brought with us: Uranda's wife, Kathy, and her baby Nancy, his secretary Grace and her little son and one or two of Uranda's faithful followers. We entered the house. A meal was on the table ready for us, consisting of fruit salad, cottage cheese, rye bread and good fresh butter. Uranda blessed the food and afterwards, in the tiny living room, invited us all to sit and hear him speak of the spirit of truth. As we listened, material barriers seemed to recede and we found ourselves joined together as if separation had never been and we were united as a whole. When Uranda finally finished what he had to say it was almost two in the morning.

There were six women in all, with two children, and accommodation being limited, Martin and I took blankets and retired to an open shed where we lay down to sleep among the farm machinery. But a wind got up and the thorny branches of the pepper trees surrounding the shed scraped the metal of the corrugated iron walls and emitted the weirdest noises. In the early dawn I distinctly felt hot breath on my forehead and, looking up, found myself gazing into the liquid brown eyes of a stray cow.

I could not compare the following few days with any others for they seemed to be unique. I felt buoyed up by a strange and holy atmosphere so formidable as to be almost frightening.

The tension upon me while in the presence of Uranda was sometimes so unbearable as to cause me to seek release in trivialities. Perhaps, too, I was afraid of coming under a hypnotic influence and kept a tight hold on my thinking. But I soon came to see that I was resisting a totally benign power, foreign to me, but into which the others could relax and allow themselves to be enfolded and become part of, so that it flowed strongly through them, unifying on all levels. They clearly felt at one with themselves and each other. This touched me as the perfect state. It had to be on a voluntary basis, of course, and the voluntary part was all-important.

The ranch house stood in the midst of a field surrounded by eucalyptus trees. Odd pieces of disused farm machinery, an out-door privy and a wood pile had been woven together into a rustic pattern by the overgrowth of tall grass and sage brush.

After breakfast Uranda seemed to wish to be alone with Martin, so I went for a walk on a neighbouring steep hill. The wind was strong and from the north. It blew up a sand storm and from the valley a brownish cloud rose towards the sky. Beyond this, and contrasting with the sub-tropical foreground, I could see distant snow peaks beckoning. I sheltered for a while from the wind behind some rocks and sat on a sand patch where I could enjoy the solitude and think. There was a quiet murmur of nearby water. A small lizard came out to watch me and a swallow-tailed butterfly settled on a rock opening out his wings. As I gradually became conscious of an inner state, I thought, 'The desert shall blossom as the rose.'

In that little white ranch house down in the valley was a man imbued with the spirit of truth, and I knew that I had come to the crucial turning point of my life. I laughed so loud that the lizard almost jumped out of his skin.

Uranda was first, last and always interested in establishing the One Christ Body on earth, a temple of human form expressing the spirit of the living God, a body of many members all united by an irresistibly cohesive force inherent in each. Of course, of course, that was the meaning of the second coming. How ridiculous I had been in thinking of a Christ descending on a cloud from above. This was a moment of birth, a sort of Christmas Day, not the return of the old, but the birth of the new in this day and age.

The idea was, perhaps, by no means new for it suggests the basis of true Christianity and, for that matter, the basis of true Hebraic worship. But the fact of the matter was that no one so far had proclaimed it in such a manner and I was beginning to awaken to the dormant giant who was now emerging in awareness – showing the true stature of the dwarf-like human personality for what it was.

The meals at the ranch were a happy experience, the food simple and organically harmonious, blessed lovingly by Uranda before being served by the ladies. The rest of the day was spent listening to Uranda until the evening sun, streaming into the little sitting room of the ranch house, would remind him that it was time again for a break and, perhaps, another meal and some exercise.

Once again, after we had eaten, we would gather together for Uranda's evening session. Strenuous as it might have seemed it achieved its purpose in releasing our minds and hearts from a domination by the material world consciousness into an indescribable freedom of swift beauty. Nevertheless, after the prolonged intensity of his presence I found that, though my mind was seething with new vistas, it had reached saturation and now recoiled. The next day when he asked me if I wanted to hear more, I admitted for the present I had had enough.

That evening he read us a paper – his lesson material seemed endless – and as soon as he had finished we discussed or elaborated and expanded the subject presented and, as we had no taperecorder, our remarks were all taken down in shorthand by two of the ladies. Of course it was mostly Uranda who spoke. He sat in a wicker rocking chair rocking himself gently with half-closed eyes, a hand passing over his forehead from time to time as he deliberated in slow measured terms. My powers of concentration were never good and often during his talks I would find my mind wandering and I would hark back to my conventional Christian upbringing with a shock and be amazed to find myself sitting there among that strange assortment of people – so racially and socially mixed, yet now united. Uranda, for instance, of German and Welsh descent, was ten years my junior, born in Marshaltown, Colorado, but brought up among the Grand Mesa Mountains. Lord Martin Cecil, an Englishman of noble birth on both sides of his family, was unquestioningly accepting Uranda's leadership.

At times I was swept on by the utter logic of the words which poured forth from Uranda's lips, while at other times I found myself rationalising and being subject to doubts. I had always expected a prophet to look like the pictures I had seen of them – men with upturned eyes and meekness in their faces suggesting weakness rather than strength. In my imagination they led conventional, blameless, almost inhuman lives; they had, in fact, no existence except as artists of the Renaissance visualised them. But the people with whom I now found myself led normal human lives. They had strong but gentle faces and determined mouths. They loved, ate and did all the things that others do, except sleep!

Compared to my habits they seemed never to go to bed. Otherwise their lives were dedicated to one ultimate purpose only, and for this they were ready to give up everything. Indeed, they would gladly yield home, comforts, riches, all in fact that stood in the way of expressing the perfect state of order which was already within them. Nothing could be more natural since order exists everywhere except in the lives of men and women. The state of order, being cohesive by nature, draws together its responsive elements and thus produces an organic whole – which Uranda called the One Christ Body.

From the Zadokite papers of Egypt, and now from the Dead Sea Scrolls, history was coming to light which gave us some inkling of the life led by the Essenes, and I was inclined to draw the parallel and see Uranda as the 'Teacher of Righteousness', in a sect that was to Christianity as the Essenes had been to the Jewish religion of those times. But it was a hasty comparison and rapidly forgotten. I was in the habit of comparing previous events as if I could relate them to the present in some fashion, oblivious to the fact that the time and place, as well as all the vibratory factors (both infinitely minute as well as immensely vast) throughout the universe combined to make each instant absolutely unique. And I saw how the character of life in form was that of perpetual animation and change in perfect balance. More and more I could see it clearly and become part of it, part indeed of the order which is eternally at hand. This was the truth. Those who spent their time delving into chronicles of the past for evidence of the truth in bygone days, had, I thought, failed to realise that it is available today in a practical form.

I was beginning to see that if I were to come, with all my failings and impurities, into the burning light of truth, I would find the difference unbearable. I would have to choose between letting the process of purification take its course or relapse into the world of compromise from which I had come.

The others at the ranch, though slightly eclipsed by Uranda and Martin, also had fascinating backgrounds. Some had salvaged their lives from marital discord, others from sickness or, like myself, had come 'out of a hunch' that every atom of my body was the evidence of order and that I did not belong to myself and never had, but was the living expression of God – that is the truth of the matter.

I did not doubt that Uranda's interpretation of certain phrases in the Bible was correct. I am not gullible by nature, but I saw danger in a drastic acceptance of his statements on their face value. By the process of putting an unorthodox interpretation on basic beliefs whether in regard to religion, history or physics, a state of such confusion could be produced in my mind that I would, no longer, know or understand anything. And my mind, being in this state of confusion, would become extremely vulnerable and easily controlled by an outside source. Likewise the process of dividing, setting one idea against another, or one person against another, or an individual against the rest, renders them prone to suggestion. I was suspicious of the techniques I had met within Europe which debunk concepts, break up petrified beliefs, or disperse groups, reforming them into patterns and formulae more easily manipulated. This, though it involves hypnosis, makes ordinary hypnotic methods look like child's play. When previously accepted standards are removed or discredited and we are left without a yardstick by which to gauge our reasoning, we are thrown into a state of perplexity and become dependent upon a leader.

I was familiar with this process in advertising, and in political propaganda, and the fact that it is becoming more prevalent does not make it right. In my view, iconoclasm is justified only where the indoctrination is for the benefit of the whole – and who is to know this? The state of order, or perfection, the heavenly state which is the full expression of Being in the universe, has to appear through man; what other possible medium is there? And this is man's service to God which he must perform to justify his existence, to fulfil his purpose as a cosmic entity. No amount of struggling or trying to accomplish it will help, it must be allowed to occur. It cannot be done in our own or another's strength, because it is already there, this ultimate state which only man can reveal.

What disturbed me most was the belief that I was being indoctrinated. Yet as I looked at it more closely I saw that the fixed beliefs which I clung to, were fixed only because I had been imbued with them during a defenceless childhood and the fact that I had already been so indoctrinated struck me as wrong. The findings of a council (which become dogma) can only apply in the moment of their emergence and are anathema to unfolding life.

Day after day, from his rocking chair, Uranda spoke to us. A bridge table before him was covered with his papers. Sometimes he read to us, sometimes he would speak without notes or else discuss the points that had been brought out. Sometimes he would kick off his shoes and smoke a cigarette. During one of these sessions I did a drawing of his head.

Uranda's car was like an elongated shooting-brake. In fact, it had been an airport limousine. It was his means of getting about and it suited him well, for he always travelled with an entourage of many others including children. It was parked under the thorn trees beside the little white ranch house and served as a sort of counsel office in which those of us who felt like discussing problems with him could speak freely on personal matters without fear of interruption.

Uranda's eagerness to heal wherever he found an opening came from a passionate desire to re-establish wholesomeness on earth. Having himself come to know that divine point of integration within himself, his purpose was to express it on all levels. His personal approach was always one of openness and of evident eagerness to heal, to bless and to comfort by exercising that universal and formidable cosmic power – 'God's love', as he called it, with which he was overflowing.

'If there is a Universe of Order,' wrote Richard Thompson, a close

associate of Uranda's, 'there must be a law upon which the Order depends and conformity with the law will bring harmony and non-conformity, discord.'

It was Sunday and we were approaching the end of our visit to Riverside. Uranda suggested a drive to Los Angeles and its surroundings which included Hollywood and other places with familiar names. The world seemed strangely unreal after the depth of communion we had experienced. I was a stranger in a strange land but with the beginnings of 'home' flowering in my heart.

I had anticipated my early return to Canada so had brought with me my travelling bag. I managed to get a seat on a night plane and, bidding farewell to the others, settled down to wait in a Los Angeles cafe for it was yet early afternoon. The cafe had been given the appearance of a grotto with vaulted ceilings from which stalactites glittered. Bird cages, containing canaries, hung among the stalactites. The birds sung to the accompaniment of an orchestra. I thought of them as perpetual captives sentenced, like man's imagination of angels on pink clouds eternally twanging harps, to a grotesque, humanly conceived heaven, longing for the fresh air and freedom of the wind, the spirit that blows withersoever it listeth according to its natural laws of life.

I had been a secret agent working for a cause I believed in, a human cause, now I would serve a universal cause, neither human nor limited in scope, the cause of all causes. My intention would be not to discover details of a political or ideological formation, but to be an agent relaying cosmic power, revealing the state of order in every aspect of life. I would reveal the cause of all causes in the form of a perpetual harmony of effects. And I would love the author of all in secret with every aspect of my being.

19

The Great Beginning

I thought of all the things in my life that had passed away and was grateful for their contribution to the present. I was aware of the worth of these events in terms of thankfulness and in the absence of resentfulness.

It was 1954 and Rosie and I were at Fairholme. We were keenly interested in the activities of our friends in what we called the Third Sacred School which we closely followed. There were regular mailings too which kept us in touch with what was current in the ministry's spiritual development. A derelict ranch in the Colorado foothills had been bought and renamed 'Sunrise Ranch' and it was hoped that before long it would flourish as the headquarters of the movement. It was little more than a dustbowl when it fell under the control of Uranda. But he predicted that there were seven springs beneath the property and followed up with this statement, 'I carry the spirit of truth and when sufficient awareness of the truth is evident among you (his followers) water, which is the symbol of truth, will appear.' Perhaps some of them found this hard to accept, but in fact water in such abundance did become available that the valley, with proper management, could only flourish.

Classes on the teachings of Uranda now took place regularly at Sunrise Ranch and the right instructors seemed to appear. Accommodation was scarce but with the frequent arrival of new members to the community housing increased. At first it was a bit primitive but, with the acquisition of a machine for making cement blocks, things began to improve.

At the conclusion of the 1954 Class period, which was six months in those days, the young ministry received its first great blow. Rosie and I and the children were at our home in the Canadian Rockies, and I recall we were halfway through lunch when the telephone rang. It was a long-distance call and I recognised the voice of Uranda's secretary Grace Van Duzen speaking from Colorado. There had been a plane

259

crash in which Uranda, his wife Kathy, Alan Ackerley (a personal friend), and two small children, had all been killed. The children had been of Grace Van Duzen and Lillian Call, Uranda's two secretaries. The impact of the crash on the system of the Third Sacred School was no less than that upon the Cessna plane as it hit the shallow waters of the bay at Oakland, California.

Shattering as it was there were those who continued to accept their responsibilities in upholding Uranda's teachings and it was at the head of this band of faithful ones that Martin now placed himself and he invited Rosie and I to attend the next Class starting in Spring 1955.

Finding a caretaker for Fairholme for six months was miraculously achieved. By chance we met an English couple in Banff who were available for exactly the required period. They moved in and we with the children and baggage piled into our Ford and drove down through Montana and Wyoming to Colorado. I shall never forget it. The snow still hung in the hollows of those endless plains. The antelope and the distant hills were reminiscent of my early days in the Mounties on the Canadian prairies. And then on arrival at Sunrise, the pang of dis-illusionment as we gazed upon our new environment.

The Ranch was still scattered with debris of broken farm machinery. Goats inhabited a pen next to the one-room cabin allotted to us. There was no indoor plumbing or sanitation yet a powerful feeling of victory dominated the scene which buoyed up our spirits and kept at bay any sense of depression.

A ranch house under a cluster of large cottonwood trees served as the kitchen and dining room, a barn was being converted into an apartment block, while to the west the foothills rose sharply to a summit called Green Ridge. However, we were warned not to take random walks in that area for fear of meeting a rattlesnake or getting lost. My sense of humour got the better of me at this instruction as I recalled the final lines of one of Hilaire Belloc's cautionary verses: 'And always keep a-hold of nurse. For fear of finding something worse.'

Ever since the days when I first met Uranda I remember vividly the salient points of his message, 'All wisdom, direction and power for living your life comes from within.' It needed no human explanation nor analysis, it only needed to be lived moment by moment, for this ground of our Being is the wellspring of life.

I miss that man who first brought me to see that truth, albeit as old as time itself, I miss his friendly spirit, his Western mode of speech and the way he sat and handled his horse. His sunny personality was most infectious, one couldn't help loving him. He lived what he preached and nothing on earth could persuade him to violate his integrity; above all he had a keen sense of humour.

Our curriculum was plain enough: the theory of his teachings in the forenoon and the practice of same in the afternoon.

In August when Class ended I returned to Fairholme alone, my marriage to Rosie, seen in the stark light of reality, disintegrated. Tough on me, tougher still on the kids but Humpty Dumpty had fallen off his dream wall and that was that. I might have managed to continue to run the place alone, but a slump on the oil market caused my tenants not to renew their lease and I was left holding the bag. With the help of Jim and Jane Lock who had been on the place as

chore boy and charwoman since the beginning, I managed to carry on for almost four years, but then my funds began to run low. Several real estate companies had found me customers but all wanted to subdivide my land and sell off freehold lots to the public and, as Fairholme was situated in the middle of one of the people of Canada's national parks, I felt under a moral obligation not to accept those offers. I simply could not do that to the place I had grown so fond of. Moreover, I thought the wild animals would be shot by unscrupulous

house owners and the beauty of the place desecrated by homes of all tastes and sizes. The dilemma went on and on while my finances grew less and less.

Then on 29 April 1958, following a long-distance phone call from the Director of Protocol in Ottawa, I was visited by a party of four men from the Alberta capital: a Cabinet Minister, Assistant Commissioner McLellen and an Inspector Porter (both from the Royal Canadian Mounted Police) and finally a member of the Albertan legislature. Princess Margaret of England, making an official tour of the Canadian West, they said, needed somewhere to stay in the Banff region. Would I consider renting Fairholme to the federal government for that purpose? This was indeed a windfall. The lease would be for five days: one day for installation, three days of Royal occupancy and a day to dismantle and evacuate. It suited me well. Moreover what better publicity could there be for a property on the market? Yes, I had made up my mind that if I were to sell Fairholme I would, for the first time in my life, have sufficient income to take the boys abroad and later support my declining years. Parting with Fairholme was perhaps the wisest move to make, albeit a very painful one. I was sixty-four years of age. This was a wonderful outworking.

The air was soon full of proposals and counter-proposals for the purchase of my home. Four or five different parties were on the hook and yet at the bottom of my heart I felt that the most fitting solution to the question was to sell Fairholme to the federal government of Canada. The Parks Department, with all its external nonchalance, was deeply concerned to incorporate all outstanding freehold lands within its boundaries. Yes, it was the right and only thing to do, but how to achieve it?

A few days later I was interviewing a very wealthy lawyer from Edmonton, who had a scheme involving the rental of Fairholme, when I was re-visited by Inspector Porter who had with him a Mr Mulligan whose job was to install a special telephone line with five outlets for the Royal visit. There would be two bright coloured phones of the latest design in the lodge, one in the cottage, and one each in the marquees, occupied by the RCMP and the Royal Canadian Army Service Corps. From this time on thing got busier and busier until by midnight I was ready for bed. In bed and with the oblivion of sleep I found peace from the restlessness of organisational fever that had invaded my home.

At 1.30 a.m. Jim and Jane Lock returned from their weekly shopping spree in Banff which they usually terminated with a couple of beers in the beer parlour and a cinema.

They parked their car at the leanto carport by the lodge and Jim was lifting the stores out of the car when he suddenly grew dizzy and collapsed. Being unable to lift him off the ground Jane came to the cottage to fetch me. I was, of course, in deepest sleep but as soon as I had put on some clothes and gone out I could see that Jim needed a doctor. I phoned the hospital in Banff and, giving directions how to get to Fairholme, went down to the bottom of the drive to guide him in. The doctor who was a recent immigrant from Northern Ireland took almost an hour to come and during that time I was able to review the situation in the light of the coming Royal visit. According to protocol I would not be able to set foot on my property during the Princess's occupancy and would therefore have to rely entirely on the Locks to represent me. Since they had been on the place since the beginning they knew all the idiosyncrasies and pecularities of the water system, garbage disposal, the feeding and care of the horses, etc. The Locks would be indispensable in my absence.

Then as I stood out on that midnight road I experienced an un-forgettable phenomenon. The sky became filled with northern lights and I found myself being encircled by a cone of light so luminous that it dazzled me. I walked around on the road to see what would happen and the apparition moved with me so that wherever I went the cone of light moved also, a hole always exactly above my head as if the cone had an open top. When I told Jane about this later she exclaimed, 'Ow! that's the sign of 'ot wevver!'

When Dr Wilson arrived he said Jim had had a mild stroke and should be moved to hospital, but by then Jim's senses had returned to him and he turned thumbs down on the idea and, as Jane said, 'Mr Jim, if 'ee says no, it's No!'

The hot weather came and the thermometer went up into the 90s and Jim lay on his cabin in the sweltering heat in the same clothes he had been wearing on the night of his stroke – but he was getting better. What buoyed him up was his determination to participate in Princess Margaret's visit as my representative at Fairholme, which indeed he succeeded in doing.

But all these excitements did not cause my interest in events elsewhere or in international politics to wane. Events in France had been riveting on Algeria, a topic no one not French understands, and on de Gaulle, a topic understood and remembered only too well in England whose minor troubles had been pushed into the shade.

The news of the Royal visit was now published in the Calgary papers with photographs and an article on the front page, and people began driving up to see where Princess Margaret would be. I accordingly closed the gate at the foot of the drive.

Miss McAuley, the head housekeeper of the Banff Springs Hotel, was now seconded from her job to manage the internal arrangement at Fairholme. We became great friends and her personality was endearing to all concerned. On 24 June I handed over Fairholme to Mr Leicester who in turn turned it over to the Banff Springs Hotel manager Mr McCartney and from that time on I was not allowed on my land. But Jim who was now back on his feet met me at the front gate. We sat together in the police tent nearby. Poor Jim seemed rather lost. Perhaps no one had time to listen to his stories which catenated on in endless sequence. I told him that at the Banff Springs Hotel everything was humming, police, press, officials photographers, cabinet ministers, the Lieutenant-Governor of the province and, of course, Premier Manning. I watched them wistfully. Peaceful Fairholme, what a cyclone had struck it.

There was an official banquet at the Banff Springs Hotel on the last day of Her Royal Highness's visit to which I was invited. I found myself talking to the French Consul at Edmonton and later to his German colleague who, on hearing my name, said, 'Ffrench? ffrench? where have I heard that name before?' to which I blandly replied, 'I'm sorry, I'm afraid I can't help you.'

The Princess was in St Stephan's Hall. We paused for drinks and so to the lobby and the Alhambra dining room where we all shook hands with Her Royal Highness. After dinner it was announced that a mountain had been named after the Princess which evoked great applause in some quarters and a bit of comment in others.

A few of us now were gathered at the Princess's end of it. Chief Inspector Crocker of Scotland Yard came and spoke to me. He had been sleeping in my bed and thanked me for the privilege of stopping in the cottage. Major Griffin, the equerry, then said something. We were at that moment all grouped in a corner which turned out to be before the door marked 'Ladies'. There was a stir, we were blocking the way. No one was embarrassed, least of all the Princess. We re-grouped further on. Griffin said one of the ladies-in-waiting wanted to see me. She later brought me a message from Hardy Amies. She asked many questions, among them why Rosie wasn't here. I explained about Martin, the 100 Mile House, and our movement or ministry and she seemed intensely interested though I put it down partly to polite-ness. The Hon. Iris Peak arrived and I was in the middle of a conver-sation with her – young, pretty, and vivacious. Then someone took me into the Princess's chamber, introduced me to the Prime Minister who, after some kind remarks about Fairholme, led me to Her Royal Highness who was sitting in a large carved chair and looked smaller and daintier than ever. She spoke to me but her words were drowned by the din and chatter of the crowd. She motioned me to a seat which was too far from her to hear what she said. But she leaned forward and thanked me for a 'perfectly lovely visit to Fairholme' which she said had been peaceful and beautiful and very comfortable. A VIP was now being marshalled toward her. I was given a rye on the rocks and made my bow, and gravitated toward Iris Peak again. The Princess made a move and the party was over.

When the glittering mass had departed from Fairholme I did my best to get things back to normal. Jane had kept things going, looked after my interests and cared for Jim as well. The next morning I made some excellent broth and gave Jane a bowl to take home to Jim. On her way out of the cottage via the basement her feet. which were uncommonly large and shod in crepe-rubber-soled espadrilles, got tangled up in a sheet she had previously thrown down the stairs for washing. I heard a thud and found her lying unconscious on the basement floor. She soon came to and kept on asking the same question, "Ow did it 'appen?' A cut on her head was bleeding freely and would need stitching. I called Dr Wilson. Jane went to hospital for a few days and enjoyed a well-earned rest. Dear simple loyal Jane. Her fall had eclipsed the whole elaborate business of the last few days from my mind.

Shortly afterwards the Parks Department made an offer for Fairholme – but it was one third less than that proffered by other bidders. Was my desire to let the Parks Department have Fairholme being taken advantage of? At all events I told them I would spilt the difference and this was then accepted. I received, in due course, the fattest cheque I had ever endorsed and the deal was closed. Ah! what a relief.

I felt easier with my money now and set to work finding lodgings or an apartment in Vancouver where the boys and I could have a home. Everywhere I went I came across the same rooted objection to children. 'Children I adore,' said they, 'but sorry, no children.' So I finally made up my mind to buy a house of my own and went to a reputable house agency in West Vancouver. It being lunch time the office was deserted except for an elderly lady who said she had the very thing I was looking for, a two-bedroom house with a southern aspect overlooking the sea in its own grounds. She locked up the office and drove me to see it. It turned out to be her own home. The house had charm and possibilities and I bought it on the spot. I had been travelling around ever since the sale of Fairholme and now wanted to settle down. Now with a place of my own my children could come and visit me. I added a studio by building on top of the garage and extended the bedroom area and the result was very pleasing.

About this time Monivea Castle fell into the hands of the Irish Free State government and its contents was sold by auction. My cousin John Blake purchased much of the family silver and most of the portraits of my ancestors and then gave the latter to me. These large oil paintings hardly fitted into my new quarters, but not knowing what else to do with them I hung them notwithstanding and they certainly leant a certain *cachet* to my new home.

I recall the prediction John Blake had made regarding our old family seat, a prediction which well might have been made of any of the old Irish estates, for they were one by one being sold as hotels, or where they had not already been burned down in the 'bad times' were being pulled down by the house-breakers and their lands sold by the lot to the country folk. Some of these noble houses have however been preserved by the Georgian Society of Ireland whose meritorious work is greatly to be praised. But the former things were rapidly passing away and the circumstances called for extreme flexibility and readjustment. With these excellent qualities there was less attachment to the things (specifically material) which were disintegrating and an increasing ability to accept the new circumstances which were opening up.

A somewhat similar state of affairs had taken place in Germany during the period of Nazi hysteria when the Germans manifested an almost unparalleled dedication to a concept, while England slept soundly, the people, the government and all, with their heads tucked firmly under their 'it-can't-happen-here' wings. Well, whatever else Peter Fleming's book, *Invasion 1940*, achieved it revealed the danger of complacency.

I lived for fifteen years at my West Vancouver house during which time I wrote and painted a great deal. Meantime the seeds of reality which Uranda had planted were sprouting. In my street alone four or five persons had got the message and opened their eyes to the fact that the truth of Being was not to be found in books, not in any institution, church or philosophy, nor in nature, nor in the abstract distances of space, nor in another human being, but was already within each person from the beginning and from which point its rule of harmony, balance and creativity was fully capable of functioning and controlling that person's life. It is a simple matter of cause and effect, or radiation and response. No use manipulating the billions of effects in the hope of achieving harmony, for the harmonious and creative tone emanates only from primary cause and cause is at the centre of all being. Therefore there was obvious truth in the saying, 'Thou shalt worship the Lord thy God and Him only shalt thou worship.' In most cases it seems that people worship anything and everything other than God, which is, of course, an invocation of effect and a denial of cause. People are beginning to see this and marvel at their blindness in not having seen it before. We are told that human beings are only using a minute part of the actual capacity of their brains. Those parts which are capable of spiritual perception have for the most part fallen into disuse, probably since man expanded his capacities for rationalisation on physical or animal levels – even here he has lost much of his intuitiveness. Uranda tells us to call to remembrance these latent capacities.

During this period I did some of my finest work in painting, including an oil called *St John*, and another, *The Twenty-Third Psalm*, which now hangs in the Lodge at 100 Mile House. It became my deep desire to stimulate the art expression of our ministry which was spreading all over the United States and Canada, South Africa and Europe, Israel and many other points including Australia and New Zealand, for it seemed to me that words alone were no longer able to reveal the subtle wholeness of spiritual awareness.

I was invited to take up permanent residence on Sunrise Ranch which is the international headquarters of our movement, and I accordingly sold my house in West Vancouver and moved down to Colorado in the United States. I was still agile and full of life but in spite of all that I was in my eighties. I picked a site on Green Ridge about 300 feet above the ranch, near enough to be able to participate in the general activities of the unit yet far enough off on my own with exquisite views from a broad balcony.

With Uranda no longer at the helm no one could have been better fitted to lead us than Lord Martin. He is deeply spiritual and accordingly wise and, in his wisdom, singleminded without being narrow in his vision. He is able to accommodate and enfold all circumstances knowing that everything in existence can be used to the glory of God. There is no fear, hatred, or judgement in him which makes him a true leader. Like an accurate compass he points only to a total response to his maker.

When I say that I have grown to love him I mean that I can respond to him in absolute reliability, for he is one with the universal order.

How do I express this love? By following his example? No, not by imitation nor by following instruction but by doing as he has done, namely, obeying the first great commandment, which means total response on all levels to the cause of all causes. That is the golden rule.

There were, of course, others whom I admired and who were true brothers and sisters, as you might say, along the way. One of these was Richard Thompson, born in 1902 in the Isle of Man, a Cambridge M.A. who had adopted the teaching profession. Richard had been a disillusioned idealist who had thrown in his lot with Social Credit but who was quick to awaken from his pipedream when he met Uranda in 1937. He was a jewel and his wife Dorothy the setting. They founded a centre for what he then called 'Ontology' in Vancouver but the name fell short of doing justice to our programme and was discarded. When Richard died in 1965 I took over the co-ordination of the Vancouver group but soon found that most of my time was spent on the road plying between my home and the 'Ontological' centre, a distance of ten miles each way.

My relief came in the form of William Bahan who with his family came from the New England states where he was well known as a successful doctor of chiropractic. Bill Bahan who was then about forty years of age was of American-Irish stock and possessed a keen sense of humour and a clarity of vision which never failed to amaze me, and this, added to his extraordinary charm, quickly brought the Vancouver centre to a new level of vibrancy. But it became evident in due course that he was of too great a calibre to waste on a city of only 365,000 inhabitants and he was given the co-ordination of the whole of the Eastern United States and Canada where he now controls over 100 groups of the Third Sacred School.

Another person, whom, incidentally, I have known since he was four years old is Martin's son Michael who shows the same qualities of leadership with which the Cecils of Burghley are renowned. He has inherited his father's sense of efficiency and accuracy together with an ability to carry through any circumstance with the same one-pointed vision and determination, sometimes referred to as the 'single eye'. The secret of success? Yes, if by success is meant the restoration of the state of order, otherwise called the divine design. The single eye is also the name of one who is not deflected from doing God's will by circumstances of a less divine nature. Michael is married to one of Uranda's daughters.

There are other outstanding people in the ministry such as Lloyd Meeker junior (Uranda's son), and my close friend Rupert Maskell, a South African by birth who represents the ministry in that continent. His following is growing so rapidly I would not venture to quote numbers. Rupert, when first I met him, was a leading figure in London's jet set and a member of one of the best-known clubs in the West End, but he saw the futility of the way things were going in postwar Europe and, hearing of the Third Sacred School, was anxious to learn more. As he said to me when we met in London in the late sixties, 'The thing makes such sense I cannot deny it without violating my integrity.'

It was around midday on a warm Sunday morning and Hyde Park seemed almost deserted. We found two chairs in the middle of a grassy expanse and sat and talked for ages until the purpose and meaning of what the ministry was all about became clear to him and clearer in my mind too.

All this while, I, who am not too good at expressing my own feelings in writing, kept in touch with Martin. I felt that my constancy in obeying the first great commandment would mean more to him in the doing than in endless written words.

It is now nearly forty years since together we went to hear Uranda speak in Vancouver and our understanding of the realm of cause, each in our different ways, has deepened and matured and clarified accordingly. There is a resonance or tonal chord which binds those who turn their faces in absolute response to God and that has always been my relationship with Martin, a mutual understanding and respect one for the other so that words are hardly necessary. Martin enjoys a good story and has a hearty laugh but small talk is not in his line.

One other person, Roger de Winton, I must mention. I met him at Fairholme in 1957 when, as guests of my tenant Tom Brook, he and his wife were spending the weekend there. I had previously met her at a party in Calgary at which time I noticed that she had trouble with her back. Now at Fairholme I spoke to Roger about it and said that I could possibly help her, for all ill conditions are effects of some wrong attitude which denies the control of the perfect state within— usually some fear or resentment, conscious or subconscious, to some condition or circumstance in one's environment. Surely that is obvious, it certainly was to Roger and he seemed to understand it already like somebody awakening to a forgotten fact. He is today one of the four members of the Supreme Council of this ministry, the others being Michael Cecil, Bill Bahan and Jim Wellemeyer who co-ordinates our international headquarters at Sunrise Ranch. I have always been very close to Roger although we may not get a chance of speaking to each other for weeks. Bill Bahan's ability to recognise skills and talents in others and his genius as a promoter brings qualities to light which would otherwise remain dormant. He told me I was a public speaker which was news to me and soon we were conducting lecture tours together all over the North American continent. One of these lecture tours on the teachings of the Third Sacred School took me 10,000 miles during which I spoke more than twenty times. I was amazed at my newly found ability to speak in public and what is more it all seemed to pour forth faultlessly without notes or rehearsal. I spoke at universities, colleges, in public lecture halls and at our centres. I spoke in French to the French Canadians and Acadians, and in Russian to the Doukhobors of British Columbia.

Richard Thompson had established contact with quantities of writers of books and articles on spiritual or esoteric subjects throughout the world. When I revisited Europe in 1954 I asked him for a list of his contacts in Great Britain and I held the first group meeting in London. This started the ball a'rolling and today our representative, Manning Glicksohn, co-ordinates several centres and groups in England, Germany, Holland, France, Italy, and elsewhere. The thing has really caught on. Indeed the ministry has centres now from Israel to South America and Australasia. So much for the release of the spoken word, but this only endorses the vibrational network as one might call it, which preceded it – the power of agreement as a vehicle for the spreading of the truth is fantastic.

It had been suggested to me that I should open up the art consciousness in the ministry for art is a very valid means of disseminating the truth.

It seemed an appropriate moment to start an art school. A disused building called Rim Rock House down by the Big Thompson waterfall near Sunrise was placed at the disposal of what we now called the Art Council. There were three active artists on this council including myself. But on 31 July 1976 a flash flood brought a wall of water fifteen feet high down the Big Thompson Canyon which took out, among many others, the bridge giving us access to Rim Rock House, and until a new bridge was built we had to rely on holding art classes and workshops in other places. Such obstacles are only overcome by agreement among the parties concerned. For some mysterious reason artists find difficulty in coming into agreement and disagreement is the subversion of order. I confess this is a riddle I have not yet solved, a riddle because, by the very nature of their calling, artists are the harbingers of order. Identity with order should be the primary purpose of our training as artists. Any run-of-the-mill art school will teach techniques, but what can we do if we have not learned to see beauty?

The reference point of beauty is within each one of us and it is our awareness of the presence of this order, harmony, balance and wholeness which is revealed through agreement. It is as simple as connecting the lamp to the main source of power and light. Beauty, in other words, comes from within.

Our consciousness begins to clarify as to the true purposes of all our activities during our lifetime just as cells in our brain awaken from their deep sleep, and awakening discover that there is nothing new in existence. All is there in reality from the beginning, harmonious in detail and in true balance. We are not talking science or logic according to human ideas of logic, or of anything the human mind has concocted, but we are looking at something real and stable and everlasting, which was, is and ever will be but which can only be experienced, and can never be explained in human terms.